Java™ *in* Distributed Systems

Java™ *in* Distributed Systems

Concurrency, Distribution and Persistence

Marko Boger
University of Hamburg

John Wiley & Sons, Ltd
Chichester · New York · Weinheim · Brisbane · Singapore · Toronto

Originally published under the title 'Java in verteilten Systemen' by dpunkt. Verlag 1999.
This edition translated by Cybertechnics

Baffins Lane, Chichester,
West Sussex, PO19 1UD, England

National 01243 779777
International (+44) 1243 779777

e-mail (for orders and customer service enquiries): **cs-books@wiley.co.uk**

Visit our Home Page on
http://www.wiley.co.uk

Other Wiley Editorial Offices

John Wiley & Sons, Inc., 605 Third Avenue,
New York, NY 10158-0012, USA

Weinheim • Brisbane • Singapore • Toronto

A catalogue record for this book is available from the British Library

ISBN 0-471-49838-6

This is the fruit of what they have planted, cultivated and grown. With great thanks I dedicate this book to Maren and Erich, my parents.

Contents

Preface

"Writing a book is an adventure. To begin with, it is a toy and an amusement; then it becomes a mistress, and then it becomes a master, and then a tyrant."
–Winston Churchill about his memoirs.

The world of software development keeps changing. On the one hand, the diffusion of **computer-assisted systems** is constantly increasing – even in chip cards, washing machines, and toasters you will eventually find a CPU. On the other hand, the **networking of computers** keeps increasing, not exclusively, but to a large extent due to the Internet. This confers a new importance on the development of **applications in distributed systems**.

Distributed systems have for a long time been employed in industry and commerce. However, while these systems were developed for highly specialized applications, and a very high cost had to be justified for their creation, distributed systems are today developing into an omnipresent infrastructure that enters more and more fields of application. While in the past only big enterprises such as banks or aeronautic enterprises were capable of investing in such efforts, today the broad mass of businesses and even private persons have the possibility of developing distributed applications.

The Internet technology, which has proved reliable for decades and has now become popular, widely diffused and easy to handle through the WWW, not to speak of the great economical significance it has acquired through intranets, extranets, and e-commerce, today provides a technology and infrastructure that foster the development of distributed applications.

In this context, the **Java** programming language is of great importance. On the one hand, Java provides the possibility to distribute applications through its portability and "download"-ability, meaning that Java code can be loaded via the Internet from a server into a browser and executed there. On the other hand it provides the possibility of developing distributed applications where the application is not executed on a single computer, but distributed over several machines.

With the combination of these two aspects, Java provides opportunities that have never before been available in any widely diffused programming language. The first aspect, downloading of Java code as applet, has been described in many books. However, the **techniques for the creation of distributed applications with Java** have until now only been dealt with under various isolated aspects, while this book represents a broad synopsis of the existing techniques for the development of distributed applications with Java.

Structure of the book

After an **Introduction**, in which the significance of Java and of distributed systems is discussed and their relationship explained, the book is subdivided into two parts.

- Part I, **Java in distributed systems**, gives a broad overview of techniques available today for use in distributed systems. The emphasis lies on the three aspects of concurrency, distribution, and persistence, which play a major role in practically every distributed system. The problem of concurrency is handled by means of Java threads. The techniques for distributed communication shown reach from sockets over RMI and CORBA down to mobile agents. Persistent storage is discussed with relational as well as object-oriented databases, and with a Java language environment which integrates persistence directly into the language. All three aspects are covered with the aid of Tuplespaces, a distributed storage mechanism for concurrent systems. Finally, Jini is introduced, an infrastructure which allows easy retrieval of services in distributed systems.

- Part II, **A distributed Java**, analyzes how far the programming of distributed systems could be simplified by an appropriate development of the Java language. To begin with, other distributed languages are analyzed and limits and possibilities of a distributed Java are derived. Subsequently, a concept is discussed that greatly simplifies the programming of distributed systems. Finally, the programming language "Dejay" – a distributed Java – is introduced, which builds on this concept, and illustrated with the aid of several examples.

The individual techniques are presented with the aid of practically relevant, yet simple examples. For a better comparison of related techniques, the same problem is solved in different chapters with the use of different techniques. Those parts of the program that actually stay the same are listed in the Appendix.

Target readership

This book originated in several seminars on the subjects of distribution, Internet, and Java at Hamburg University and the author's research work in the field of programming languages for distributed systems. It is addressed to different groups of readers:

- Students with previous knowledge of Java who are interested in the programming of distributed systems. The book can be very well used as accompanying material for a lecture, a practical course, or a seminar.

- Programmers who wish to take a look at different programming techniques for distributed systems. The book presents the current state of the art in the programming of distributed systems and provides a good possibility for comparison.

- Decision makers with a programming background who wish to get a feeling for the spectrum of different available alternatives for the design of a distributed system.

- Researchers who wish to get acquainted with the state of the art of this technology and want to get to know new, innovative techniques.

For all presented techniques, the most important concepts are listed and illustrated with the aid of simple examples. In no case is a programming interface covered in its whole breadth and depth. This book does not replace a reference manual. Instead, it offers what reference manuals cannot offer: a broad overview of a subject area in a reasonable depth.

Conventions

This is a book about Java; therefore, quite a lot of Java code will appear. Most examples have been kept as short as possible, to emphasize the essential aspect and not let it disappear in a jumble of code. Therefore most examples do not have a graphical interface, but work with the text console as an input and output medium.

Representation of code

Java code and identifiers, such as class or method names inside the text, for example when we talk about a TestClass, or source code fragments and screen input and output, are represented in a Sanserif font. Methods are quoted in the body text with empty parentheses (someMethod()), independently of whether they require parameters or not. When the text refers to specific areas in a source code fragment or an already quoted source code fragment is extended with some new lines, this text is in addition printed in **bold**.

```
class TestClass {
  public static void main (String[] args) {
    System.out.println("Hello World");
  }
}
```

Code segments whose width exceeds the normal body text or which go over several pages are enclosed in two horizontal lines.

Representation of input and output

Input, such as calls of the javac Java compiler, is marked with a prefixed greater than symbol.

```
> javac TestClass.java
```

Screen output of the system, which is often the result of screen input, is marked with a prefixed vertical bar.

```
> java TestClass
| Hello World
```

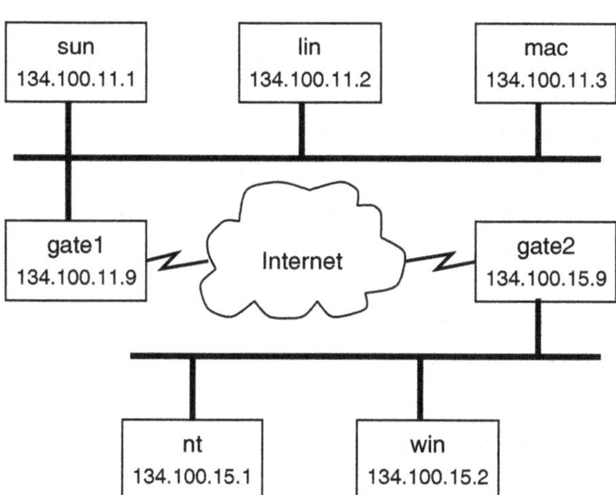

Figure 1 *Computers and network structure used in the examples.*

Since this book deals with distributed systems, many examples require several computers for the execution of one application. Therefore, we will be using a heterogeneous network, composed of two subnetworks connected via the Internet, and including different computers. In this sample network shown in Figure 1, the computers have a (fictitious) IP address and a name.

These names stand symbolically for different hardware platforms and the corresponding operating systems which were effectively available as test computers for the program samples. The names used are sun, lin, mac, nt and win, plus gate1 and gate2 as gateways into the Internet. Where necessary, these names or IP addresses are used in the text, in the program samples, and before items of input and output to differentiate between the machines. The following example, in which a message is sent from the sun computer to the lin computer and displayed there, illustrates this convention:

```
sun> java Talker
sun| sending Message "Hello World" to 134.100.11.2

lin> java Listener
lin| received Message "Hello World" from 134.100.11.1
```

Home page and source code

As it should be with a book in which the Internet plays a major role, this book has a home page which can be reached under the URL http://www.dpunkt.de/produkte/dejay. There you can find excerpts from this book, the presumably inevitable *errata*, plus the source code for the examples.

Dejay (a distributed Java which is presented in the second part of the book) has its own domain. Information, additional documentation, and the source code are freely available under http://www.dejay.org.

Acknowledgements

This book has been entirely produced with freely available software. The operating system employed was Linux with the newly developed KDE graphical user interface. As a text processing program, kLyX, a program that fully exploits the possibilities of LaTeX, but hides its complexity behind an easy to handle and helpful interface, has been of great value. The graphics were created with xfig. The programs were mainly created with Sun's JDK version 1.1.7 and are fully compatible with JDK 1.2 (or Java platform 2). For some chapters (Jini and parts of Tuplespaces), JDK 1.2 is required. I would like to thank all of the people who have been involved in the development of this software and made their knowledge and their skill available in such an unselfish way to the general public.

Most of this book originates from my teaching activities in the field of distributed systems at Hamburg University. A special mention goes to the practical course "Internet", the seminar "Objects in distributed systems", and the project seminar "Implementation of open distributed software applications". The many students who participated and taught me to teach, critically and constructively commented on my lessons, helped me with their own contributions, inspired me with new ideas and identified some bad ones, read my manuscripts, sought and found errors, reminded me of flaws and suggested improvements, all deserve a hearty thank you. Special thanks go to all those who have directly supported my work with their seminar papers and theses. A major role in the development of Dejay was played by Jan Raap, Thorsten Sturm, Tobias Baier, Nils Poppendiek, and Per Fragemann. A special mention goes to Marco Kaiser, who supported me strongly and reliably in many respects. For a critical review of the manuscript I would like to thank Prof Dr Claudia Linnhoff-Popien, Dr Christian Zeidler, Stefan Middendorf, and Uta Arnold.

Thanks go also to my colleagues of the distributed systems working group for a very good atmosphere, many talks and discussions, support and help. My deep respect is due to Prof Dr Winfried Lamersdorf who, with great commitment and farsightedness has allowed, accompanied, and fostered my work.

Finally, I would like to thank the team of dpunkt.verlag, in particular Christa Preisendanz, for good cooperation during the production of this book.

Hamburg, August 1999, Marko Boger

1 Introduction

"The Network is the Computer"
– Scott McNealy, CEO of Sun Inc.

Distributed software applications are difficult to develop. They are large and complex – but they are important and increasingly employed. Terms such as Internet, intranet and extranet, e-commerce and virtual private network prove that this is the case. Developers, however, struggle with the heterogeneity of hardware, high transmissions times during remote communication, failure and unreliability of system components, and many other problems.

At the end of the 80s, Sun wrote the motto "The Network is the Computer" on their banners. Their vision is to make networks and distributed systems as simple and reliable as we have become accustomed to from normal computers.

An essential corner stone on the way to this goal is Java. This language breathes the spirit of this vision. Java helps to reduce the complexity of distributed systems by integrating important mechanisms for programming of distributed systems directly into the language, and it overcomes the heterogeneity through its platform independence. Sun's youngest brainchild, Jini, too is an important step on the way to fulfilling this vision. In this book, building blocks from the Java environment, which are available to developers on this way, are introduced, from threads to Jini.

The introduction will first shed some light on the significance of Java and the significance of distributed systems. Subsequently, three aspects will be discussed that are to be blamed for the fact that distributed applications are so difficult to develop: concurrency, distribution, and persistence.

1.1 The significance of Java

Originally, when we first collected ideas for this book, the title was to have been "Objects in Distributed Systems". But, at a second look at the topics to be dealt with, most of them turned out to revolve around the Java language. We can no longer imagine object-oriented programming in distributed systems without Java.

Since its introduction as a Beta version in 1995, Java has experienced a boom similar to no other language. Java's popularity has a number of good reasons, the most frequently mentioned being portability, the security concept, and the browsing ability. With these three aspects alone, Java already offers advantages that have never before been combined in such a way in any other language and that make it appear as an almost ideal language for today's needs in the age of the Internet. In Java, programs can be written that can be downloaded from the Internet with a (Java-savvy) browser and run as applets within a Web document and that can, for example, manage the interaction with the user or the interactive representation of information.

Java for applets

But Java offers far more than this, as it is developing into a truly universal language which finds its application in many areas. It is no longer only used for animating Web pages, but extends its range of activity from programming of Smart Cards to large applications on high-performance parallel computers. Java has strongly established itself in the world of distributed systems.

Portability of Java

Java offers a decisive advantage for the development of distributed applications: Java is portable. Java code is independent from the hardware platform and can be distributed across a network, dynamically loaded and linked. Applications written in Java run on all kinds of platforms, from high-performance computers via PCs down to modern telephones or washing machines. Java also offers fundamental technics which are rather important for programming of distributed systems, such as a relatively simple connection to sockets, a simple mechanism for splitting concurrent threads (which, for

Integration of important techniques

example, listen to a socket port), and a mechanism for remote method invocation (RMI).

Java and the Internet

It is frequently stated that Java owes its popularity to the Internet. Usually, this does not mean the Internet as a whole, but its most popular part, the WWW, which is only one besides many other services such as e-mail or FTP. At the beginning of the WWW, static contents used to be described in HTML, the Hypertext Markup Language, and were made easily accessible by browsers supporting HTML. However, the emphasis lay on the word static. Although contents could be put relatively quickly on a Web server and called up online, these pages, as a mixture of graphics and text, were static under three aspects:

Applets for animating Web sites

First of all, graphic and text elements were firmly positioned relatively to each other. Except for the fact that one could change the size of the browser's window, the Web pages were as static as newspaper pages. Java attracted great attention and popularity with the animation of small graphics, similar to thumbnail movies, or with tickers, which can move text messages across the screen. This was made possible through applets, small applications that can be embedded in an HTML page and loaded and executed in the browser over the Internet. For a long time, Java had the fame of being a pure applet language which otherwise could not offer many new features.

Java for designing interaction

Secondly, HTML lacked the possibility of interaction. At first, the user could only follow specified links, that is, shortcuts in the sense of a hypertext system, which allowed the user to *browse* through the text structure provided. However, no data could be entered and transferred from the user back to the server, so no real interaction could take place. In a very short time, a quick and easy solution to this problem was found: FORMs were introduced in HTML, which allow simple ways of data input, such as the specification of a search string or a name, and the Common Gateway Interface (CGI) made it possible to transmit such data back to the server. These data can be interpreted on the server side by programs that have access to this CGI interface. At the beginning, these programs were mostly written in C, later in Perl,, a language which has now become the most popular CGI language. This form of interaction is, however, very limited, and remains restricted to simple text entry fields or simple buttons or switches. Here, Java offers a multitude of possibilities for creatively designing the user interface on the browser.

Most surprisingly, the importance of this did not seem quite clear to the developers of Java. The first version of the user interface control, the Abstract Windowing Toolkit (AWT), was hacked together in just a few weeks and had to be thoroughly revised from version 1.0 to version 1.1. Nevertheless, the achievement of the AWT developers should not be underestimated, since they had to find an abstract interface which could be implemented both on UNIX interfaces, such as X11 or Motif, and on Macintoshes and Windows PCs. After all, these interfaces were simple enough to allow plain user interfaces to be programmed quickly and elegantly, which accounted for one part of Java's popularity. But the demands on the power of graphic user interfaces increased quickly, so that a fundamental re-design became necessary. In the change from JDK 1.0 to 1.1 and then to 1.2, special attention was paid to this area. Today Swing, the successor of AWT, provides developers with a very powerful library with which very elegant and complex user interfaces can be created. However, the development goes on, and the next step can already be foreseen. Currently, techniques are being developed which allow the creation of so-called *thin clients* which can be loaded via a network and communicate with a server that manages and processes the application data. The swing components themselves are divided into a client side and a server side, which makes the clients' code size substantially smaller than that of complete applications and minimizes the communication effort with the remote server.

The third aspect, namely why HTML pages are static, has to do with the actual production of the pages. At the beginning of the WWW, HTML was programmed by hand. Applications were put on the market very quickly, with which it was possible to produce a layout of HTML pages in WYSIWYG style (what you see is what you get), so that production became faster and easier, but these generated pages too were stored and thus became static with regard to their content. To make the content itself dynamic, whether to be able to present the latest data on the Web page, or to be able to generate pages on purpose which could answer a query, HTML code must be generated by means of a program. This is frequently programmed in the same languages used to access the CGI interface, for example to create a reply to a query transmitted via CGI. Here too, Perl is very popular. Perl is an interpreted, untyped language which, despite simple language constructs, can reach enormous power. Complicated processes, such as the transformation of character strings from one format into another, can be described in only a few lines of code. Perl is very suitable for processing character strings, and thus also for production of HTML pages. However, Web sites are no longer what they used to be, namely simple text documents by researchers and statements by individualists in a virtual world, but have become serious applications and information media used to offer merchandise, carry out commercial transactions, and provide all sorts of services. Such applications are large and complex. Untyped languages such as Perl, and even typed, but not object-oriented languages such as C, are hardly suitable to make such applications manageable and serviceable. This is where Java is deemed to have a great potential – as a language which combines the advantage of object-orientation with suitable techniques for the Internet. Java is used to write Web applications on the serve side which are either embedded in HTML (Java Servers Pages) or which generate HTML code and pass it on to a Web server (servlets). And even Web servers themselves are written in Java.

Java on the server side

Thus, in many different ways, Java offers the possibility to turn the static WWW into a dynamic one: for an all-singing, all-dancing interactive and individually generated Web, thank Java. However, Java is not only used for the Internet, but it is also gaining more and more acceptance as a universal programming language in all application areas. Also, the definition "platform-independent" acquires a new meaning with Java. Frequently, this term is understood to mean that a program can be developed under UNIX and run on Windows and MacOS computers, which is certainly an important feature of

Java as a universal language

Java. But currently Java is no longer used only on PCs, but covers a spectrum from miniature devices to high-performance computers. This spectrum, which ranges from very small system sizes, such as chip cards, to massive parallel computers, and from systems close to the user, such as PCs, telephones or PDAs, to systems which are far from the user, such as controls or routers, is shown in Figure 1.1.

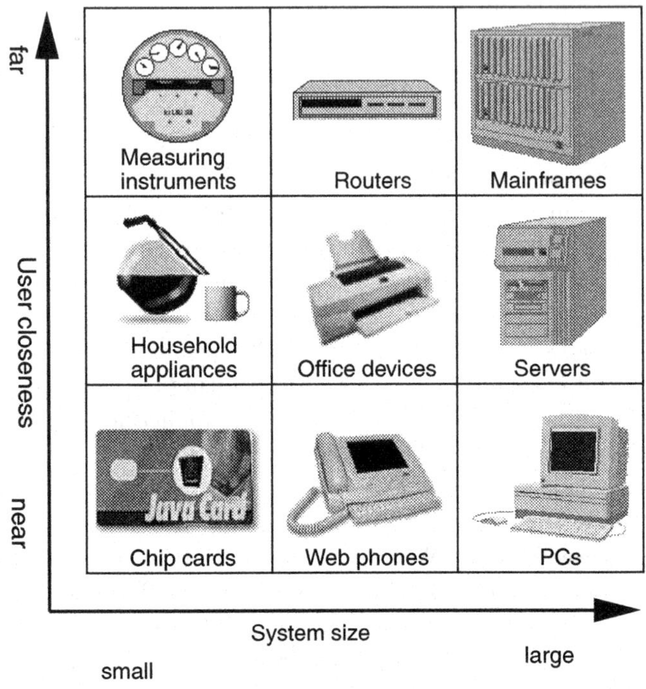

Figure 1.1 *Different computer-controlled systems, where Java finds its use.*

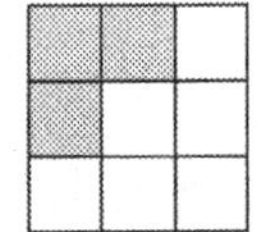

Java was first developed for small devices, ...

Originally, Java was developed to be used in small devices, such as top-boxes, measuring and control systems, and routers. In 1990, Sun Microsystems started a project named "Green Project", under the direction of James Gosling. At first, the project dealt with consumer electronics, interactive TV, and top-boxes, for which the OAK programming language was developed, which was to solve the problem of heterogeneity of these devices and which could be loaded onto these devices from a network. The Java language emerged from this project.

Java had its breakthrough in the PC world, that is, as shown in Figure 1.1, on the diametrally opposite side. The platform-independence, originally developed for small devices, made Java *the* language for the Internet because here, PCs with different architectures and practically unsurmountable system differences were used, which lacked a common programming language. The concept of the Java Virtual Machine which needs to be developed once for every platform, but then makes it possible that application programs need to be developed only once for this machine, allows the deep gaps between different hardware systems to be bridged. By integrating this virtual machine into Internet browsers, programs can be loaded from the Internet and started within a Web site. Initially, this made it possible to achieve some fancy effects, but the real advantage lies in the fact that finally a possibility had become available for the programming of clients.

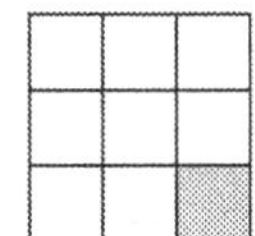

... then conquered the PC ...

After Java had taken the client side by storm, it is now slowly beginning to conquer the server side as well. Here, the advantage of platform-independence is no longer that important, because it is much easier to develop or port server programs to a dedicated platform, while the disadvantage of being slow is quite serious. However, with the aid of just-in-time compilers or platform-specific compilers, Java can slowly make up for this disadvantage. In the form of servlets, which can be loaded and called from an HTTP server before a corresponding tag is sent in an HTML page, Java again shows its full potential: servlets, like applets, can be loaded and linked dynamically via the Internet by means of URLs, but this time on the server side, and can thus produce Web information dynamically, for example.

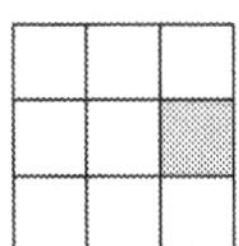

... and then the server.

However, Java is also present on devices as small as chip cards. A slimmed-down version of the Java Virtual Machine can run on a chip card and can then be programmed with Java independently from the manufacturer. Today, the ranges of application of the JavaCard concept are still limited by the slow execution time of Java byte code; thus, for example, cryptographic algorithms cannot yet be efficiently programmed on

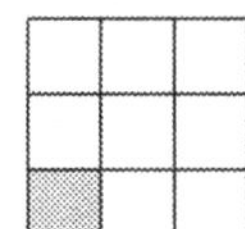

There is Java for chip cards, ...

the JavaCard. This technology is deemed to have a great potential in the foreseeable future.

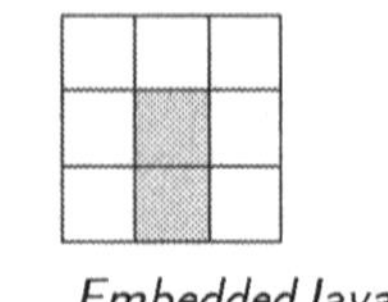

... EmbeddedJava and PersonalJava, ...

For somewhat larger devices, which can house a full processor but do not require the full functional range of Java, EmbeddedJava and PersonalJava were developed. In future, small devices such as household devices or office machines, which until now did not contain any or only highly specialized hardware, will be programmed with Java using the Java Chip. Typical application areas for these techniques include Web telephones, office and household appliances, as well as mobile devices.

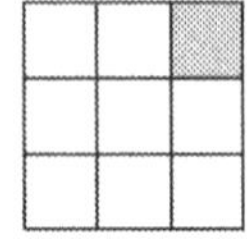

... and even Java for mainframes.

Today there are even projects to link mainframe computers into the Java world or to have Java itself run on mainframe computers. Although nowadays Java is still considered slow in execution and at first seems to have little to do with high-performance computing, it offers nevertheless a great potential for this. The Java Grande Forum, a consortium which pushes Java's further development into a high-performance language, places Java as the potentially best language existing so far for this area, even though there are still some problems to overcome.

Thus, Java is used on a very large spectrum of hardware platforms and finds ever greater diffusion and acceptance in all fields. However, this book is not only about programming of individual systems that can run in isolation on one of the many possible plattform, but it is about the cooperation of several program parts over a network: it is about programming of applications in distributed systems with Java.

1.2 The importance of distributed systems

Definition of a distributed system

This book defines a distributed system as a combination of several computers with separate memory, linked over a network, and on which it is possible to run a distributed application. Computers in the context of this book are understood as devices on which at least one Java Virtual Machine exists and which are capable of communicating over a network. This network is usually stable, even if single devices may fail (for example by switching them off), and the devices should each have a permanent identification within the network. A reconfiguration of the system takes place in a controlled way and not spontaneously, as is the case with mobile systems.

Definition of a distributed application

A distributed application is an application which consists of several parts of a program communicating with each other, which cooperate to carry out a common task. Typically, but not necessarily, the parts of the application are distributed across several computers. The distribution can also be simulated on one computer. In this case, however, information is not transmitted via a common memory or address space, but with the aid of techniques of remote communication.

Until the beginnig of the 80s, most computer systems were centralized mainframe installations, which different users could access via a text terminal. With the introduction of personal computers, these were at first replaced by single-user workstations, which provided the individual user with a cheaper and easier-to-use computer, but which cut them off from the possibility of using shared resources, such as central printers or communication via the computer. The development of technologies for networking such PCs finally made the construction of local networks possible. Even in the field of high-performance computing, the trend is moving from large central systems to networked distributed systems.

Advantages of distributed systems

Distributed systems, as opposed to centralized systems, have a whole series of advantages, some of which will be mentioned here:

Inherent parallelism

- In distributed systems, many computers can work together at the solution of a problem simultaneously. The prerequisite for this to happen is that a task can be split into a number of small subtasks and can therefore be handled in parallel. Obviously, there are also centralized parallel computers which can handle this type of task, but these are extremely expensive and specialized. PCs, on the other hand, can nowadays be found on almost every office desk, are often networked, and do nothing throughout most of the day. This potential can be used by distributed applications. For example, moving images or cryptographic problems can be solved elegantly by computer collectives or by computer clusters connected spontaneously over the Internet.

Scalability

- Distributed systems are much easier to scale, compared to centralized systems: in central systems, where the work is carried out by large and expensive specialized computers, as it is still frequently the case in many computer centers of banks, meteorological institutes or industrial enterprises, an increase of computing power as a reaction to rising demands will usually not be able to exceed a factor of 2. On the other hand, in distributed systems, computer nodes can be added or removed, according to the needs.

Resource sharing

- In distributed systems, expensive resources such as printers, or centralized resources such as databases, can be used by many decentralized devices.

Fault tolerance through replication

- Distributed systems can increase reliability through replication. Computers in critical installations, which must not fail under any circumstances, such as flight control systems, can be protected by a second computer which carries out the same calculations. If the main computer fails, the second computer steps in and immediately carries on with the critical calculations.

Inherent distribution

- In many applications, distribution is simply a natural feature of the application. In chemical process control facilities, or in traffic control systems, data are gathered at different measuring facilities and transferred to central computers, only to be sent back again to distributed regulators, which are often located in the vicinity of the original measuring stations. Through a distributed *processing* of such data, communication cost and complexity of such applications can be greatly reduced.

Current distributed systems are often very expensive and highly specialized facilities. This is an aspect that Java will change.

Using Java and the Java chip, it will be possible to connect even very simple and cheap devices to a communication network and assign them independent processing units and programs. Thus, for example, light switches and sensors in a household or office could communicate with the heating control or the automatic illumination of a building. The application areas of distributed systems are numerous. Distributed applications are developed and employed, for example, in the fields of electronic commerce, automation techniques and workflow control systems, as well as in computer-supported cooperative work (CSCW).

Integration of highly different systems

Also, as the degree of networking increases, the necessary infrastructure becomes better and cheaper and advances into more and more areas. Besides the Internet, other networks are being created which work with the same techniques as the Internet. Corporate networks closed to the general public, the so-called Intranets,, provide a fast, reliable and secure communication infrastructure within enterprises. Special networks, called Extranets are also set up between branch offices of global organizations, or between cooperating companies. But the same techniques are increasingly used even in very small networks. Nowadays, in a modern car, for example, you will find up to 50 individual processors, which are partly connected and communicate with each other through so-called Controller Area Networks (CAN) .

1.3 Concurrency, distribution, and persistence

Development and programming of distributed systems are substantially more complex than the programming of local applications, as they are typically used on standard workstations. Of course, even the development of sequential programs is quite complex, but through distribution, several dimensions of complexity are added. While local sequential programs can be executed only on exactly one computer, be controlled only by one single user, and their data can be stored in a file without major difficulties, distributed applications run on several

Complexity of distributed applications

spatially distributed computers, need to communicate over a relatively slow and potentially unsecure network, are used by several users simultaneously, and access and security of shared data need to be secured through transactions, and a consistent central or distributed data management needs to be guaranteed.

This book addresses three of these aspects in particular: concurrency, distribution, and persistence.

Concurrency is the actual or apparent parallelism of control flows. Concurrency can occur either between different processors, as in a multi-processor system, or on a single processor. Modern processor architectures allow several processes to be executed simultaneously on one processor. Obviously, these processes do not really run simultaneously, but are allocated staggered time slices of the processor's computing time. For the user, however, these processes appear to be running in parallel. There are two types of such processes. On the one hand, they can be completely isolated from each other, so that they each have a separate execution environment. In this case, they are called heavyweight processes. On the other hand, several control flows can be processed within one execution context, the so-called lightweight processes, which can cooperate with each other through a common address space. In Java, lightweight processes, known here under the name of threads, have received a user-friendly integration: programmers can immediately produce and manage them within the language. On the other hand, several processors can nowadays be integrated into a computer system by modern computer architectures and operating systems, which gives rise to a real parallelism. Concurrency shall be understood in this context as a generic term for apparent or simulated parallelism obtained through several processes, and real parallelism obtained by using several processors.

Distribution is the logical or physical spatial distance of objects from each other. Two objects, which cannot use the ordinary method invocation for their communication, but need to employ mechanisms of remote communication, are distributed with respect to each other. This is the case when they are located on different computers and therefore are spatially separated. But also when they are located on the same computer, but in different address spaces (in different heavyweight processes), they are (logically) distributed. Obviously, different objects that have nothing to do with each other, but are located on several computers, are also distributed with respect to each other, but are of no great significance for us. Here, distribution shall be understood as the separation of objects that stand in relation to each other. Between these, there is the problem of how they can locate each other, access each other, and communicate with each other.

Persistence is the long-term storage of data or objects on non-volatile media. Data or objects, which are not explicitly saved in some form or the other, no longer exist after a program is terminated. They are described as transient. However, much data needs to be retained, even when the program is terminated or the computer is shut down. Therefore, such data needs to be stored in some way or other in order to be available again when the computer is re-started. In this case, we speak about persistent data or objects. Persistence achieves the distribution of data or objects in time.

These three aspects of distributed programming are relatively independent from each other and are dealt with using totally different techniques. Therefore, we could describe them as being orthogonally related to each other and talk about dimensions. Nevertheless, at least in many cases, they must be dealt with simultaneously. These three dimensions are shown in Figure 1.2.

Techniques for all three subject areas will be presented in this book. With regard to concurrency, Java threads, basic problems and techniques of synchronization, as well as frequent

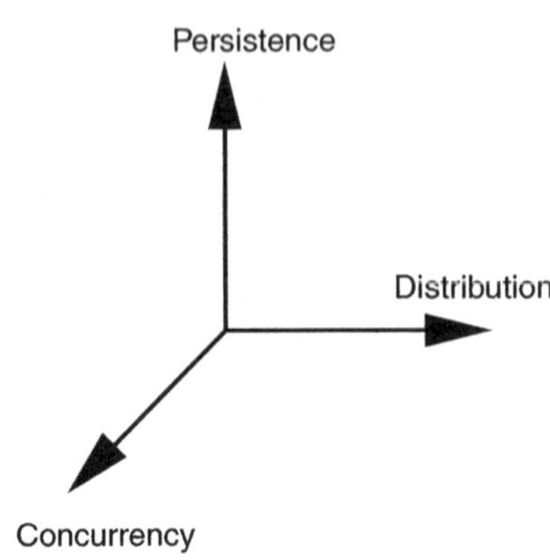

Figure 1.2 *Dimensions of distributed programming.*

patterns of concurrency, as they often occur in distributed systems, will be explained.

Distribution or, we should say, how to overcome it, is the main topic of this book. The communication of programs in distributed systems can be solved in extremely different ways which, in the end, all boil down to the same thing: in the last analysis, bits and bytes are shifted across a network. However, this simple data communication can be abstracted on different levels. On the lowest level, we find the mechanism of transmitting data streams via *sockets*. Here, data is transferred from one computer to another, without further interpretation. All subsequent mechanisms build on this one; however, they confer specific semantics to the transmitted data and relieve programmers from a large part of work, so they can concentrate better on their real tasks. From the programmer's point of view, it is preferable not to have to communicate from one computer to another, but from object to object, as it happens in object-oriented programming. This mechanism is *RMI*, the Remote Method Invocation, which will be presented subsequent to the sockets. However, this mechanism only works when the same semantics is used on both sides, which means i practice that the same language must be used and the location of the remote object is known. When you abstract further and conceal location and language of a remote object, you arrive at *CORBA*, the Common Object Request Broker Architecture. Here, the programmer can use a remote object without knowing where

Abstraction levels of remote communication: ... Data transmission, ...

... Remote Method Invocation, ...

... transparency of location and language, ...

it is and in which language it has been implemented. The next step of abstraction consists in the possibility of changing the position of an object at runtime, which is described as migration. A system which makes this possible is *Voyager*, which can do much more than this, but is presented here specifically under this aspect. And when objects not only let themselves be moved, but do so on their own (autonomously), we talk about *mobile agents*, which will be introduced in two variations.

... migration of objects, ...

... up to autonomous migration.

Fundamentally, there are three techniques for permanent storage of data, that is, for persistence. The most basic one, the simple storage of serialized data streams into files, will not be treated here. The most widely diffused and reliable technology is represented by relational databases which store data in tables that can be connected with each other. These permit the search for data through structured enquiries with SQL. They also permit the coordination of access by several users and the compliance with the so-called ACID principles (Atomicity, Consistency, Isolation, Durability). For Java, access to relational databases is standardized by the Java Database Connectivity (JDBC). However, the storage of data in tables means a rupture with object-oriented programming languages which no longer deal with data, but with encapsulated objects. To avoid this, object-oriented databases were developed which fit much more seamlessly into languages such as Java. Finally we will examine whether persistence can be integrated as an integral part into a programming environment such as Java. If this works out well for all data elements, it is described as orthogonal persistence, which is currently being put into practice in the PJama project.

Techniques of persistence: ...

relational, ...

... object-oriented ...

... and orthogonal.

These three dimensions and their respective techniques are pointed out in Figure 1.3 and represent the structure of the first part of the book. At the end of the first part, tuple spaces will be described as yet another technique that presents elements of all three dimensions. Finally, an infrastructure is presented which enormously simplifies the localization of services in distributed systems and thus solves one of the most essential prerequisites for distributed applications – the Java Intelligent Networking Infrastructure, in short Jini.

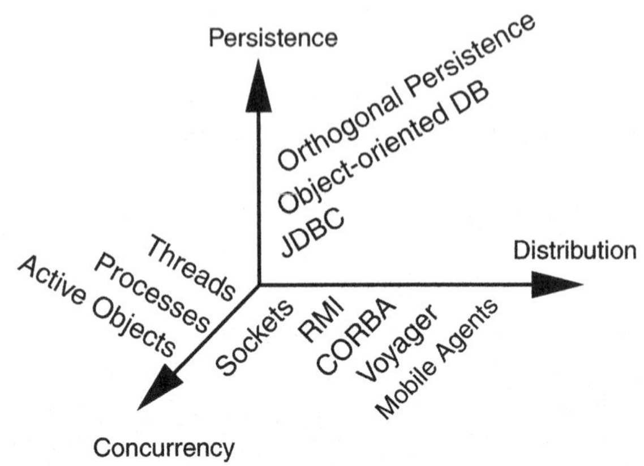

Figure 1.3
The subjects of the first part of this book.

In the second part, a possible way to unify the three dimentions will be shown. To clarify this, an analogy with the origin of object-oriented programming languages will be put forward. In procedural programming, for example with languages such as Pascal or C in their original forms in which at first purely sequential and local programs were developed, we can also recognize three dimensions, which had to be coped with in the same way, using different techniques. These are

data structure, which is built out of base types, arrays, structs, and records,

functionality, which is established in procedures, and

modularity, which is expressed in files, program packages, and libraries.

These three dimensions were combined into one concept by object-orientation – the class. A class (strictly speaking its instance, the object) contains a data structure and links it inseparably with its functionality, which is also described as encapsulation, representing at the same time a mechanism for modularization. The combination of the previously separated three aspects into a single concept considerably simplified programming, setting free capacities for dealing with new aspects, such as concurrency, distribution, and persistence. We are not

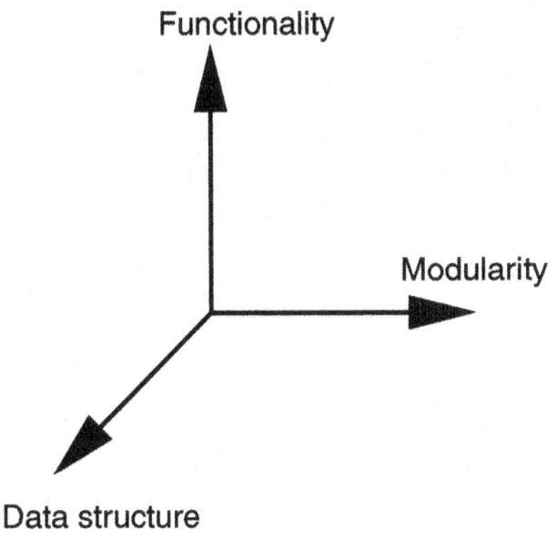

Figure 1.4 *Dimensions of procedural local programming.*

saying that this would not be possible using procedural languages, but object-oriented languages have proved more productive and of easier maintenance for such complex areas. If we now succeed in combining these three aspects, concurrency, distribution, and persistence, in one concept as well, this could mean a further considerable simplification of programming, especially for distributed applications which are perceived as very difficult to program. A concept which eventually makes this possible and which has been put into practice in a Java dialect will be introduced in the second part of the book.

1.4 References

This book presents a wide spectrum of techniques used to develop distributed applications. However, distributed applications are highly complex and have many aspects which cannot be all considered here. For these topics, you need to refer to specific literature.

A topic which finds much too little space in this book for the importance it has is the problem of security. This is a very difficult and multi-faceted topic, which deserves to be dealt with in specific books and would by far exceed the scope of this book. Furthermore, security is not a self-contained subject, orthogonally related to the other topics such as concurrency, distribution, and persistence, but it is a topic which is ubiquitous and deeply interwoven with all three areas and requires permanent attention, and great experience and care. Aspects of security in general are discussed in [Birman 1996], special aspects of Java in [Oaks 1998].

An aspect which is only marginally touched in this book is the mobility of devices. A variety of mobile devices are quickly entering the market, from simple devices such as pagers, the ubiquitous mobile telephone, down to pocket-size, fully-fledged PCs. These will increasingly establish themselves in the world of distributed systems, and will become integral components of distributed applications. In many ways, they can be considered as perfectly normal devices in a distributed system. But mobile devices have some peculiar features and constraints, such as higher communication costs, temporary accessibility, limited memory capacity and computing power, and the need for different forms of interaction due to their usually reduced size, which will not be dealt with any further in this book.

We will also only marginally deal with the underlying techniques of data communication and data transmission. This area is at present undergoing an incredible expansion, which will enormously accelerate the diffusion of an infrastructure so essential for distributed systems. Thus, for example, new solutions for the problem of the "last mile" are in sight, for example by transmission over power supply systems available in every household and over easy-to-install radio LANs. Satellite communication makes this infrastructure ubiquitous on a worldwide scale. For an overview of network technology, [Siegmund 1999] is highly recommended.

The discussion about algorithms for distributed systems has also found only little space in this book. Here, you should refer to the books by [Lynch 1993] and [Tel 1994].

Finally, this book presupposes a certain familiarity with the Java programming language. Readers who would first like to get acquainted with the subject matter are recommended to read [Winston and Narasimhan 1996] as an easy introduction, [Eckel 1998] as an extensive textbook, and [Middendorf and Singer 1999] as textbook and reference. Current experiences with Java are documented in [Maffais *et al.* 1999].

Part I

Java in Distributed Systems

2 Concurrency in Java

Concurrency is often described in the literature as a topic associated with operating systems or computer architecture and it is therefore dealt with in the context of the corresponding lectures and textbooks. Concurrency, at operating system level, has always been considered necessary for the administration of resources used by several processes, such as fixed storage media or printers. Concurrency appeared closely linked to computer architectures which support parallel processing, for example in parallel computers with several CPUs or vector processors with several arithmetic units within one CPU.

This has changed with Java. Concurrency, in the form of lightweight processes is directly supported in Java, independently from the hardware and the operating systems on which the Java Virtual Machine is running. Concurrency has become a topic for software engineering. The complexity of programming of concurrency has been considerably reduced with Java. Programs in which concurrency is required can be developed with Java on one platform and be used on a different one.

Application areas for concurrency

Concurrency is used in different contexts and to solve different tasks:

- In modern operating systems, simultaneous execution of several programs on one computer is possible. Mostly, this happens with one heavyweight process each per program. When executing several Java programs on a Java Virtual Machine, however, lightweight processes are split off.

- Mutually independent tasks within one program can be processed in parallel relatively easily. It is true that no acceleration is achieved (when using one CPU), but the CPU is not blocked by major tasks until the task has been completed. In this way, for example, high-quality word-processing programs can simultaneously prepare for printing, carry out the spelling check, and display the help system.

- A task that can be subdivided into several partial tasks is carried out faster in parallel, by splitting it across several CPUs. This obviously requires suitable hardware, but thanks to modern chip architecture and operating systems, multiprocessor systems are increasingly used as servers and desktop workstations. The art lies, however, in splitting the problem into subtasks, which are ususally not completely independent from each other and therefore require an increased effort of coordination.

- Processes in blocking wait states which are, for example, waiting for an external event, can be isolated from the main control flow, so that this can carry on functioning. This occurs quite frequently in distributed systems and will be illustrated with the aid of several sample programs in the course of the book.

- Interactive programs are a special case of a situation where waiting processes appear very frequently. The program waits for the user's input, but it also needs to carry on with its other activities. Without the possibility of expressing concurrency in the language, interactive programs are substantially more complicated to develop.

Working with concurrency is not a simple matter and there are good reasons why it has so far been left to the experts. Concurrency is full of hidden traps which are unknown in sequential programming.

For simple tasks, Java offers simple solutions, for example for the creation of a new lightweight process, but the difficulty lies in working out the details, and the combination of simple tasks quickly turns into a series of highly complex problems.

Thus, the complexity does not (any longer) lie in the programming interface, but in the matter itself. The following is a list of problems which may be encountered:

Problems caused by concurrency

- When at the same time one of two (or more) processes wishes to access a resource which is reserved by the other process and vice versa, we reach what is described as a *deadlock*. For example, if process A keeps a resource x reserved and needs the resource y to continue, which is kept by process B, which in turn is waiting for x, and if no other mechanism is provided to prevent and solve deadlocks, both process A and process B will become blocked in their waiting states.

- *Livelocks* are a related problem. In a livelock, a process is waiting for an event which will not occur or for a resource which will never be provided. A process A checks a condition c, until the condition is fulfilled. If this is never fulfilled, A is blocked and will not make any further progress.

- If a resource is available but is not equally distributed, we use the term *unfairness*. This may even be a desired effect. If, for example, process A requires resource x for a longer period of time, while processes B and C also need x, but each time only for a short time, it is more sensible that processes B and C will be given precedence over A, so that the system as a whole makes faster progress, even though this means that A is going to be treated unfairly. However, if too many processes are allowed precedence over A so that A cannot make any progress and is practically left without resources, this causes a problem, called *starvation*.

- The result of computing operations can depend on the sequence of the execution of different processes. In this case, we speak of a *race condition*. Such errors are difficult to detect, since they appear only occasionally (transient faults) and the execution sequence is nondeterministic.

The example of the dining philosophers ...

Edsger W. Dijkstra has presented a problem in which many of these issues can occur simultaneously: the *dining philosophers* problem. Five philosophers are sitting around a table. A bowl of rice is on the table, and one chopstick is between every two philosophers. To eat the rice, the philosophers need to use both the left and the right chopsticks. When they are no longer hungry, they put the chopsticks back and begin to think, until they get hungry again and start once more to get hold of the chopsticks.

... demonstrates many of these problems.

The following problems may arise. If every philosopher takes the right chopstick, so that none of them can take a left stick any longer, a deadlock occurs. If one or more philosophers who got hold of two chopsticks put them back only after a longer time, this creates an unfair distribution of the food. If a philosopher does not put his chopsticks back at all, or a philosopher always lacks either the right or left chopstick, a philosopher may suffer starvation. Naturally, in an implementation, the chopsticks are not physically present, but are represented by a data object. When two philosophers reach for the same chopstick simultaneously and neither of them succeeds in time to register in the data object that it has been assigned, they will both be under the impression that they own this chopstick – and we have a program error through a *race condition*.

This problem of the five philosophers is frequently discussed in the literature and is considered a standard example of the problems occurring with concurrency. For various implementations in Java see [Hartley 1998], for example.

2.1 Threads in Java

Java supports concurrency in the language itself with the aid of lightweight processes. In most languages used previously, this was possible only by direct access to operating system libraries, which made working difficult and portability next to impossible. Java enables concurrency not only independently from the platform and with immediate language support, but also makes things fairly simple.

The core of this concept is the class java.lang.Thread. This class enables us to start, to interrupt, to wake up, to slow down, to accelerate and to terminate a lightweight process. A handful of other useful classes, such as the Runnable interface, help with the use of this class. The concept is supported by methods which are defined in the parent class of all objects, java.lang.Object, as well as through two keywords, synchronized and volatile, which are an integral part of the language.

Lightweight processes are often described as threads, a term intended to refer to the "control thread". This term is also common in Java and will be used in the following text. There are two possibilities for creating a new thread. The simpler way consists in deriving a class from the Thread class and creating an instance of this derived class. The inheriting class must mandatorily implement the run() method. This method, which is called by the system, must specify what is to be executed in the new thread. It represents the root method of this thread. After the creation of an instance, the start() method must be called, which causes a new thread to be split off within the system and the run() method to be started in this thread. Parameters to be passed to this new thread cannot be passed through run(), but only through the constructor of the derived class of Thread.

Two ways to create threads:

by inheritance ...

```
class ExampleThread extends Thread {
  int parameter;
  ExampleThread (int param) {
    parameter=param;
  }
  public void run() {
    // what should the new thread perform?
    ...
  }
  public static void main(String[] args) {
    // instantiating and starting the sample thread
    ExampleThread t = new ExampleThread(42);
    t.start();
  }
}
```

Since this procedure makes use of inheritance, and Java allows only simple inheritance, a second variation is needed, which avoids direct inheritance. A thread can also be created without having to resort to inheritance. However, in order to know what it is supposed to execute, the thread needs a class which contains a run() method. For this purpose, a class is written which implements the available Runnable interface. This interface marks the class as one that contains the run() method, so that the thread can call it. An instance of this class can be passed to its constructor during creation of a thread, and this in turn calls the run() method. In this way, it is possible to assign a thread to a class which inherits from an arbitrary class.

... and by passing.

```
class ExampleRunnable extends SomeClass implements Runnable {
  int parameter;

  ExampleRunnable (int param) {
    parameter=param;
  }

  public void run() {
    // what should the new thread perform?
    ...
  }

  public void main(String[] args) {
    // instantiating Runnable and starting the thread
    ExampleRunnable r = new ExampleRunnable(42);
    new Thread(r).start();
  }
}
```

The Thread class makes it possible to access the state of this thread and to affect it. With sleep(), a thread can be delayed for a given time. By calling the suspend() method, it is interrupted for an unspecified time, and by calling the resume()method, it can be woken up and reactivated.

A simple program will be introduced to demonstrate threads. The example used here is an algorithm which checks whether a number n is a prime number or not. The algorithm used is based on a procedure which was developed in ancient times by the Greek philosopher *Eratosthenes* and is therefore known as the *Sieve of Eratosthenes.* This procedure is frequently mentioned in the literature on concurrency and parallel programming, see for example [Chandy and Misra 1996]. The algorithm generates a list of all numbers that may be used as divisor of the number to be checked, takes the smallest prime number known to it and eliminates all multiples of this number from the list. At the end, only prime numbers remain in the list, which can then be output. This procedure is represented visually in Figure 2.1. The set of numbers to be considered trickle like grains of sand through a sieve. If the number to be checked falls all the way through the sieve, then it is a prime number, otherwise it is not. The sieve consists of several filters which filter out the multiples of a prime number from the set of numbers. If a number falls through all of the filters, then it has no divisor but itself and one and is therefore a prime number.

Sieve of Eratosthenes

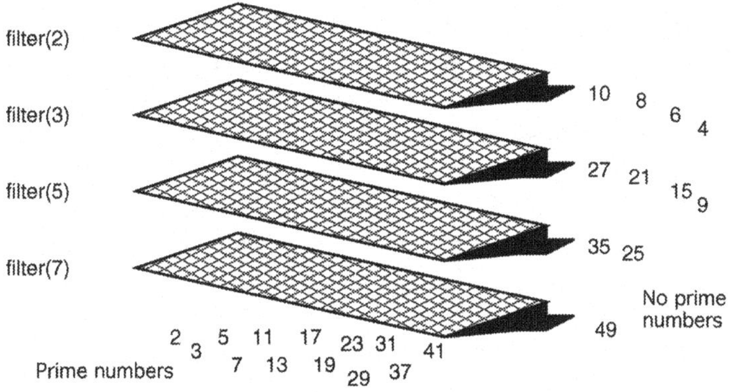

Figure 2.1 *Calculation of the Sieve of Eratosthenes.*

This procedure is now implemented with the PrimCalculator and Sieve classes. The PrimCalculator class starts with an arbitrary int-number as argument and applies the isPrim() method to it. This creates a sieve and follows the procedure described above.

```
public class PrimCalculator {

  public boolean isPrim(int n) {
    Sieve sieve = new Sieve(n+1);
    return sieve.isPrim(n);
  }

  public static void main(String[] args){
    int n = Integer.parseInt(args[0]);
    boolean result = (new PrimCalculator()).isPrim(n);
    System.out.println("Value "+ n +" is" + (result?"":" not") +" a prim");  }
}
```

The Sieve class generates a BitSet in which each number is represented by one bit and in which initially all bits are set (apart from the bit for 0 and 1, which are not dealt with by the algorithm). The isPrim() method now uses the filter() method to eliminate all multiples of 2, then fetches the next prime number with the aid of the nextPrimAfter() method and carries on in this way. It terminates when the numerator is greater than the number to be checked, since a divisor cannot be greater than the root of this number. Finally, a check is made as to whether the bit for the number to be checked is still set or not. If this is the case, it is a prime number, otherwise it is not.

```
public class Sieve {
  private int number;
  private int rootN;
  private java.util.BitSet bitset;

  public Sieve (int N) {
    number = N;
    rootN = (int) Math.sqrt((double) number);
    bitset = new java.util.BitSet (N);
```

```
    // Preparing the list of numbers
    for (int i=2; i < number; i++) {
      bitset.set(i);
    }
  }

  public boolean isPrim(int n) {
    for (int aPrim=2; aPrim<=rootN; aPrim=nextPrimAfter(aPrim)) {
      filter(aPrim);
    }
    return bitset.get(n);
  }

  // delete all multiples of prim from the set of numbers
  private void filter(int prim) {
    int counter = prim;
    while (counter<=number){
      bitset.clear(counter);
      counter = counter + prim;
    }
  }

  // find the next prime number after prim
  private int nextPrimAfter(int prim) {
    int i = prim+1;
    while(!bitset.get(i) && prim < number) {
      i++;
    }
    return (i);
  }
}
```

Parallelization of the algorithm

Until now, this program was purely sequential. But the algorithm can be improved in different ways when using threads. At first, it should be modified in such a way as to check several numbers concurrently. To do so, the mechanism described above is not changed, but only triggered repeatedly. For this purpose, the PrimCalculator class is turned into a class that supports threads and started repeatedly by its own main() method.

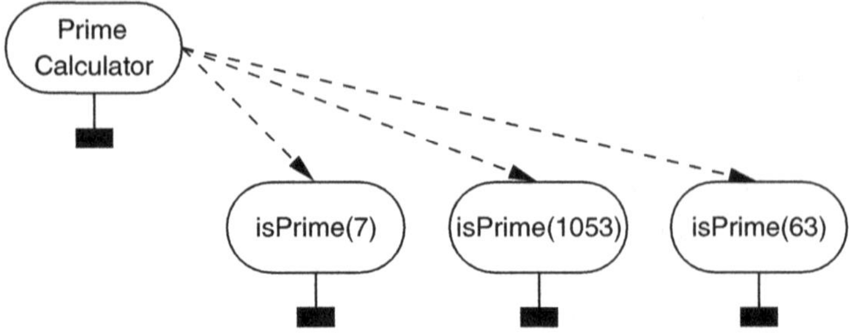

Figure 2.2 *PrimCalc with several threads.*

```
public class PrimCalculator extends Thread {
  int n;
  PrimCalculator (int n) {
    this.n = n;
  }

  public void run() {
    Sieve sieve = new Sieve(n+1);
    boolean result = sieve.isPrim(n);
    System.out.println("Value "+ n +" is" + (result?"":" not") +" a prime");
  }
  public static void main(String[] args) {
    for(int i=0; (i<args.length); i++){
      int n = Integer.parseInt(args[i]);
      (new PrimCalculator(n)).start();
    }
  }
}
```

When calling this version, an arbitrary number of different numbers can now be specified. For each argument, a new thread is started which checks for the prime property of this number.

```
sun> java PrimCalculator 7 1057 983 63
sun| Value 7 is  a prime
```

```
sun| Value 63 is not a prime
sun| Value 983 is  a prime
sun| Value 1057 is not a prime
```

However, until now, only a parallelization of different tasks has been achieved. It should be noted that the results are not ouput in the order in which the corresponding threads have been started. On the whole, the calculation is not carried out faster, however, some results can be already output while others are still being calculated. The check for number 63, for example, which would be checked as the last number in sequential processing, does not need to wait in concurrent processing until 983 and 1057 have been processed, but is checked simultaneously and, since the process takes less time for 63, the result is available sooner.

The sequence of output depends on the operating system used. In operating systems which do not support any preemptive multi-tasking, threads are completely processed one after the other in the order in which they have been created. Since the Java Virtual Machine cannot be better than the underlying operating system, the Java standard does not prescribe any implementation either. This is what causes different behavior of Java programs on different platforms.

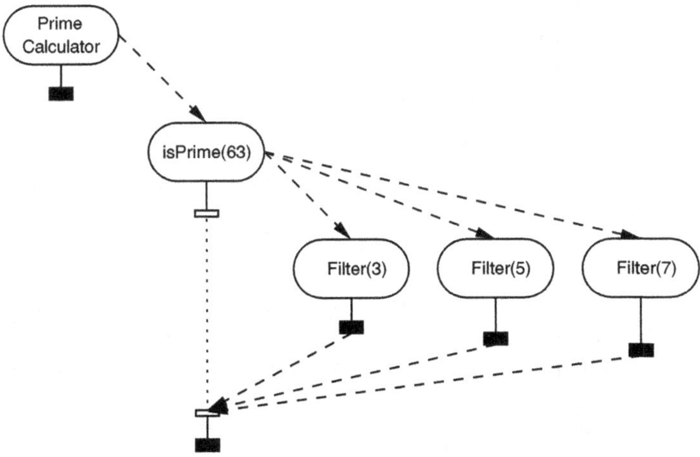

Figure 2.3
PrimCalc with internal parallelism.

Would it now be possible to parallelize the calculation itself? To achieve this, we introduce a new mechanism into the calculation. Filtering out the multiples of a prime number from the set of numbers is now taken over by a new class, the filter. Every new filter is executed in its own thread, so that the multiples of 3, 5, 7, 11, 13, etc. are filtered out simultaneously. Until now, this filering was carried out sequentially by the Sieve class, by calling the filter() method. We will now change this mechanism and execute a new filter with its own thread for every new prime number. To do this, the following Filter class is used. In order to demonstrate the second method of starting a thread, too, this class does not inherit from Thread, but implements the Runnable interface.

```
public class Filter implements Runnable{

  int prim;
  java.util.BitSet bitset;
  int number;

  public Filter(int p, java.util.BitSet b, int n) {
    prim=p;
    bitset=b;
    number=n;
  }

  public void run(){
    int counter = prim;
    while (counter < number){
      bitset.clear(counter);
      counter = counter + prim;
    }
  }
}
```

Evidently, the Sieve class must now be adapted in order to create and start this filter. The question of whether a number is a prime number or not can obviously be answered only after all filters have completed their task, as shown in Figure 2.3.

Thus the thread in which the isPrim() method runs must wait for the filter threads to terminate. There are a number of possibilities for this: for example, the Thread class provides a method named join(), which blocks the calling thread, until the thread for which this method was called is terminated. However, since we need to wait for many threads and not just for one, we will choose another mechanism. Java provides the possibility of managing threads in groups, called ThreadGroups. Threads can be assigned to such a ThreadGroup and then managed together. For example, it is possible to determine the number of currently active threads in a group. We will choose this mechanism to wait for the termination of all filters: we create a ThreadGroup and assign every filter of a sieve to this group. When the number of threads in this group is zero, the result can be read out.

ThreadGroup

```
// in class Sieve ...
public boolean isPrim(int n) {
  ThreadGroup group = new ThreadGroup("Filter"+n);
  for (int aPrim=2; aPrim<=rootN; aPrim=nextPrimAfter(aPrim)) {
    Filter filter = new Filter(aPrim, bitset,number);
    (new Thread(group,filter)).start();
  }
  System.out.println("Started "+group.activeCount() +" Filter");
  while (group.activeCount() > 0) {
    try {Thread.sleep(100);} catch (InterruptedException e) {}
  }
  return bitset.get(n);
}
```

Thus we finally arrive at the following output, which shows the concurrency in this example:

```
lin> java PrimCalculator 171 83
lin| Started Thread for 171
lin| Started Thread for 83
lin| Started 12 Filter
lin| Started 8 Filter
lin| Value 171 is not a prime
lin| Value 83 is a prime
```

2.2 Synchronization mechanisms

As we have seen, the creation of new threads is relatively simple in Java. However, the temporal synchronization of threads and the synchronization of access to shared data or other resources is a difficult matter. A variety of synchronization techniques is available, but the right choice requires skill and experience. We will now present some of these techniques.

2.2.1 Monitors

A monitor is a critical section, which may always be entered only by one caller. Monitors are supported directly by Java and are built directly into the language. Every object in Java is assigned one monitor. Methods which should fall under the management of this monitor are labeled with the keyword synchronized.

```
public class ExampleMonitor {

  public synchronized int exclusiveMethod() {
  // what should the exclusive method do?
  ...
  }

  public int reentrantMethod() {
  // this method can be used several times simultaneously
  ...
  }
}
```

If the exclusiveMethod() method is called by several threads, then only one thread at a time can be processed. All other processes must wait and are managed in an internal queue of the object. On the other hand, if the reentrantMethod() method is called repeatedly, all calls can enter the object without obstacles.

2.2.2 Semaphores

Semaphores are a special type of counter variable which represent one of the most important, well-known and common mechanisms for synchronization. They are very flexible and powerful; all other synchronization mechanisms can be implemented with semaphores. However, they are also very sensitive to errors, and errors in synchronization can be fatal and bring a whole system to a total lock. They are a fundamental constituent for synchronization; however, one should generally rather use higher concepts, such as monitors or ReadWrite-Locks, which will be introduced in the following section.

Semaphores were initially developed by Dijkstra. A semaphore contains a fixed number of tags, which are frequently interpreted as entry ticket or permission. These tags are represented by the counter variable. To access an area protected by semaphores, a tag needs to be taken. If there was a tag and it was taken, the counter variable is decremented. If no tags are available (the counter variable is zero), the caller waits until a tag is put back into the semaphore. By putting the tag back, the counter variable is incremented. A very clear (and also frequently occurring) situation are semaphores with exactly one tag. In this case, only one caller can enter the critical section, and only after this caller has put the tag back can the next caller enter the area. Such semaphores are also called binary semaphores or locks.

In the original version of Dijkstra's semaphore, the methods to take a tag and put it back are called P() and V(), a notation frequently used also in the literature. Dijkstra is Dutch, and P and V stand for the Dutch words "proberen" and "verhogen". These names and their abbreviations are quite unfortunate and (for non-Dutch speakers) not really self-explanatory. The semaphores used here are based on a collection of classes to be used for synchronization by Doug Lea, who makes them available publicly and free of charge. In [Lea 1998], these methods are called acquire() and release(). This collection contains more than 60 classes and is highly recommended to everybody dealing with synchronization. Part of this library is used here and will also be briefly discussed.

Because of its great importance, the interface that provides the Semaphore class will be presented in more detail and excerpts of it will be listed further below. It should be noted that Semaphore itself is implemented as a monitor in which some methods are exclusive, while others may be entered repeatedly. When creating a semaphore, the number of tags (called *permits* in the program listing) is specified. When calling acquire() we try to take a tag, which thus corresponds to P(). If no tag is available, this call is blocked until a tag is available again. In case one wishes to wait for a tag only for a specific period of time, there is the attempt() method which can be set to the maximum waiting period in milliseconds. Since these methods are blocking, it is clear that they must not fall under supervision of the monitor, since only one caller at a time would be able to call this method. By calling release(), a tag is put back. To be more precise, the internal counter of the semaphore is incremented, which means that a release() can be called without the caller having taken a tag. This can be very useful; however, it is also a frequent source of errors in the programming of semaphores.

```
package EDU.oswego.cs.dl.util.concurrent;

public class Semaphore implements Sync {

  public Semaphore(int initialPermits) {...}

  public void acquire() throws InterruptedException {...}

  public boolean attempt(long msecs) throws InterruptedException {...}

  public synchronized void release() {...}

  public synchronized void release(int n) {...}

  public synchronized int permits() {...}
}
```

Semaphores will be shown here in a short but typical example, to clarify their use. In the following program segment, a semaphore is used as a simple lock. For this purpose, a semaphore is created as a global variable of a class and initialized with one tag. Then, this tag can be requested by means of acquire() inside a method (here, for example, in someMethod()) and be released again by means of release(). As long as the tag is held, other requests must wait, which allows a critical section to be protected.

```
import EDU.oswego.cs.dl.util.concurrent.*;

public class SemaphoreDemo {

  Semaphore semaphore = new Semaphore(1);

  public void someMethod() {
    try {
      semaphore.acquire();
      // Critical by Semaphore protected area
      ...
    } catch(InterruptedException e) {
      System.out.println(e);
    }
    semaphore.release();
  }
}
```

In general, however, this functionality should be realized by implementing a lock, such as the ones we can find in [Lea 1998]. We will introduce a variation to this in the following section.

2.2.3 ReadWriteLock

As already mentioned, semaphores should be handled with great attention and a better mechanism should be used, which builds up on semaphores but which remains hidden under a special interface. There is a large number of more specialized mechanisms (see [Lea 1997]), such as

- Locks or mutex, which achieve mutual exclusion,
- Barriers, which block an area until a condition arrives and then let pass all waiting processes,
- Countdowns, which can only be passed after n tags have been deposited,
- Latches, which block until they are triggered once and can then freely be passed.

Different types of access

Here, we present one of the most frequently used models, the ReadWriteLock. Often, a distinction must be made between two types of access to a critical section: in the first type, several or even an unrestricted number of access operations are permitted, typically for reading the data. This kind of access is known as read access or *reader*. The other type of access operation may only take place individually and with exclusion of the first type, and typically access the data for writing. This kind of access is known as write acess or *writer*. In order to guarantee the readers a consistent view of the data, both groups are authorized only in mutual exclusion, and only one writer type is allowed.

A ReadWriteLock consists of two coupled locks, one for the readers and one for the writers, which can be accessed separately. A reader tries to take a tag by calling rwLock.readLock().acquire(); a writer by calling rwLock().writeLock().acquire(). With different variations of the ReadWriteLock, different priorities can be specified. Practically, the "right of way" to access a critical section can be controlled. If the writers are to have a high priority, a writer must wait until the readers already present within the critical area have exited it, but newly arriving readers are blocked and must wait for the writer. If the readers are to have a higher priority, all arriving readers can have precedence over the writer. This means that an arriving writer must wait until there are no more readers wishing to enter the critical section. If both are to have the same priority, the FIFO (First In First Out) strategy is applied. In the following example, the reader has the highest priority, which is why we use a ReaderPreferenceReadWriteLock.

However, this mechanism cannot only be used to synchronize read and write access, but also to implement execution models. This will now be used to provide a more elegant solution to the algorithm on page 33. In particular, it should be garanteed that all filters of the sieve have terminated their task before the sieve reads out the result. For this purpose, the filters receive one read tag each, and the sieve tries to obtain a write tag (without attempting to write anything, this is just to specify the execution order).

```
import EDU.oswego.cs.dl.util.concurrent.*;

public class Sieve {
  ...

  private ReadWriteLock rwLock;

  public boolean isPrim(int n) {
    rwLock = new ReaderPreferenceReadWriteLock();
    for (int aPrim=2; aPrim<=rootN; aPrim=nextPrimAfter(aPrim)) {
      Filter filter = new Filter(aPrim, bitset,number,rwLock);
      (new Thread(filter)).start();
    }

    try {
      rwLock.writeLock().acquire();
      boolean result = bitset.get(n);
      rwLock.writeLock().release();
    } catch (InterruptedException e) {}
    return result;
  }
  ...
}

public class Filter implements Runnable{
  ...
  private ReadWriteLock rwLock;
```

```
  public Filter(int p, java.util.BitSet b, int n, ReadWriteLock rw) {
    prim=p;
    bitset=b;
    number=n;
    rwLock=rw;
  }

  public void run(){
    try {
      rwLock.readLock().acquire();
    } catch (InterruptedException e) {}
    int counter = prim;
    while (counter < number){
      bitset.clear(counter);
      counter = counter + prim;
    }
    rwLock.readLock().release();
  }
}
```

2.3 Concurrency and distribution

Threads, as we have discussed them so far, principally provide concurrency within a program and on a computer. They are not a mechanism for distribution. It is, for example, not possible (without further ado) to create a thread on a different computer. Nevertheless, concurrency is a very important element of distributed programming. Two models will be introduced in the following two sections, which have great relevance for communication in distributed systems.

2.3.1 Servers and handlers

A model which is frequently found on the server side of a distributed system is that of *server and handler.* A server is a program which provides services, such as expensive calculations or database access to other programs. A server receives a request from a client and it processes it. Since servers usually run on centralized, well equipped and expensive computers (which are themselves also called servers, but this is a term pertaining to a different language level), they are supposed to perform these services not only for one, but for a whole series of clients. This requires an architecture in which the server does not process one task completely and then wait for a new one, but where it remains always available and can accept several tasks at a time.

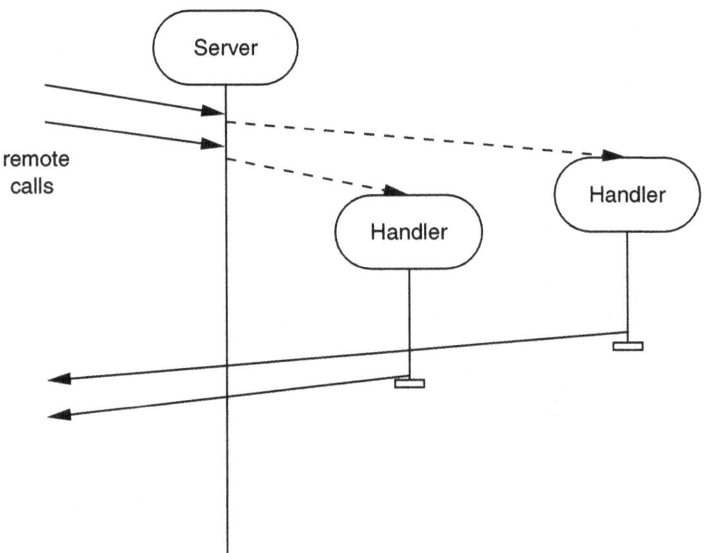

Figure 2.4
The server passes calls on to the handler.

Threads are employed to achieve this goal. The server does not perform the task on its own, but delegates this to another class, which runs in its own thread. Therefore, the server needs only a very short time to accept a task and to pass it on, and then is directly available again. The class which executes the real task is known as *handler*.

The following two classes represent exactly this model, although in a very simple version. In addition, the network connection for incoming requests is simulated by a keyboard input, since network connections will only be discussed in the next chapter.

```
import java.io.*;

public class Server extends Thread {

  public Server() {
   this.start();
  }

  public static void main(String[] args) {
    new Server();
  }

  public void run() {
    while (true) {
      System.out.println("waiting for new task");
      try {
        System.in.read();
      } catch (IOException e) {
        e.printStackTrace();
      }
      Handler handler = new Handler();
    }
  }
}

public class Handler extends Thread {

  public Handler() {
    this.start();
  }

  public void run() {
    System.out.println("Doing some work ...");
    // an entire task could be completed here
    ...
```

```
    try {
      Thread.sleep(1000);
    } catch (InterruptedException exc) {
      exc.printStackTrace();
    }
    System.out.println("... done");
  }
}
```

2.3.2 Asynchronous calls

A model which is frequently found on the client side is the asynchronous call. With a normal (synchronous) call, the caller must wait until the called process has completed the task assigned to it, and is blocked for all of this time. This is the standard semantics of a method call. However, sometimes the caller is supposed to continue its task while the call is being processed. This happens rather frequently in parallel systems, where these calls are used to distribute subtasks of problems across different processors. This model plays a very important role in distributed systems too, since communication times themselves are already relatively long, which is added to the aspect of parallelism.

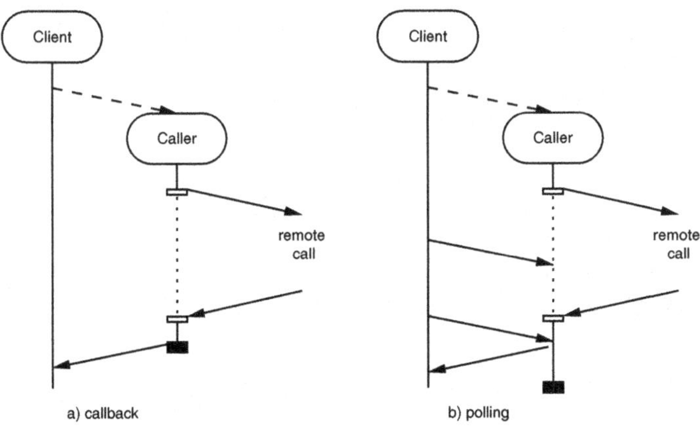

Figure 2.5 *Simulation of an asynchrous call.*

As we are going to see later, there are systems which directly support asynchronous calls. In Java, however, method calls are always synchronous, and the asynchronism must be obtained by concurrency. For this, an additional thread is created, which can execute a method call synchronously, but concurrently to the main activity thread, as shown in Figure 2.5.

Since the main activity thread, which is represented here by the Client class, does not wait for the result, another mechanism is required to get hold of the result. Principally, there are two possibilities to achieve this. One is that the client can continuously ask the object that provides the asynchronous call (the caller), whether the result has already arrived. If this is not the case, it can take care of other things. However, if the result has arrived, it can read and utilize it. This procedure is called *polling*. The other possibility is that the caller calls a method of the client as soon as it has received the result. This is known as *callback*. In the following example, both procedures are outlined; the remote call is simulated again by a keyboard input.

```
public class Client {

  public Client() {
    Caller caller = new Caller(null);
    while(caller.returned()==false) {
      System.out.println("Do some other work ...");
      try {
        Thread.sleep(1000);
      } catch (InterruptedException e) {
        e.printStackTrace();
      }
    }
    System.out.println("Received Result");
    Caller caller2 = new Caller(this);
    System.out.println("Do lots of other work");
  }
```

```
  public void callback() {
    System.out.println("Received Result");
  }

  public static void main(String[] args) {
    new Client();
  }
}

import java.io.*;

public class Caller extends Thread {

  Client client;
  private boolean returned = false;
  public Caller (Client cl) {
    client = cl;
    this.start();
  }

  public void run() {
    // Here could be remote call
    System.out.println("Press button");
    try {
      System.in.read();
    } catch (IOException e) {
      e.printStackTrace();
    }
    returned = true;
    if (client != null) {
      client.callback();
    }
  }

  public boolean returned() {
    boolean result = returned;
    returned = false;
    return result;
  }
}
```

2.4 References

Since threads are an integral part of the Java language, an introduction to programming with Java threads can be found in every good Java textbook and reference manual, such as [Middendorf and Singer 1999] or [Eckel 1998]. Books dealing exclusively with threads in Java are [Oaks and Wong 1997], [Hartley 1998], and [Magee and Kramer 1999]. A practice-oriented book on this topic is [Kredel and Yoshida 1999], which is suitable for practice because it is based on concrete tasks. A very high quality book, in which models of concurrency are discussed and demonstrated in Java, is [Lea 1997], which is very instructive for advanced programmers. Lea is also the author of the Java library for synchronization, parts of which we have presented earlier in this chapter ([Lea 1998]).

3 Java sockets

The basic prerequisite for programming in distributed systems is the possibility to transfer data from one part of a system to another. From the programmer's point of view, such data is provided as bits and bytes, as ASCII characters, or even as objects and should be transferred from one computer to another. For the transmission, physical media such as copper wires or fiber optic cables are available over which electrical signals or light waves are sent and received. The gap between the representation of data at the programming level and at the physical level is closed by protocols, a kind of linguistic convention between the individual devices involved in the data transmission. The Internet is a network of networks where different kinds of physical signal carriers, network topologies and network protocols are employed. The protocol family which is used on the Internet and which combines the different protocols of the subnetworks it consists of is TCP/IP.

A connection over a TCP/IP network is represented by two sockets which are each identified by an IP address and a port number. Thus sockets represent one of the most basic techniques for communication in distributed systems. All other methods discussed later on in this book are internally built on this mechanism, but most often cover it completely. Therefore, this mechanism will be presented in this chapter.

3.1 TCP/IP

The TCP/IP protocol family has its roots in a project of the US American forces. The "Advanced Research Projects Agency" of the US Ministry of Defense, in short ARPA, created the

The ARPANET

ARPANET, a network whose aim was to enable a secure and reliable data communication which also worked in critical situations. The basic technology was to be a packet-oriented network, where a data stream is subdivided into small portions which can be transmitted over the network independently from each other. Unlike a connection-oriented network, where a dedicated connection between two computers is established, this technology has the advantage that the communication is not necessarily interrupted even when a network node fails, since the individual packets can be rerouted via other paths and possibly lost packets may be still stored on the last but one node and may thus be resent or rerouted via a different path. A description of the history of the ARPANET, which is definitely worth reading, can be found in [Hafner and Lyon 1997].

3.1.1 The protocol layers

The transmission of data is technically subdivided into layers – on the one hand, to reduce the complexity and, on the other hand, to keep the layers interfaceable with each other. Therefore, a higher layer can be built on different underlying layers, but does not have to know their internal functioning but only the interface that this layer provides to the higher layers. The actual data transfer occurs only on the lowest layer; however, logically speaking, one layer communicates with the corresponding layer of the same level on the opposite side, using the lower-level layer. Communication on one level is specified by a protocol, a kind of convention through which the exchange of data is controlled. The International Standardization Organization (ISO) has developed a standard for communication in open distributed systems, but unfortunately the standardization process took so long that, in practice, the standard itself is not employed, but the techniques on which it is based. Although this standard, the Open System Interconnection Model (OSI model), has encountered great attention, it has never been successful in its pure form. The most popular protocol suite is TCP/IP, which leans strongly on the OSI model (malicious tongues say it is the other way round). The OSI model is a layer model and includes the following seven layers:

The Physical layer as the lowest layer determines how data is transferred via the transmission media, glass fiber cable or copper wires, for example. Here, a conversion of data from a digital form into a physical form it is carried out, such as a modulation of the signal as a voltage or as a light impulse.

The Data Link layer provides the transmission of data blocks between two network nodes and carries out error correction procedures inside such blocks. In local area networks (LANs), Ethernet, Token Ring or FDDI are used on this layer. In wide area networks (WANs), mostly the X.25 protocol or ATM are used. ATM can be employed both in local and wide area networks, and it is particularly suitable for services that require a service guarantee, such as the transmission of speech.

The Network layer performs the transfer of packets across several network nodes, and also provides the routing of paths through the network from the sender to the receiver. In the Internet, this layer is used for the IP (Internet Protocol).

The Transport layer provides error-free transmission of data from sender to the receiver, via a so-called "end to end" connection. It accepts messages, splits them into packets of suitable size and also provides a correctly ordered and error-free reconstruction of the massage before submitting it to the next higher layer on the opposite side. Thus the transport layer provides a high-quality service which often suffices as an interface for applications. In the Internet, this corresponds to the TCP protocol (Transmission Control Protocol).

The Session layer further abstracts from connections to sessions. For a session, this layer can internally build up several connections, share connections, re-establish interrupted connections, and so on.

The Presentation layer is responsible for a uniform representation of data. On the Internet, the responsibility for the format used usually lies with the application, so that this layer is often not occupied.

The Application layer contains the programs that make use of data communication.

The ISO layer model is certainly very important and influential, although the standardization (as frequently happens) was slower than the practical development, so that this layer model is oriented as much towards the practical solutions as it tries to influence them. The most important practical protocol stack is without doubt TCP/IP. The TCP/IP protocol suite fits more or less into this standard, as shown in Figure 3.1, although the particular mapping cannot be very exact. The protocol suite consists essentially of three protocol elements, the Internet Protocol (IP), the Transmission Control Protocol (TCP), and the User Datagram Protocol (UDP). TCP is a reliable protocol which guarantees the delivery of data packets and also puts them together in the right order, thus offering a connection-oriented service. UDP, on the countrary, does not give these guarantees, but it is more efficient and frequently used with applications which put high demands on transmission power, but can accept reductions in transmission quality, such as in the transmission of image or sound data in real time. The IP corresponds to the network layer of the OSI model and is responsible for addressing, routing, and transport of the data packets.

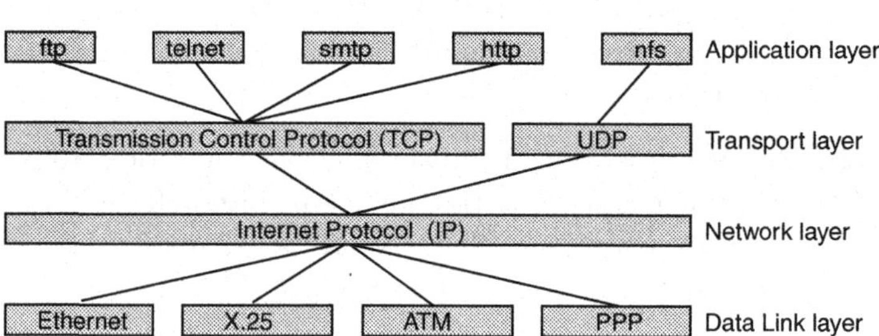

Figure 3.1
TCP/IP architecture in the OSI layer model.

3.1.2 Ports

Computers connected to a TCP/IP network are identified by their IP address. This kind of addressing is, however, too coarse, when processes need to be addressed that communicate with each other via the network. To be able to address such a network service on a particular computer, a port number is required in addition to the IP number. These 16-bit numbers are managed by the operating system and allocated to processes when these want to use the network. Many important services have a standardized port; port number 25, for example, is reserved for telnet.

If a connection to a service is to be opened between one computer and another, such as data transfer via FTP, the local process is assigned a port number. The remote service can then uniquely identify this process in connection with the local IP address in the entire network.

However, if a server process is started on a computer, such as a Web server, the system links it to a fixed port. The server then waits as a background process for incoming connections addressed to this port number.

3.2 Sockets

Ports represent communication points which obviously are not sufficient for the communication because they still require a communication channel which represents a connection between the two ports. Such communication channels are provided by sockets. Strictly speaking, a socket is an endpoint of a communication connection between two computers. It is identified by the IP address and the port number. From the programmer's point of view, a socket represents the mechanism to transfer data from one computer to another. Originally, sockets were developed for BSD Unix, but are today available on all platforms and represent, according to today's programing standards, the most fundamental communication mechanism.

In the days when sockets used to be part of the operating system and had to be invoked via system-specific libraries for C

Sockets with C++

or C++, programming of distributed applications was really hard. Access was different from operating system to operating system, often even from version to version, so that these programs were anything but portable. A certain standard is represented by the BSD UNIX socket interface, whose use is, however, quite arduous.

Sockets with Java

This has changed with Java. The Java programming interface for sockets completely abstracts them from the underlying operating system, thus significantly increasing their ease of use. The Socket class is contained in the java.net package and can be easily instantiated with a call to the constructor. Parameters to be specified are the IP address and port number of the opposite side's socket. Thus, on the opposite side, a socket must be already set up which can react to the connection request. For a number of important services, servers provide such sockets on standardized port numbers. To set up a user-defined socket on a server, you need a ServerSocket, which is also available in java.net.

```
int port = 1234;
ServerSocket server = new ServerSocket (port);
```

When a connection to this server is established, the server must react by accepting the connection set-up (accept()) and providing a new socket especially for this connection. Frequently, the server will be set to wait for further connections in an endless loop. The accept() method blocks until a new connection request arrives.

```
//Server
int port = 1234;
ServerSocket server = new ServerSocket (port);
while (true) {
  System.out.println("Waiting for client...");
  Socket client = server.accept();
  System.out.println("Client "+client.getInetAddress()+" connected
}
```

After a ServerSocket has been set up on the server computer, a client can address it and establish a connection.

```
// Client
Socket server = new Socket("sun",1234);
System.out.println("Connected to "+server.getInetAddress());
```

Finally, to be able to exchange data over these sockets as well, Java uses streams, which will be explained in the following section.

3.3 Streams

Streams are an abstraction for arbitrary data streams, whether from or to a socket, the console, the file system, or a storage medium. Streams therefore play a very important role in Java and time and again appear all over the place. Examples which show their omnipresence are screen output and keyboard input of text. The command line System.out.println() will be familiar to everyone who has had anything to do with Java. If we take a thorough look at this line and delve a bit deeper, we come to the following conclusion: the System class is a class of the java.lang package, which can be used to request information about the current system and to control basic services, such as the garbage collector. This class contains the static fields in, out, and err, which denote the standard input and output devices. Upon request, these fields return a stream or, more precisely, subclasses of it, such as out in case of a PrintStream.

There are streams for input, the InputStreams, and streams for output, the OutputStreams. All other streams are derived from these two classes contained in the java.io package. InputStreams and OutputStreams cannot be instantiated directly (they are abstract classes), but only through their children, which then describe a data stream into or out of something concrete, such as the file system or the console.

The program fragments of the previous section will now be extended to be able to transfer a couple of bytes of information. To do this, the client asks a socket to pass it an OutputStream, and then sends a byte array in this stream. On the other side, the server asks for an InputStream, reads it into a byte array and outputs the content.

Remote time request

As a first simple application for sockets and streams, we are now going to show a program which, upon demand, transmits the current time. This application can be easily extended to a message ticker, a chat application, or similar, which we will do later, but let's first return to the very principle of transmitting data. The program is called TimeServer. It creates a ServerSocket with a fixed port number of 1234 and then waits for incoming requests via the accept() method. When one arrives, a socket and thus a connection with the client is created (whose IP address is displayed for control). Then the current time is fetched, converted into a string and then into a byte array, and finally transferred via the socket connection by means of an OutputStream.

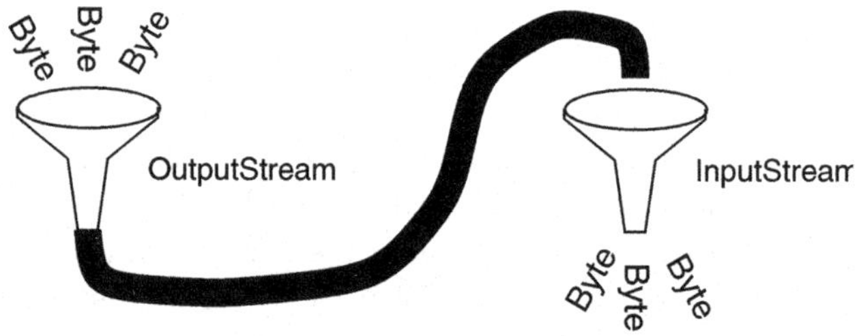

Figure 3.2
Streams.

```
// Time Server
import java.net.*;
import java.io.*;
import java.util.*;

public class TimeServer {
  public static void main (String args[]) throws IOException {
    int port = 1234;
    ServerSocket server = new ServerSocket(port);
    while (true) {
      System.out.println("Waiting for client...");
      Socket client = server.accept();
      System.out.println("Client from "+client.getInetAddress()+" connected.");
```

```
        OutputStream out = client.getOutputStream();
        Date date = new Date();
        byte b[] = date.toString().getBytes();
        out.write(b);
      }
    }
}
```

A suitable client might look as follows: the TimeClient connects with the TimeServer by creating a socket with its IP address and port number. It reads a byte array from an InputStream, converts it into a string and outputs it.

```
// TimeClient
import java.net.*;
import java.io.*;

public class TimeClient {

  public static void main (String args[]) throws IOException {
    Socket server = new Socket("sun",1234);
    System.out.println("Connected to "+server.getInetAddress());
    InputStream in = server.getInputStream();

    byte b[] = new byte[100];
    int num = in.read(b);
    String date = new String(b);
    System.out.println("Server said: "+date);
  }
}
```

The above programming yields the output:

```
sun> java TimeServer
sun| Waiting for client...

lin> java TimeClient
lin| Connected to 134.100.11.1
```

sun| Client from 134.100.11.2 connected.
sun| Waiting for client...

lin| Server said: Fri Jul 31 13:49:05 GMT+03:30 1998

Thus, streams provide a simple mechanism for the transmission of data. However, only bytes and byte arrays can be transported via streams. To extend their functionality and to be able, for example, to transfer strings without having to convert them to byte arrays, Java provides the concept of filters, which will be described in the following section.

3.4 Filters

In the same way as in a sieve or in photography, streams can be connected in series and combined with each other. Actually, they are also called filters in Java. For InputStreams and OutputStreams, the FilterInputStream and FilterOutputStream classes are provided, which at first do not offer any further functionality than that of passing on incoming and outgoing information virtually unfiltered. FilterInputStream and FilterOutputStream themselves are children of Input/OutputStream, so that they can be used again by another filter exactly like a simple stream, allowing such filters to be cascaded.

Now, to extend the functionality of streams, a class can be derived from these filter streams which provides additional methods or implements methods of the superclass in a different way. Java already provides a number of such filters, so that filter classes are readily available for the most common applications.

For the transmission of simple types such as int, long, String, etc. the DataOutputStream class is available, which contains a write methode for each of these types, for example writeInt(), writeLong(), and writeChar(). For the transmission of strings, usually the UTF-8 format is employed, which transfers the characters in Unicode, for which a writeUTF() method is available. Correspondingly, a DataInputStream exists, with methods such as readInt(), readLong(), and readUTF(). These

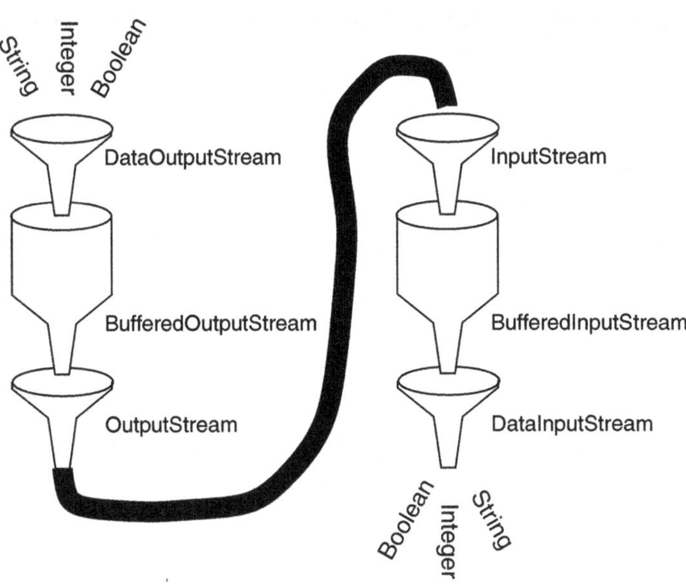

Figure 3.3
Filters for streams.

classes essentially perform the conversion of these types into byte sequences, which are then transferred by simple streams, and vice versa carry out the reconstruction of the correct type from the transferred byte sequence.

Data buffering

To make the transmission of data more efficient and resource-saving, a data transmission should not be triggered for every arising byte, but the data should be intermediately stored in a buffer and be transmitted only when an adequate quantity has been reached. A filter which provides this functionality is the BufferedOutputStream, which by default holds an intermediate memory of 512 bytes, and triggers the transmission of data only when the buffer is full or when the transmission is explicitly triggered with a flush() command. Such a buffered filter also exists on the receiver's side, the BufferedInputStream.

Another filter which is, for example, used with the above-mentioned console output by means of System.out is the PrintStream, equally a child of FilterOutputStream.

With these filters it is now possible to write the above example in a simpler and more efficient way by placing a buffered stream and a DataOutputStream in front of the true Output-Stream of the socket.

```
// TimeServer with Filter
DataOutputStream out =
new DataOutputStream( new BufferedOutputStream( client.getOutputStream()));
Date date = new Date();
out.writeUTF(date.toString());
out.flush();

// TimeClient with Filter
DataInputStream in = new DataInputStream( new
BufferedInputStream( server.getInputStream()));
System.out.println("Server said: "+ in.readUTF());
```

3.5 A chat system with sockets

As an example of a simple but meaningful application of sockets, we are now going to present a chat system. A chat is a textual conversation between several participants communicating with each other. Participants must register for a chat, which is offered by a server, and can then send messages to this chat and follow all messages sent to this chat. These chats are not only very popular on the Internet, but they also belong to the typical applications in distributed networks and have requirements that are no longer quite trivial.

Every participant builds up a communication connection to the server. The server manages the connections and sends incoming messages to all participants. With regard to sockets, which represent only individual point-to-point connections, this means that the servers must simulate a multicast by many individual unicasts. Techniques for a real multicast, which make the programming of this application easier, will be introduced later.

In addition, the server has to be reachable at any time. If it receives a message, it must create a new thread, which undertakes the processing of this message.

Three classes are required for this chat system: a ChatClient on the client side, a ChatServer on the server side, and a ChatHandler, which undertakes the processing of the message for the server. To keep the example as short as possible, the graphical user interface of the client side is separated from the ChatClient class. The class responsible for the interface, that is, the ChatFrame class, is listed in the Appendix and is also used by examples in other sections. The classes EnterListener and ExitListener, which react to the closing of a window, are listed in the Appendix as well. EnterListener waits for input in the graphical interface, which is terminated by pressing the Enter key, reads the input and sends it to the ChatClient by means of the sendTextToChat() method. ExitListener listens to the closing of the input window and then calls the disconnect() method to give the client the possibility to unregister properly from this chat.

First, we show the ChatClient class.

```
import java.net.*;
import java.io.*;
import java.awt.event.*;

public class ChatClient {

  public ChatFrame gui;

  private Socket socket;
  private DataInputStream in;
  private DataOutputStream out;

  public ChatClient(String name, String server, int port) {

    // Create GUI and handle events:
    // After text input, sendTextToChat() is called,
    // when closing the window, disconnect() is called.
    gui = new ChatFrame("Chat with sockets");
    gui.input.addKeyListener (new EnterListener(this,gui));
    gui.addWindowListener(new ExitListener(this));
```

```
    // Create a socket, register, and listen to the server
    try {
      socket = new Socket(server,port);
      in = new DataInputStream(socket.getInputStream());
      out = new DataOutputStream(socket.getOutputStream());
      out.writeUTF(name);
      while (true) {
        gui.output.append("\n"+in.readUTF());
      };
    } catch (Exception e)  { e.printStackTrace(); }
  }

  protected void sendTextToChat(String str) {
    try {
      out.writeUTF(str);
    } catch (IOException e) {  e.printStackTrace(); }
  }

  protected void disconnect() {
    try {
      socket.close();
    } catch (IOException e) {
      e.printStackTrace();
    }
  }

  public static void main (String args[])throws IOException {
    if (args.length!=3)
      throw new RuntimeException
        ("Syntax: java ChatClient <name> <serverhost> <port>");
    int port=Integer.parseInt(args[2]);
    ChatClient c=new ChatClient(args[0], args[1], port);
  }
}
```

On the server side, the program is divided into two parts, on the one hand, the ChatServer which accepts the calls and, on the other hand, the ChatHandler, which is passed a single call by the ChatServer and processes it. The ChatServer waits for new, incoming socket connections, reads the name of the new client via this socket and then starts the ChatHandler, which takes care of the further connection, so that the server can again reply quickly to other connection requests.

```
import java.net.*;
import java.io.*;
import java.util.*;
public class ChatServer {

  public ChatServer (int port) throws IOException {
    ServerSocket server = new ServerSocket (port);
    while (true) {
      Socket client = server.accept();
     DataInputStream in = new DataInputStream(client.getInputStream());
      String name = in.readUTF();
      System.out.println ("New client "+name+" from " +
client.getInetAddress());
      ChatHandler c = new ChatHandler (name, client);
      c.start ();
    }
  }

  public static void main (String args[]) throws IOException {
    if (args.length != 1)
      throw new RuntimeException ("Syntax: java ChatServer <port>");
    new ChatServer (Integer.parseInt (args[0]));
  }
}
```

The ChatHandler is implemented as a thread, so every new handler has its own control flow and they can be executed concurrently. At creation time, the handler initializes its socket connection with the client for which it is responsible. Together, the handlers manage a global list (vector), in which each of them registers, thus being able to reference all others. This is required to simulate a broadcast. The handler waits for incoming contributions of the client by constantly trying to read from the InputStream. When it receives a message, it sends it to the OutputStream of every handler in the global list.

```
import java.net.*;
import java.io.*;
import java.util.*;

public class ChatHandler extends Thread {

  Socket socket;
  DataInputStream in;
  DataOutputStream out;
  String name;
  protected static Vector handlers = new Vector ();

  public ChatHandler (String name, Socket socket) throws IOException {
    this.name = name;
    this.socket = socket;
    in = new DataInputStream (new BufferedInputStream
       (socket.getInputStream()));
    out = new DataOutputStream (new BufferedOutputStream
       (socket.getOutputStream()));
  }

  public void run () {
    try {
      broadcast(name+" entered");
      handlers.addElement (this);
      while (true) {
        String message = in.readUTF ();
        broadcast(name+": "+message);
      }
    } catch (IOException ex) {
      System.out.println("-- Connection to user lost.");
    } finally {
      handlers.removeElement (this);
```

```
        broadcast(name+" left");
        try {
          socket.close ();
        } catch (IOException ex) {
          System.out.println("-- Socket to user already closed ?");
        }
      }
    }

    protected static void broadcast (String message) {
      synchronized (handlers) {
        Enumeration e = handlers.elements ();
        while (e.hasMoreElements ()) {
          ChatHandler handler = (ChatHandler) e.nextElement ();
          try {
            handler.out.writeUTF (message);
            handler.out.flush ();
          } catch (IOException ex) {
            handler.stop ();
          }
        }
      }
    }
}
```

At start-up, the server receives a port number as parameter, while the ChatClient is started with user name, server name and port number of the chat service and creates its graphical interface.

```
sun> java ChatServer 1234

lin> java ChatClient marko sun 1234

win> java ChatClient tom sun.vsys.informatik.uni-hamburg.de 1234

sun| New client marko from 134.100.11.2
sun| New client tom from 134.100.15.2
```

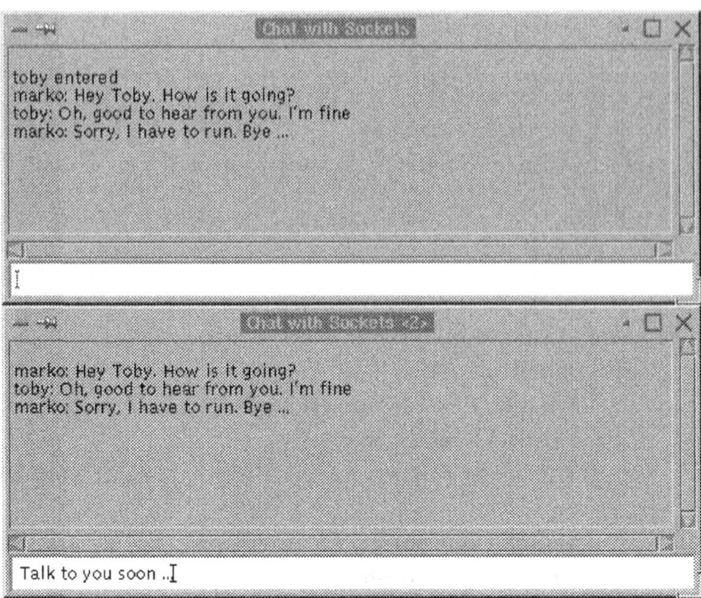

Figure 3.4
A simple user interface of the chat.

3.6 Multicast

Besides the sockets which serve for a point-to-point communication, Java also provides a multicast socket which can be used to communicate with a group of communication points. Obviously, this is not an invention of Java, but is already available at the Internet protocol level, but Java offers a relatively simple and platform-independent interface to this service. However, unlike a point-to-point connection in which the TCP protocol can easily correct small errors such as lost packets – the receiver simply asks the sender to send the lost packet again – in a multipoint connection many of these errors cannot be remedied that easily. If one of the many receivers does not receive a packet, it cannot simply arrange a new transmission of this packet to all receivers. However, since it is the very task of the TCP protocol to provide a reliable service, which cannot be expected at all in this case, the IP Multicast is based on IP, but uses a different transport protocol, namely the UDP, which delivers individual packets, called datagrams, and is not concerned with error correction.

Error correction

Multicast communication uses IP addresses of a particular class (class D) which are not linked to host computers, but are exclusively reserved for multicast communication. These addresses lie in a range between 224.0.0.1 and 239.255.255.255, where the addresses up to 224.0.0.255 are reserved for the transmission of multicast routing information. All other addresses can be freely used for group communication. All participants in such a communication group must first register with the group to be able to join the communication. Subsequently, messages can be sent to all group members or received from others. To end the membership in the group, the participant must sign out.

Applications

Applications for a multicast are, for example, multimedia conferences on the Internet. Especially in the transmission of video or audio data, a casual loss of data can easily be overcome; in any case, a later completion of the data is of no use when video or audio data are played directly upon their reception, as is usually the case in real-time communication. Transmission of identical data to many receivers is more efficient via a multicast than via individual point-to-point connections, since the data is sent only once over a communication thread as one broadcast. The routers can decide whether they need to transmit a multicast message; the information as to whether a receiver is registered for a multicast address is at their disposal. In addition, multicast messages can have a restricted "Time-To-Live" (or TTL) which corresponds to the number of routers to be passed. When this "Time-To-Live" is set to one, for example, the message is transmitted only inside the local network. If this value is not explicitly set, a default value of one is used, so that the messages remain confined to the local network.

Since JDK 1.1, Java provides support for multicast sockets in the java.net package. To write messages to a multicast group, first a MulticastSocket must be created for a suitable port.

```
InetAddress group = InetAddress.getByName("226.1.3.5");
int port=6789;
MulticastSocket socket = new MulticastSocket(port);
```

The sender does not necessarily have to be registered for a group, it can simply send datagrams to a multicast address. To do this, it produces a DatagramPacket, assigns it to a data buffer, fills it with a byte array and sends it through the prepared socket.

```
byte[] buffer = new byte[500];
DatagramPacket datagram = new DatagramPacket(buffer,buffer.length, group,
port);
datagram.setData(new String("Hello World").getBytes());
socket.send(datagram);
```

To receive a datagram, the receiver must register with a group, by creating a MulticastSocket on a port (by the way, the same as the sender's) and registering it with the multicast group with a call to the joinGroup() method.

```
int port 6789;
MulicastSocket socket = new MulticastSocket(port);
InetAddress group = InetAddress.getByName("226.1.3.5");
socket.joinGroup(group);
```

It then waits for a datagram. Realistically, this would happen in an endless loop in a thread created especially for this purpose, in order not to block the remaining application. The messages are transferred as byte streams. To be able to interpret the information in the datagram, the receiver must know the structure of the information to be expected, that is, it has to build up the same data structure as the sender, creating it from the byte stream via an appropriate interpretation.

```
while (true) {
    socket.receive(datagram);
    String message= new String(datagram.getData());
    System.out.println("Datagram received from
        "+datagram.getAddress().getHostAddress()+" saying: " + message);
}
```

3.6.1 A chat system with IP multicast

Communication via IP multicast will also be demonstrated with the aid of a complete program, again with the chat example. This example will also be found again in the subsequent chapters, which allows the techniques in use to be easily compared.

As opposed to socket communication, the implementation of a chat system with multicast no longer requires a server to receive and forward the messages, but to send them directly to anybody listening on the corresponding IP address. Thus, only one class, ChatClient, is required, which is symmetric for all communication partners.

When closing the connection, in contrast to the socket variant, the client does not need to sign out from the server.

```
import java.net.*;
import java.io.*;

public class ChatClient {

  ChatFrame gui;
  String name;

  InetAddress group;
  MulticastSocket socket;
  int port = 6789;

  public ChatClient(String name) {
    this.name = name;

    // Create GUI and handle events:
    // After text input, sendTextToChat() is called,
    // when closing the window, disconnect() is called.
    gui = new ChatFrame("Chat with IP-Multicast");
    gui.input.addKeyListener (new EnterListener(this,gui));
    gui.addWindowListener(new ExitListener(this));
```

```
    try {
      socket = new MulticastSocket(port);
      group = InetAddress.getByName("226.1.3.5");
      socket.joinGroup(group);
      gui.output.append("Connected...\n");

      // Waiting for and receiving messages
      while (true) {
        byte[] buffer = new byte[1000];
        DatagramPacket datagram = new DatagramPacket(buffer,buffer.length);
        socket.receive(datagram);
        String message = new String(datagram.getData());
        gui.output.append(message);
      }
    } catch (IOException e) {
      e.printStackTrace();
    }
  }
  public void sendTextToChat(String message) {
    message = name+": "+message+"\n";
    byte[] buf = (message).getBytes();
    DatagramPacket dg = new DatagramPacket(buf,buf.length,group,port);
    try {
      socket.send(dg);
    }
    catch (IOException ex) {
      System.out.println(ex);
    }
  }

  public void disconnect() {}

  public static void main(String args[]) {
    if (args.length!=1)
      throw new RuntimeException ("Syntax: java ChatClient <name>");
    ChatClient client = new ChatClient(args[0]);
  }
}
```

3.7 iBus: a reliable multicast

Multicast is attributed a growing importance in the programming of distributed applications and, in particular, also in the currently emerging intranets. However, in the form multicast has been introduced in the previous chapter, it does not fulfill the particular requirements of reliability and usability. Therefore it is not surprising that research and development projects are seeking multicast extensions and improvements.

One extension, based on the IP multicast, but adding some missing qualities, is the iBus ([Maffeis 1997], [Softwired 1998]), a software package by Softwired Inc., developed by Silvano Maffeis. Since May 1999, iBus has been available in version 2.0 and is subject to payment for commercial projects. A free licence is available for teaching and research institutions. The API used here is still based on the last completely free version (version 0.5) which, in principle, differs only very little from the verion 2.0. iBus provides a range of additional functionalities and should be understood more as communication middleware based on IP than as a mere extension of multicast. It offers a configurable protocol with which the programmer can decide whether quality of the transmission service, efficiency or security is more important. Protocol modules can be used to build different, application-oriented protocol stacks which reach from a simple, unreliable multicast transmission, as shown in the previous chapter, to reliable, compressed, and encrypted transmissions. Furthermore, not only byte streams can be transferred, but also arbitrary (serializable) Java objects. The socket interface of Java, as discussed in the previous sections, is completely covered, although the transmission is based on just this in a very direct way. IBus, as sockets, is used for data transmission and not, as many of the following techniques, for remote method calls.

In iBus, all data to be transmitted is encapsulated in a `posting`, a class which represents a dynamically expandable container of serializable Java objects. A posting can be created, filled with arbitrary Java objects, and then transmitted via the network.

```
import iBus.*;

Posting posting = new Posting();
posting.setLength(3);
posting.setObject(0, new Integer(1));
posting.setObject(1, new String("Hi, I am an iBus message!"));
posting.setObject(2, new Date());
```

To send this posting, you need a protocol stack on the one hand and, on the other hand, a special iBus URL, to which it can be sent. A stack can be assembled from various existing protocol objects and can even be extended by user-defined ones. There is a whole series of such protocol objects. The simplest one is the IPMCAST, which provides the functionality of java.net.MulticastSockets. The extensions will be discussed later; now, we first create such a simple stack:

```
Stack stack = new iBus.Stack("IPMCAST");
```

While in MulticastSockets, messages are simply sent to a multicast IP address, there is a more refined mechanism in iBus, namely the creation of channels, specified by a URL (*universal resource locator*) and consisting of an IP address, a port and a subject identifier. They have the form ibus://<ip address>[:port]/<subject> and are created as follows:

```
iBusURL url = new iBusURL("ibus://226.1.3.5/Talk");
```

The IP address can, but need not, be a multicast address, so that iBus can be used to implement both a multicast and a point-to-point communication. With such a channel, an application can register, and send or receive messages. Sending and receiving parties are internally distinguished by iBus, so that two methods exist, namely registerTalker() and registerListener(). If both stack and URL are present, the registration can be carried out and the posting can be sent. Since iBus differentiates between unidirectional and bidirectional communication, also known as Push&Pull technology, it uses the push()method to send a posting. Via push, information is sent by the sender without request, while pull offers the possibility to request information explicitly.

```
stack.registerTalker(url);
stack.push(url, posting);
```

Interested receivers can register for a channel by means of a subscribe() method. Therefore, the receiver has to know the channel's URL, and it must provide a class that implements a Receiver interface. This receiver provides one method each for handling the Push&Pull messages (dispatchPull() and dispatch-Push()), as well as an error() method for error handling. One receiver can be registered with several channels, just as several receivers can be registered with one channel. The receiver has to know the data structure of a posting it expects, to be able to parse it and react accordingly. For the postings created above, the receiver might look as follows:

```
class MyReceiver implements Receiver {

   public void dispatchPush (iBusURL channel, Posting posting) {
      int seq = ((Integer)posting.getObject(0)).intValue();
      String message = (String)posting.getObject(1);
      Date date = (Date)posting.getObject(2);
      System.out.println("*** Received Message: "+message
                        +" (Seq: "+seq+" at "+date.toString()+")");
   }

   public Posting dispatchPull (iBusURL channel, Posting request) {
      //No pull messages are expected in this application
      return new Posting();
   }

   public void error (iBusURL channel, String details) {
      System.out.println(details);
   }
}
```

Thus to register with a channel, you need a stack which implements the same protocol stack at the sender's and the receiver's ends, a URL of the channel, and an implementation of a receiver.

```
Stack stack = new iBus.Stack("IPMCAST");
iBusURL url = new iBusURL("ibus://226.1.3.5/Talk");
MyReceiver receiver = new MyReceiver();
stack.subscribe(url,receiver);
```

3.7.1 The protocol stack

In the above example, a very simple protocol stack was used, which provides about the same functionality as a MulticastSocket. One of the most important advantages of iBus is, however, that this protocol stack can be assembled as required from a collection of protocol objects. As the following examples show, highly different demands can be made upon the quality of a transmission.

- For the transmission of audio streams, which are immediately played back when the data arrives, it is important to use a simple stack which does not unnecessarily delay the playback. If single data packets are lost, this is usually barely audible or can be interpolated by the listener.

- When transmitting software or application data such as, for example, an update of Java applications installed on several computers within an intranet, the time needed for this transmission plays a secondary role, but the loss of even a small quantity of data is fatal and not to be tolerated. For this purpose, a secure transmission is required.

- If the size of the data to be transmitted is very large, too large to fit in a datagram packet, the data has to be split up and then reassembled again. Usually, datagrams have a size of up to 8192 bytes, which is fully sufficient for the transmission of messages in a news ticker or in a blackboard system, but this is not sufficient for the transmission of sound tracks or software packages.

- Data worth being protected for an enterprise, such as customers or sales data, requires encryption.
- When the transmission time is relatively expensive, it may be worth compressing the data to be transferred. Depending on the nature of the data, this can cause a reduction of the transmission volume by a factor of 2 to 20.
- Application servers which need to provide an extremely high availability are frequently replicated. This means that their data stock is completely mirrored on one or more identical servers so that, in the event that the main server fails, these servers can step in and the overall system can continue to run. Such systems are, for example, employed in banks and in nuclear power plants.

For this and other cases iBus offers the possibility to create special protocol stacks that fulfill these requirements. These are built up modularly from protocol objects and can be organized in different ways.

The most important protocol objects are the following:

- IPMCAST provides the functionality of the two classes `java.net.MulticastSocket` and `java.net.DatagramSocket` and, as the lowest element, forms the base of most protocol stacks. IPMCAST can also be used alone and then behaves like a normal multicast.
- LOCALBUS is a local alternative to IPMCAST which is used when the multicast should only be used within a virtual machine. Thus, for example, several applets all running within one browser (within one HTML page, for example) or several applications communicating with each other on one computer, can use iBus as a kind of event bus.
- TCP provides TCP/IP connections under iBus.
- REACH controls and checks the membership in a channel. This layer sends a short signal in regular intervals,

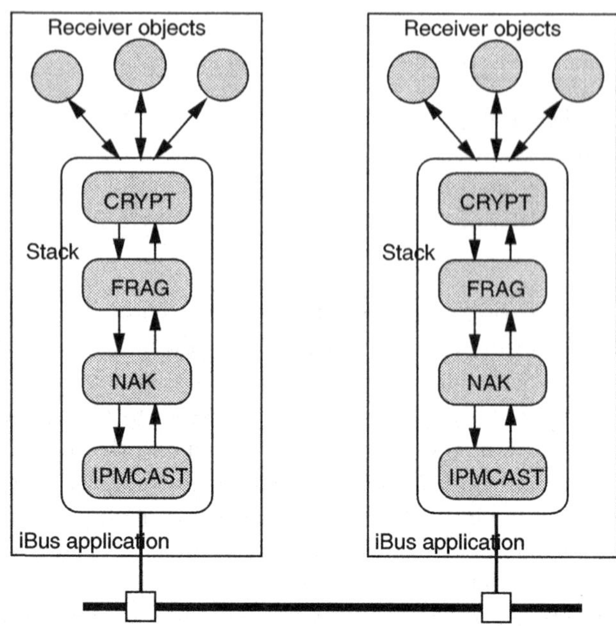

Figure 3.5
Example of an iBus protocol stack.

a so-called *heartbeat*, which can be used to detect new members or the absence of previously present ones, thus creating a picture of the attainable members. In addition, it enables the recognition of failures.

- NAK looks after the delivery of lost messages through negative confirmation. If the receiver notices that a packet is missing out of a sequence of packets, it reports this to the sender and the packet is delivered again.
- FRAG provides the possibility of fragmenting large messages into small packet sizes adapted to the communication protocol, and putting them back together in their correct order. This is necessary for all messages which, for example, exceed the UDP datagram size, such as files, audio or video streams, or images.
- PULL enables an explicit request for information, so the transmission can be also triggered by the receiver.
- CRYPT allows encryption and deciphering of sent data.

When creating a new stack, the creation method of Stack is passed a list of colon-separated protocol objects as a string.

```
Stack s1 = new Stack("FRAG:FIFO:REACH:IPMCAST");
Stack s2 = new Stack("FRAG:FIFO:NAK:REACH:IPMCAST");
Stack s3 = new Stack("NAK:REACH:IPMCAST");
```

For frequently used protocol stacks, an alias can be defined to replace this string. Thus the stack "PULL:FRAG:FIFO:NAK: REACH:IPMCAST" is available in the alias Reliable. New, user-defined protocol objects can also be created. For the compression of data to be transferred, for example, it is important to have a precise knowledge of the data structure in order to reach the highest compression rate possible. Therefore, it can be sensible to create a user-defined protocol object COMPR and combine it with the suitable protocol objects.

```
Stack s4 = new Stack("CRYPT:Reliable");
Stack s5 = new Stack("COMPR:Reliable");
Stack s6 = new Stack("Vsync");
```

These protocol stacks can be employed for the most varied needs in all sorts of applications. An application may well manage different protocol stacks, but has to make sure that the same stack is used with sender and receiver. Stack s1, for example, can be used to transfer audio streams, s2 to send out software updates, s3 for a blackboard system, s4 to transfer critical data and s5 for data to be compressed. A protocol stack suitable for the replication of server data, a concept also known as virtual synchronism, is still to be developed under the alias Vsync, as in stack s6.

3.7.2 A chat system with iBus

The chat example will also be used to show reliable multicast via iBus. Unlike multicast via IP, handling and transmission of objects is significantly simpler in iBus, since with iBus objects can be sent as such and need not be manually converted into a byte stream first. The real advantage, however, is that a reliable service is provided without having to bother about details. In this example, we use the predefined protocol stack Reliable, which ensures a reliable transfer.

In the constructor, the user interface and its control, as well as the stack are initialized and the connect() method is called, which takes on the registration with the communication channel. The graphical user interface (GUI) is again implemented by the same class, ChatFrame, that has already been used in the previous examples on chats and will thus not be listed here. The events that go out from the GUI when a message is entered and the window is closed are intercepted by the EventListener and ExitListener classes, which are each registered with the GUI as EventListener. These classes are also listed in the Appendix.

```
import java.io.*;
import iBus.*;

public class ChatClient {

  ChatFrame gui;
  Stack stack;
  iBusURL url = null;
  ChatReceiver receiver = null;

  public ChatClient() {
    // Create GUI and handle events:
    // After text input, sendTextToChat() is called,
    // when closing the window, disconnect() is called.
    gui = new ChatFrame("Chat mit iBus");
    gui.input.addKeyListener (new EnterListener(this,gui));
    gui.addWindowListener(new ExitListener(this));
    stack = new Stack("Reliable");
    try {
      url = new iBusURL("ibus://226.1.3.5/Chat");
      receiver = new ChatReceiver(this);
      stack.subscribe(url,receiver);
      stack.registerTalker(url);
    } catch (Exception ex) {
      ex.printStackTrace();
    }
  }
```

```
  void sendTextToChat (String str) {
    Posting posting = new Posting();
    posting.setLength(1);
    posting.setObject(0,str);
    try {
      stack.push(url,posting);
    } catch (Exception e) {
      e.printStackTrace();
    }
  }

  void disconnect() {
    try {
      stack.unregisterTalker(url);
    }catch (Exception ex) {
      ex.printStackTrace();
    }
  }

  void connect() {
    try {
      url = new iBusURL("ibus://226.1.3.5/Chat");
      receiver = new ChatReceiver(this);
      stack.subscribe(url,receiver);
      stack.registerTalker(url);
    } catch (Exception ex) { ex.printStackTrace(); }
    gui.input.requestFocus();
  }

  public static void main(String[] args) {
    if (args.length!=1)
      throw new RuntimeException ("Syntax: java ChatClient <name>");
    ChatClient chat = new ChatClient();
  }
}
```

ChatReceiver has to implement the Receiver interface and therefore the dispatchPush() and dispatchPull() methods. Incoming messages are delivered to the receiver as postings via the Push method, from which it can read the messages. A possible implementation looks as follows:

```
class ChatReceiver implements Receiver {

  ChatClient app;

  public ChatReceiver (ChatClient app) {
    this.app = app;
  }

  // The Receiver methods

  public void dispatchPush (iBusURL source, Posting posting) {
    String message = (String)posting.getObject(0);
    app.gui.output.append(message+"\n");
  }

  public Posting dispatchPull (iBusURL channel, Posting req) {
    return null;
  }

  public void error (iBusURL channel, String details) {
    System.out.println(details);
  }
}
```

3.8 References

The standard reference about the basics of network technology is [Tanenbaum 1996]. In this book, the ISO OSI layer model and basic techniques are treated in all their aspects. For special information about TCP/IP we recommend [Stevens and Wright 1994]. A book which is specifically concerned with multicast is [Wittmann and Zitterbart 1999]. Books which explain socket communication in Java are [Hughes *et al.* 1997] and [Neimeyer 1998].

Further information on iBus [Softwired 1998] can be found on Softwire's Web site (www.softwired-inc.com). iBus is a commercial product, but it can be downloaded from the Web server for evaluation purposes and use by educational institutions. A good introduction is offered by [Altherr *et al.* 1999].

4 RMI

Sockets, which we have already introduced in the last chapter, are a simple, solid and flexible technology for data communication in distributed systems, and represent a sufficient solution for many applications. However, since sockets are restricted to the transmission of data and leave the semantics of this data unconsidered, protocols which provide the semantic interpretation of this data must be developed on the application level. The development of such protocols is often time-consuming and prone to errors. Furthermore, object-oriented programming languages already provide a framework for semantics of data – the objects. In local applications, objects communicate with other objects via (sematically loaded) methods. Therefore, it would be desirable, for the distributed case, to have a similar, consistent communication paradigm available, which would permit the remote call of methods. For this purpose, Java provides the Remote Method Invocation, in short RMI.

Remote Procedure Call

In the 80s a technology was developed for the procedural programming paradigm to call procedures on remote computers, the Remote Procedure Call (RPC). It allows the call of procedures located in another process space on the same machine or on a remote computer. There are several technical hurdles to overcome: in the local case, data is simply passed as a reference (frequently described as pointer) which refers to the physical memory address. Such references have no (or, at least, no correct) meaning in a different address space. Therefore, in the distributed case, the referenced data needs to be passed as a copy. On the other hand, in communication between heterogeneous computer architectures, we can no longer rely on the fact that the internal representation of data on another computer is the same as on the original computer. In addition, data to be copied must be converted into a platform-independent data format, such as XDR (External Data Representation), developed by Sun for this purpose, and then converted back into an internal representation on the receiver's side.

External Data Representation

This technology was quite successful and was (and still is) employed in many distributed systems. The Distributed Computing Environment (DCE) of the Open Software Foundation (OSF), for example, is based on this technology and, building on it, offers a middleware platform for distributed systems, which provides a fully developed security concept, the management of network structures in logical cells, a time, file, and directory service, and other basic services. But due to the boom of object-orientation, the RPC became obsolete only shortly after it had been developed.

OSF/DCE

The adaptation of this concept to object-orientation is more complicated than one would initially suspect, since further technical problems are getting in the way. In object-oriented languages, references are not treated as physical memory addresses, but as logical addresses, so that it is desirable to maintain this concept seamlessly also in a distributed scenario. Equally, memory management via garbage collection must be maintained in an object system such as Java even when the objects are referenced from remote systems.

With the Remote Method Invocation (RMI), Java provides such an object-oriented mechanism which represents a solution for remote method calls. Since JDK version 1.1, it has become an integral part of the Java language.

4.1 The architecture of RMI

RMI is a Java mechanism for calling methods of objects which do not run on the same Java Virtual Machine. Here the RMI offers full transparency, so that, after a first initialization, a call can be used in exactly the same way as in the local case. The RMI is structured in several layers, with the highest layer covering the underlying layers, such as socket communication and serialization and deserialization of parameters and results.

In RMI there is always one service provider, the *server*, and one service receiver, the *client*. Although both are normal objects implemented in Java, at least the server must be indicated as such and be prepared for remote access before it can be used by the client. While in non-distributed systems the relationship between two objects is symmetrical (each object can call another one as long as it has a reference to it), in RMI this relationship is asymmetrical.

Client and server

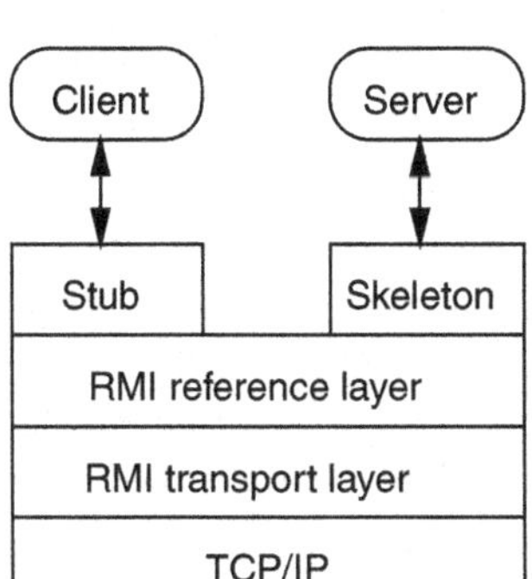

Figure 4.1
The layers of the RMI architecture.

The server must document the interface it provides for remote access in an interface description derived from the Remote interface. From this description, additional classes are created by a special compiler, which internally take care of communication handling between client and server, the stub and the skeleton. The stub is a placeholder object, which offers the same interface as the server object and passes a call on to its server object. It must either be stored on the client's computer or loaded at runtime by the server computer by means of the RMIClassloader. The skeleton remains on the server side and takes the calls of the stub, processes them, forwards the call to the server object, waits for the result, and sends it back to the stub. Stub and skeleton together form a protocol layer in the RMI architecture. The underlying reference layer (see Figure 4.1) is used to find the respective communication partner. Another part of this layer is the name service, the registry. The transport layer, which must not be confused with the transport

Stub and skeleton

layer of the ISO/OSI model, communication connections are managed, and the communication itself is handled. This layer relies on TCP/IP.

Class dependence

Since distributed objects cannot behave in the same way as local objects RMI objects do not inherit directly from the java.lang.Object class, but from java.rmi.RemoteObject. This causes some methods from java.lang.Object to be overloaded to adapt them to the conditions in distributed systems. From this class, in turn, the class java.rmi.UnicastRemoteObject is derived, which provides a service with point-to-point connections. An object to be accessed by RMI must inherit from this class. The interface that wants to offer this object for remote access must be separately specified in an interface definition. This interface definition is the basis for the creation of stubs and skeletons, so that only methods indicated here are available on a remote computer. To ensure that all these RMI services can be handled generically, this interface must extend the java.rmi.Remote interface. Overall, this leads to the inheritance hierarchy shown in Figure 4.2.

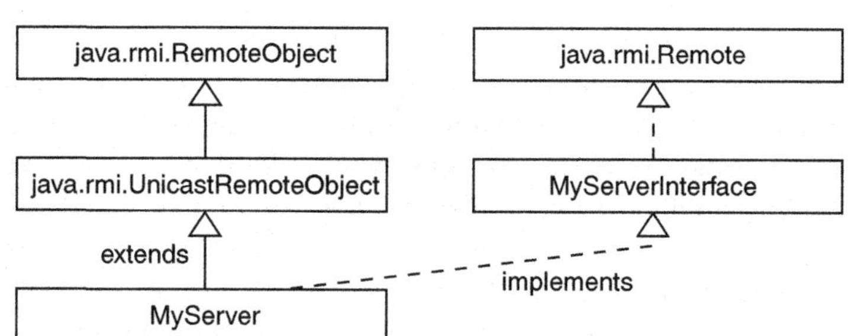

Figure 4.2 *The RMI inheritance hierarchy for Server objects.*

Things are, instead, relatively simple for the client. But clients, too, need to be modified compared to the local call. On the one hand, they must intercept the additional exceptions which may occur in distributed communication. On the other hand, they must establish an initial connection to a remote object.

4.2 A simple example

To clarify the principle of RMI and the necessary steps, we first write a very simple local program, which will then be distributed. In this program, there are two classes: a *bat* and a *ball*. The bat beats the ball, that is, the bat calls the hit() method of the ball, and the ball issues the message that it has been hit.

```
public class Bat {

  public void play(Ball ball) {
    ball.hit();
  }

  public static void main(String args[]){
    Ball ball= new Ball();
    Bat bat= new Bat();
    bat.play(ball);
  }
}

public class Ball {

  public void hit() {
    System.out.println("ball has been hit");
  }
}
```

In the local case, the above program simply outputs the following line:

```
sun> java Bat
sun| ball has been hit
```

In order to distribute this program, the ball should be started as a server on a different machine. To do this, it must first be modified.

4.2.1 The server

First of all, the server must notify the services it wishes to provide for remote access, to an interface called RemoteBall in this example. This interface must be derived from the Remote class and contain the methods which should be remotely accessed, in this case hit(). Since additional error sources may occur at the remote call of this method, which are indicated by a RemoteException, the methods must include a specification that they can pass this exception on.

```
import java.rmi.*;

public interface RemoteBall extends Remote {
  public void hit() throws java.rmi.RemoteException;
}
```

The actual server object, the Ball, must not only implement the interface, but also inherit from RemoteObject or a subclass of RemoteObject. The only subclass implemented in JDK 1.1 is the UnicastRemoteObject class, which enables a point-to-point communication. In the constructor of the Ball class, the constructor of the UnicastRemoteObject superclass must be called via super() so that it initializes correctly. Here too, exceptions may occur, so that the constructor as a whole may create a RemoteException. Once a ball has been produced, it can be registered in the Registry by calling Naming.rebind().

```
import java.rmi.*;
import java.rmi.server.*;

public class Ball extends UnicastRemoteObject
  implements RemoteBall {

  public Ball() throws RemoteException {
    super();
  }

  public void hit(){
    System.out.println("Ball has been hit");
  }

  public static void main(String args[]){
    try {
      Ball ball = new Ball();
```

```
            Naming.rebind("Ball", ball);
        } catch (Exception e) { e.printStackTrace(); }
    }
}
```

Now the stub and skeleton of the Ball class need to be created. This is carried outby the rmic program that takes a compiled class as a parameter which, as the Ball class, is prepared for distribution.

```
sun> rmic Ball
```

This creates the classes Ball_Stub.class and Ball_Skel.class. The skeleton is required on the server side and is usually available to the server. The stub, on the other hand, is required on the client side. The stub is either provided to the client as a file, or the client must load this file over the network. In this case, a SecurityManager must be set up for the client's system to supervise the transmission of the code. The client can do this by means of System.setSecurityManager (new RMISecurityManager()), and then load the code.

But let us first continue with the server. Before the server can be started, the instance responsible for name service and acceptance of enquiries, the rmiregistry, must be started. Then the server can be started, and we can look after the client.

```
sun> rmiregistry
sun> java Ball
```

4.2.2 The client

The client too needs to be prepared for remote access. But in contrast to the server, the client does not need to inherit from additional interfaces or superior classes. To be able to find the server, the client consults the name service on the server's computer and, using the name under which the server is registered there, asks for the required service. All this is done with one call to Naming.lookup(), passing the method a URL of the type rmi://some.server.com/ServiceName as a parameter.

As a result, a reference to an object of the type RemoteObject is returned, which must be restricted to the correct type (*casting*) to be able to use the specific methods of the service. This reference can be then used in the same way as a local reference. Only the additional exceptions, which may occur though the remote call, need to be intercepted.

```
import java.rmi.*;

public class Bat {

  public Ball ball;

  public void play(RemoteBall ball) {
    try {
      ball.hit();
    } catch (RemoteException e) {
      System.out.println(e);
    }
  }

  public static void main (String args[]){
    Bat bat = new Bat();
    try {
      System.setSecurityManager (new RMISecurityManager());
      RemoteBall remoteBall= (RemoteBall)
         Naming.lookup("rmi://sun.informatik.uni-hamburg.de/Ball");
      bat.play(remoteBall);
    } catch (Exception e) {
      System.out.println(e);
    }
  }
}
```

Starting this program on an arbitrary computer (here, on the win computer) that has a TCP/IP connection with the server computer (here, sun) leads – mind you, on the server computer – to the following output:

```
win> java Bat
```

```
sun| Ball has been hit
```

4.3 A chat system with RMI

To be able to point out the advantages and differences of RMI over a socket communication, we will again use a chat system for the demonstration. This application is subdivided into the ChatServer and the ChatClient. As opposed to what happens in the sockets example, where server and client simply replace strings and interpret these (via the agreed protocol) as chat contributions, here a ChatServer provides its services to the clients with a well-defined interface. The server registers its service with the local name server and waits for calls. A client can make use of this service by addressing the corresponding name server, building up a reference to the server object, and then using the interfaces as if it were a local object. The accompanying interface definition of the ChatServer, here called IChatServer, looks as follows:

```
public interface IChatServer extends java.rmi.Remote {

  public void login(String name, ChatClient newClient)
    throws java.rmi.RemoteException;

  public void logout(String name)
    throws java.rmi.RemoteException;

  public void send(Message message)
    throws java.rmi.RemoteException;
}
```

It should be noted that not only strings, as in the socket example, but also objects can be transferred here: when calling the **send** method, the client passes the server an object of **Message** type which, in this example, is a very simple object containing only two strings, one for the name of the client and one for the message. This is, however, where the advantage of object-orientation over pure data transmission becomes apparent. When, in socket communication, the data structure changes, the conventional protocol might need to be changed both on the server and the client side, since these directly handle and interpret the agreed data types. With RMI, instead, the Message object can be changed alone or simply extended by inheritance so that, in a good design, fewer and smaller modifications are needed.

An object will also be passed when the login method is called. However, this object of ChatClient type is different from Message or String, as we will soon see. The client describes itself in this object and transmits it to the server at registration time. The server, however, requires not only a description of the client, but rather a reference to it, in order to deliver messages which, in this example, should obviously also be transmitted via RMI method calls. Therefore, the ChatClient object must also be an object marked as Remote. Normal objects, such as String or Message are copied when they are passed as parameters in a method call. Objects which implement the Remote interface are instead passed as reference, more precisely, as remote reference. The server can then call remote method calls on the ChatClient object via RMI and thus transmit it new chat participants (receiveEnter()) and new contributions (receiveMessage()).

```
public interface IChatClient extends java.rmi.Remote {

  public void receiveEnter(String name)
    throws java.rmi.RemoteException;

  public void receiveExit(String name)
    throws java.rmi.RemoteException;

  public void receiveMessage(Message message)
    throws java.rmi.RemoteException;
}
```

After the interfaces of both server and client have been specified, they can now be implemented. Both ChatClient and ChatServer are listed.

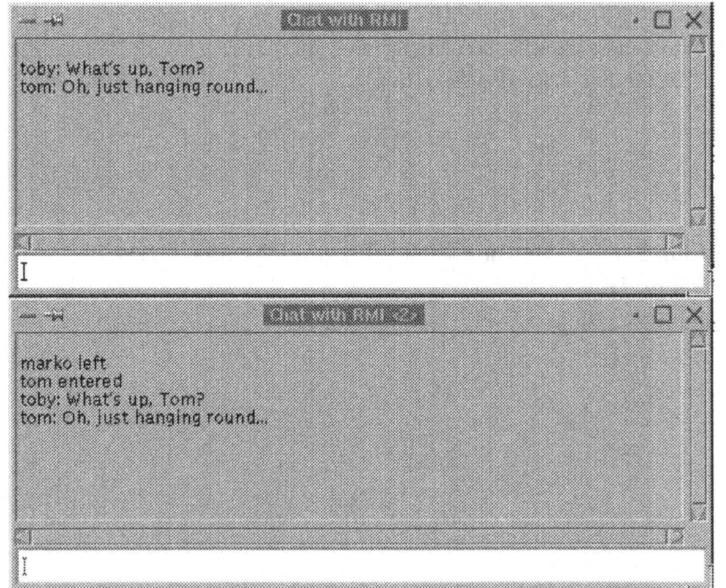

Figure 4.3
Screenshot of a chat with RMI.

```
import java.rmi.*;
import java.rmi.server.*;

public class ChatClient extends UnicastRemoteObject
                        implements IChatClient{
  ChatFrame gui;
  String name;
  IChatServer server;
  String serverUrl;

  public ChatClient(String name, String url) throws RemoteException {
    this.name = name;
    serverUrl = url;
    connect();
    // Create GUI and handle events:
    // After text input, sendTextToChat() is called,
    // when closing the window, disconnect() is called.
```

```
      gui = new ChatFrame("Chat with RMI");
      gui.input.addKeyListener (new EnterListener(this,gui));
      gui.addWindowListener(new ExitListener(this));
   }

   private void connect() {
      try {
         server = (IChatServer) Naming.lookup("rmi://"+serverUrl+
               "/ChatServer");
         server.login(name, this);
      } catch (Exception e) {
         e.printStackTrace();
      }
   }

   protected void disconnect() {
      try {
         server.logout(name);
      } catch (Exception e) {
         e.printStackTrace();
      }
   }
   protected void sendTextToChat(String text) {
      try {
         server.send(new Message(name,text));
      } catch (RemoteException e) {
         e.printStackTrace();
      }
   }

   public void receiveEnter(String name) {
      gui.output.append(name+" entered \n");
   }

   public void receiveExit(String name) {
      gui.output.append(name+" left \n");
   }
```

```
  public void receiveMessage(Message message) {
    gui.output.append(message.name+": "+message.text+"\n");
  }
  public static void main(String[] args) {
    try {
      //Usage: UserName ServerUrl
      new ChatClient(args[0],args[1]);
    } catch (RemoteException e) {
      e.printStackTrace();
    }
  }
}
```

By its very nature, the implementation of the server is somewhat more complicated. It keeps contacts not only to one remote object, but maybe to quite a number of ChatClients, to which it needs to forward incoming messages. To manage the clients, we use a hash table, in which clients are entered with their names as keys (whose uniqueness is tacitly assumed). From this table, an Enumeration is created when required, which is processed sequentially, returning one client every time, who is then sent a message. In this way, all clients are informed when a new user logs in or out, or when a message comes in. The server keeps the remote references, so that the call is carried out via RMI. Since the ChatClient can also be called by the server (*callback*), the ChatClient too is implemented as an RMI server.

```
import java.rmi.*;
import java.rmi.server.*;
import java.util.*;

public class ChatServer extends UnicastRemoteObject
                        implements IChatServer {

  public synchronized void login(String name, IChatClient newClient)
    throws RemoteException {
    Enumeration enum = chatters.elements();
```

```
    chatters.put(name, newClient);
    // make login known to all clients
    while (enum.hasMoreElements()) {
      ((IChatClient) enum.nextElement()).receiveEnter(name);
    }
    System.out.println("new client "+name+" is logged in");
  }

  Hashtable chatters = new Hashtable();

  public ChatServer() throws RemoteException {
  }

  public synchronized void logout(String name) throws RemoteException {
    chatters.remove(name);
    Enumeration enum = chatters.elements();
    // make logout known to all clients
    while (enum.hasMoreElements()) {
      ((IChatClient)enum.nextElement()).receiveExit(name);
    }
  }

  public synchronized void send(Message message) throws RemoteException {
    Enumeration enum = chatters.elements();
    while (enum.hasMoreElements()) {
      ((IChatClient)enum.nextElement()).receiveMessage(message);
    }
  }

  public static void main(String[] args) {
    try {
      ChatServer server = new ChatServer();
      Naming.rebind("ChatServer", server);
    } catch (Exception ex) {
      ex.printStackTrace();
    }
  }
}
```

These programs can be compiled independently from each other, provided that the definitions of ChatServer and ChatClient are known. Both must run through the rmic compiler to create both the stubs and the skeletons. The following inputs compile and start the server on the sun computer, and one client each on win and lin.

```
sun> javac IChatServer.java ChatServer.java Message.java
sun> rmic ChatServer
sun> rmiregistry &
sun> java ChatServer

win> javac ChatClient.java ChatFrame.java Message.java
win> rmic ChatClient
win> java ChatClient marko sun.informatik.uni-hamburg.de

lin> javac ChatClient.java ChatFrame.java Message.java
lin> rmic ChatClient
lin> java ChatClient tom sun
```

Subsequently, the user is provided with an interface similar to the one shown in Figure 4.3.

4.4 References

It is still difficult to find literature about RMI. In most of the standard books about Java, the topic is no longer mentioned, and in some books about networks or distributed programming, it is not yet found since it has been available only with JDK 1.1. In [Farley 1998] and [Hughes *et al.* 1997], for example, only a general outlook can be found. The only book published until now that deals exclusively with the subject of RMI is [Downing 1998], which provides a good entry together with extensive explanations and a reference section. The specification can be looked up under http://java.sun.com/ or in the JDK documentation, where a small introduction can also be found in the Java Tutorial.

5 CORBA

One of the most important efforts of the software industry in the field of distributed systems is the creation of a language-independent, standardized programming system named CORBA (Common Object Request Broker Architecture). More than 800 industrial enterprises have got together in an organization with the aim of jointly developing this project. This organization, which manages the standardization of CORBA, is the Object Management Group (OMG). The OMG has set itself the task of making network-transparent communication between heterogeneous systems possible on the basis of object-oriented software components. In this process, the OMG understands itself as a supervisory body which controls and supports the standardization, but does itself not implement this standard.

The vision behind CORBA

The vision of the OMG is to create an overall architecture in which different software components can communicate with each other as transparently as possible and in heterogeneous environments. The heterogeneity covers the type of networks, computer architectures, and operating systems, up to programming languages. For this overall architecture the OMG has coined the name Object Management Architecture (OMA). The heart of this architecture is what everybody is currently talking about: CORBA.

CORBA is not a language, but a middleware platform. It represents an infrastructure for the programming of distributed systems, but you cannot program in it. To program, you need a programming language supported by CORBA, such as C, C++, Smalltalk, Ada, and obviously Java. The greatest advantage of CORBA is that you can write different parts of an application in different languages, and that nevertheless all parts can cooperate with each other. To achieve this, the different parts are defined in a largely language-independent notation, the Interface Definition Language (IDL), which is then translated by a compiler into the appropriate target language in which these interfaces will finally be implemented. These interfaces can then be accessed by other components, not only locally, but also remotely via a communication network.

This chapter introduces the OMG, CORBA, the functioning of CORBA, and the IDL. With the aid of an example, the development of a CORBA application will be demonstrated, making use of the CORBA implementation by Visigenic (now Inprise). To start with, the OMG and the standardization process will be presented, which will help you to assess the significance of CORBA.

5.1 The structure of the OMG

The OMG differs substantially from other standardization bodies. As opposed to the ISO, it does not represent a Government institution. Nor does it develop a special product, unlike the Open Software Foundation (OSF) which, for example, has both standardized and implemented the DCE (Distributed Computing Environment).

Based on members' proposals, the OMG defines specifications, which are then standardized, made freely available to the public, and can finally be implemented by members or by third parties. This gives rise to a multitude of products showing different qualities, such as runtime behavior or pricing, but always presenting the same interface and the same external behavior. These products compete with each other on the market and must try to prevail over other implementations. This is supposed to improve innovation and interchangeability of components.

The OMG's bodies

The OMG is governed by a Board of Directors which is elected by the members. The Architecture Board controls the technical work of the subordinate groups. The OMG's main bodies are the Technological Committees (TCs), to which the standards are submitted, and which harmonize and finally decide them. There are two TCs, reflecting the structure of the OMA: the Platform TC determines the general infrastructure and controls its further development, while the Domain TC is responsible for the special, domain-specific questions.

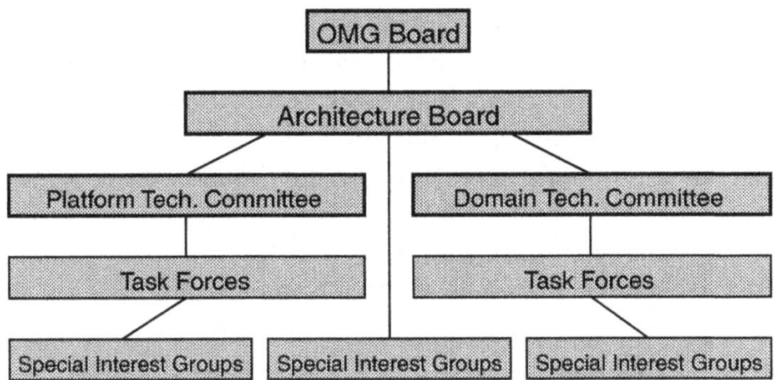

Figure 5.1
The structure of the OMG.

The TCs are further subdivided into Task Forces (TFs) and Special Interest Groups (SIGs). The actual work of preparation and submission of the requests, harmonizing of the answers, and elaboration and supervision of the standards is carried out in the Task Forces. The Special Interest Groups are prevailingly a discussion forum for the preparation of new requests.

Only members are allowed to submit proposals for new standards or extensions and participate in the voting. Further committees, for example, are concerned with the coordination with other standardization bodies.

5.2 The standardization process

The standardization process of the OMG is quite noteworthy, since it relatively quickly drives the members to an agreement, forces them to a certain degree of cooperation and at the same time pushes the conversion of the proposals into merchantable products.

From the RFI ...

When a new standard is to be created, a Task Force formulates a Request for Information (RFI) in which the members are asked to state their fundamental position towards the problem in question. After an evaluation of the answers, the

Task Force prepares a Request for Proposal (RFP), in which the members are asked to elaborate a solution for the open question. Only those solutions are accepted as an answer to an RFP that are guaranteed to be further developed into a merchantable product by the members proposing the solution in the form of a Letter of Intent (LOI).

... to the product

The time scale of the individual steps is fixed, so that usually not more than two years pass between an RFI and the availability of a merchantable product. This is exceptionally fast for a standardization process. ISO standardization processes may take up to eight years. Furthermore, the enterprises are forced to cooperate with each other, so that answers to an RFP usually bear a whole series of company names.

5.3 OMA – the overall architecture

The OMA represents the framework in which the vision of the OMG is to be put into practice. The heart of this architecture is constituted by the Object Request Broker, a kind of software bus that connects the individual parts or components of the architecture transparently with each other. Objects may address other objects via this bus and send them messages in the sense of object-orientation. Thus objects get into contact as clients with other objects that serve them as servers. This Object Request Broker is at the origin of the name CORBA, which is the acronym for Common Object Request Broker Architecture.

Besides the CORBA bus, the overall architecture is subdivided into further sections. On a lower level, basic services needed by every object are combined into what is known as CORBAservices. On a higher level, superior services are available called CORBAfacilities. Here, a distinction is made between services that are trade-independent and those that are trade-specific. The first are known as horizontal, the second as vertical services. The objects of the actual applications can make use of these services via the Object Request Broker (ORB). The following list explains the individual service groups in more detail.

CORBAservices. The CORBAservices represent fundamental services, as they are used by every application and

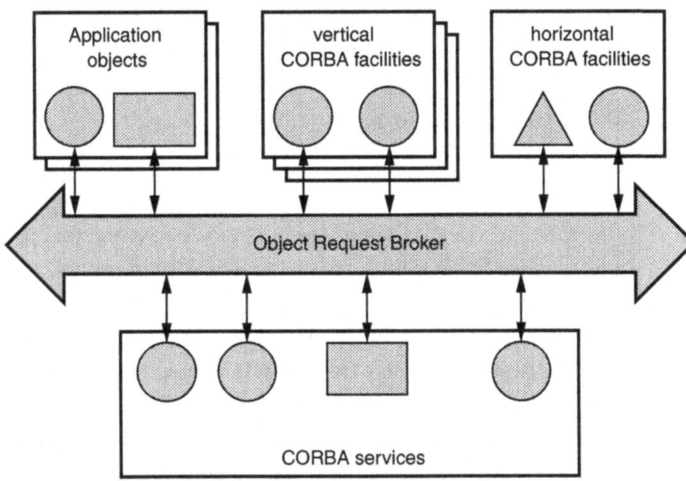

Figure 5.2 The Object Management Architecture (OMA).

even by nearly every object. As all CORBA services, they are defined and standardized in IDL and can be addressed and used via the ORB. Examples of CORBAservices are:

- Lifecycle Service
- Relationship Service
- Naming Service
- Trader Service
- Security Service
- Persistence Service
- Concurrency Control Service

CORBAfacilities. The CORBAfacilities are subdivided into a horizontal and a vertical layer. The horizontal layer of the CORBAfacilities includes services that are trade-independent. In every trade there are documents, for example, which are combined out of text, images, tables, and so on. Such documents are processed by the horizontal services. These are, in turn, subdivided into four segments that are concerned with the following four subfields:

- User Interface
- Information Management
- Task Management
- System Management

The vertical CORBAfacilities provide services for specific trades. Such standard services are being developed in a whole range of industrial branches. In part, such services have emerged from trade-specific standards and been incorporated into the CORBA standards in close cooperation with the OMG. Vertical services are, for example, being developed for the health service, and for banking, petrochemical, and telecommunication areas.

5.4 The CORBA architecture

CORBA is an architecture, not a piece of software or a programming language. This architecture consists of various components which are shown in Figure 5.3 and will be briefly discussed in the following section. The heart is the Object Request Broker (ORB), which is responsible for accepting a request of a CORBA object, the *client*, to another CORBA object, the *server*, to locate the server, forward the call, and deliver the answer back to the client. For the client, the process of locating the server is hidden, it has merely a reference to the server object without knowing where this object is actually located.

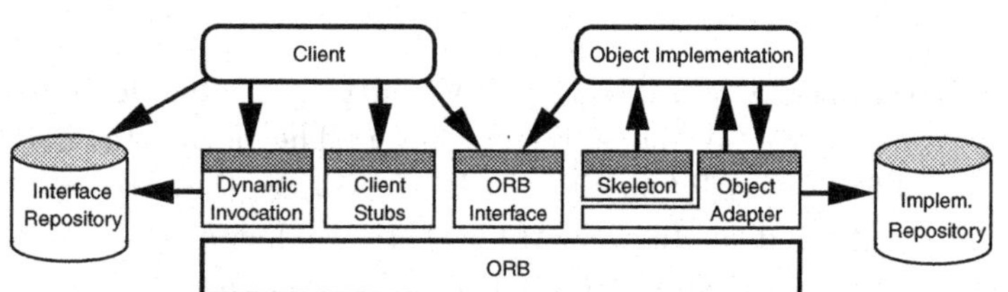

Figure 5.3 *The CORBA architecture.*

The client side

The client does not directly address the ORB. On the client's side, there is a representative for the server object, the client stub, which offers the client the same interface as the server object itself. The client stub takes over the task of communicating with the ORB.

There is yet another mechanism that the client can use to access a server object, namely one that does without a representative of the server object, the stub. This is particularly sensible when the interface of the server object was not known to the client at compile time. In such cases, CORBA provides a dynamic mechanism, the Dynamic Invocation Interface (DII).

CORBA standard operations can be directly accessed by a client via an ORB interface. In particular, this is used for starting and initializing the ORB.

The Interface Repository contains the description of all registered objects, their methods, and their attributes. Via a programming interface, the client can access the repository and read the interface of the objects contained in it.

The server side

On the side of object implementation, that is, the server, the object adapter represents the direct interface with the ORB. It contains calls for objects from the ORB, starts and instantiates the object implementations, where required, and passes the call to the object implementations. The object adapter registers the classes it supports and their object implementations in the implementation repository. It assigns unique object references for new instances and manages them. CORBA prescribes one standard object adapter (the Basic Object Adapter, BOA) for each conformant ORB implementation. An implementation may, however, contain additional object adapters; one adapter that has equally been standardized by now is the POA (Portable Object Adapter).

The Implementation Repository provides a name service which can be used to query which classes are supported on a server and which objects are instantiated, and manages their object references. Here, additional information can be stored which may, for example, serve for security support or accounting.

The Broker

The Object Request Broker is defined in the CORBA standard through its interface. It may be implemented in different ways by different manufacturers, as long as the interface corresponds to the standard. Consequently, ORB implementations may be rather different. There are ORBs based on libraries which are linked to the stubs or skeletons; there are ORBs built upon a daemon mechanism; and there are those that are centrally managed by a server machine.

To be able to address an object, each object is assigned a unique reference. This reference is the information required to identify and address an object via an ORB. This reference is assigned to the object by the ORB at creation time and remains valid as long as the corresponding object exists, even if the object changes location.

Making the reference known

This reference can be made available to other objects which can then use it to access the object. This can happen in various ways: a reference can be stored in a file or in a database and be read by a client, or the client can resort to a service that provides object references, such as, for example, the naming service or the trader service. A naming server can create a mapping of a name to a reference. A trader can offer different objects with the same service, but different conditions, or with different quality features, letting the client choose one of these objects or making a suitable choice for the client.

Calls via CORBA

Once a client has obtained a reference to an object, it can call up operations on this object. Two mechanisms are available to the client for this purpose: the dynamic call via the DII or the static call via the client stub. The DII is used, for example, when the type of the object to be called was not known at compile time. The simpler and more frequent case, however, is the call via a stub. Since the stub represents a placeholder of the object on the client's side, the object call functions, from the client's view, exactly like a local call.

The stub packs the parameters in a suitable form (*marshalling*) and refers this call to the ORB which then forwards it to the object adapter. The object adapter activates the object, even creating a new instance if required, and hands the call over to the skeleton. This unpacks (*demarshalling*) the parameters and calls the object implementation (see Figure 5.4). The result of the call is then packed, sent, and unpacked in the opposite direction and finally delivered back to the client.

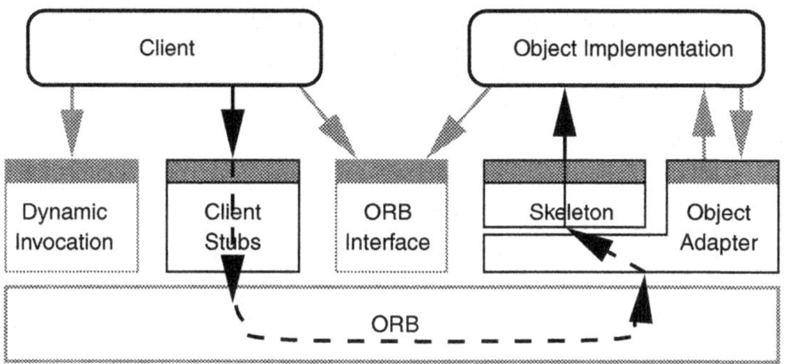

Figure 5.4
The pathway of a request.

5.5 IDL

The Interface Definition Language (IDL) is used to desccribe objects together with their methods and attributes. IDL has been designed as an interface description language, which is independent from the languages in which these interfaces will actually be implemented. This confers on the IDL a central role in CORBA. IDL makes it possible that client and server may be programmed in different languages, not even having to know in which language the relative counterpart has been programmed. Syntactically the IDL is oriented towards C++, but has been extended by several elements and has no algorithmic components.

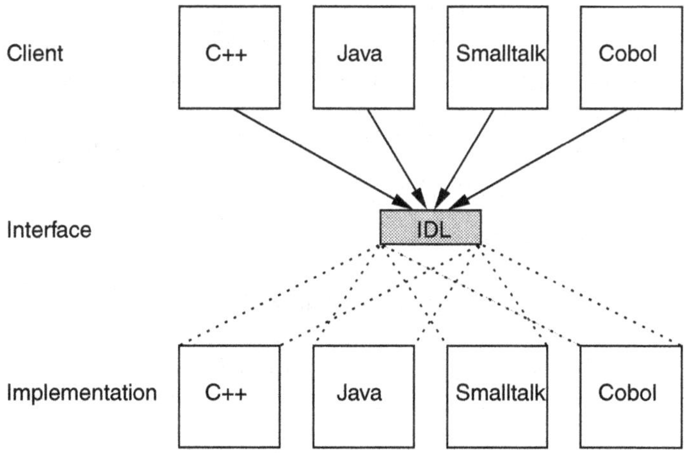

Figure 5.5
The role of the IDL.

Specifications in IDL consist of module, constant, type, interface, and exception definitions. The following paragraphs will introduce the syntax of IDL without, however, getting into all of the details.

Definitions in IDL are subdivided into modules. Each module constitutes a namespace (*scope*), in which identifiers of types, constants, attributes, and so on, are defined. Inside the namespace the identifiers must be unique names. Names from a different namespace, that is, from a different module, can also be referenced, by addressing the namespace through the name of the module and separating namespace and identifier with two colons.

```
<namespace>::<identifier>
```

Through the connection of namespace and identifier, names are also globally unique, so that CORBA services can be uniquely referenced even in very large networks such as the Internet. All further declarations must be defined inside a module.

The most important element in IDL is certainly the declaration of interfaces. Interfaces can be derived from other interfaces by inheritance, even by multiple inheritance, where it is the programmer's very own task to resolve the naming conflicts caused by inheritance. Then, an interface provides a series of operations. Each operation has a signature which consists of the name of the function, a result type, and a parameter list. The parameters in the list consist of a parameter name, its type, and one of the attributes `in`, `out`, or `inout`. An `in` parameter is only transmitted from the client to the server, an `out` parameter is only transmitted from the server to the client, and an `inout` parameter can be transmitted in both directions. Such declarations are more or less of the following form:

```
module <identifier>
{
  interface <identifier> [:<inheritance>]
  {
    [<op_type>]<identifier>([in|inout|out] <parameter>);
  }
}
```

Besides the operations, it is also possible to define attributes. These begin with the identifier attribute and are then declared by a type and a name. Attributes that may only be read are given the additional identifier readonly.

```
module <identifier>
{
  interface <identifier> [:<inheritance>]
  {
    attribute <type> <identifier>;
    readonly attribute <type> <identifier>;
    [<op_type>]<identifier>([in|inout|out] <parameter>);
  }
}
```

Operations can trigger exceptions, as they are known from Java or C++, which must be indicated in the signature of an operation in IDL. For this, an operation definition may contain a raises clause which lists the exceptions. Exceptions must also be declared before they can be used. They can be defined either at module level or inside an interface. In contrast to Java, an exception can be assigned a context which can describe the caused error message more precisely.

```
module <identifier>
{
  exception <exception_name>;
  interface <identifier> [:<inheritance>]
  {
    exception <exception_name>;
    [<op_type>]<identifier>([in|inout|out] <parameter>)
      raises <exception_name> [{<context_type>
                                <context>}];
  }
}
```

The simple data types used in IDL correspond more or less to those of Java, such as, for example, boolean, char, int, or float. Unfortunately, not all types have an exact counterpart, thus, for example, in IDL a long must be used instead of a Java int.

IDL offers the possibility of building more complex data types out of these simple types by means of a type system as it is used in C++. For this purpose, simple data types are combined into structs or unions and given a specialized name by means of typedef. IDL also includes enumerations, which exist in C++ but not in Java, constants, and multi-dimensional arrays.

```
module <identifier>
{
  struct <struct_name>
  {
    <type> <identifier>;
    <type> <identifier>;
  };
  union <union_name> switch(<type>)
  {
    <type> <identifier>;
    <type> <identifier>;
  };
  typedef <type> <identifier>;
  enum <type> {<identifier>,<identifier>};
  const <const_declaration>;
  interface <identifier> [:<inheritance>]
  {
    struct ...
    const ...;
    [<op_type>]<identifier>([in|inout|out] <parameter>);
  }
}
```

Our example will once again be a chat. Since CORBA is a typical client/server infrastructure, the example will be implemented as a client/server architecture. On a server machine, a ChatServer is to be started on which individual ChatClients can log on and off. For this purpose, the ChatServer provides the operations login() and logout(), in which the client must specify its name and, when logging in, also a reference to itself. After the login, the client can use the send() method to send messages to the chat, where a message consists of the client's name and a String and is passed in a struct Message. The client should always be informed of logins and logouts of other participants and be able to receive the messages sent. Thus the IDL interface of such a service might look as follows:

```
module Chat {

  typedef string Name;

  struct Message {
    Name name;
    string message;
  };

  exception UnknownName {};
  exception Reject {string reason;};

  interface ChatClient {
    void receiveEnter(in Name name, in ChatClient chatter);
    void receiveExit(in Name name);
    void receiveMessage(in Message message);
  };

  interface ChatServer {
    const short MaxClients = 20;
    readonly attribute short numOfClients;
    void login (in Name name, in ChatClient chatter) raises (Reject);
    void logout (in Name name);
    void send (in Message message);
  };

};
```

5.6 The IDL compiler

Once such an IDL interface has been defined, it can be processed with the IDL compiler which, depending on the complexity of the example and the CORBA product used, generates at least the following output.

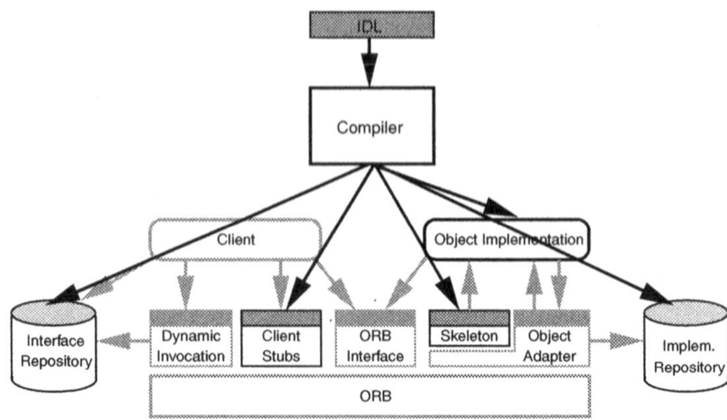

Figure 5.6
The IDL compiler.

- A client stub is generated which performs a mapping of the programming language constructions to the constructions in IDL, then translates these IDL constructions into an on-the-wire format, and can also call the ORB. Equally, it must be able to unpack the result from the on-the-wire format and translate it back into constructions of the target language.
- A skeleton is created as the corresponding counterpart on the server side, which unpacks the information it receives from the client stub and transmits it by means of an upcall to the called object.
- The IDL compiler equally creates an implementation frame of this object, which needs to be filled in by the programmer.
- Fourth, the compiler generates everything that is registered in the Interface and Implementation Repositories, and even takes care of the registration.

In the following, we will use the CORBA implementation by Inprise (formerly Visigenic), which is called VisiBroker and is one of the most important and easy implementations in particular for the Java area. VisiBroker's IDL compiler for Java has the name idl2java. With the call

```
sun> idl2java chat.idl
```

the following Java files are created:

```
sun| Traversing chat.idl
sun| Creating: Chat
sun| Creating: Chat/NameHolder.java
sun| Creating: Chat/NameHelper.java
sun| Creating: Chat/Message.java
sun| Creating: Chat/MessageHolder.java
sun| Creating: Chat/MessageHelper.java
sun| Creating: Chat/UnknownName.java
sun| Creating: Chat/UnknownNameHolder.java
sun| Creating: Chat/UnknownNameHelper.java
sun| Creating: Chat/Reject.java
sun| Creating: Chat/RejectHolder.java
sun| Creating: Chat/RejectHelper.java

sun| Creating: Chat/ChatClient.java
sun| Creating: Chat/ChatClientHolder.java
sun| Creating: Chat/ChatClientHelper.java
sun| Creating: Chat/_st_ChatClient.java
sun| Creating: Chat/_ChatClientImplBase.java
sun| Creating: Chat/ChatClientOperations.java
sun| Creating: Chat/_tie_ChatClient.java
sun| Creating: Chat/_example_ChatClient.java

sun| Creating: Chat/ChatServer.java
sun| Creating: Chat/ChatServerHolder.java
sun| Creating: Chat/ChatServerHelper.java
sun| Creating: Chat/_st_ChatServer.java
sun| Creating: Chat/_ChatServerImplBase.java
sun| Creating: Chat/ChatServerOperations.java
sun| Creating: Chat/_tie_ChatServer.java
sun| Creating: Chat/_example_ChatServer.java
```

At first sight, this seems to be an incredible lot of files for so short and simple an IDL. But each of these has its reason for being there, which we will now briefly discuss. Each file contains a Java class that plays its own special role.

The XXXHolder and XXXHelper classes are internal auxiliary classes for a class XXX, which are chiefly responsible for the mapping operations from IDL to Java. These files will be explained in more detail in the next section. Such auxiliary classes are also created for the ChatClient and the ChatServer. In addition, for the latter, the even more important files _st_ChatClient.java and _st_ChatServer.java are created, which contain the stub classes needed on the client side. Let us take a closer look at the stub of the ChatClient. For each operation of the ChatClient in the IDL, it contains a method which essentially forwards the call to the CORBA system and ensures correct handling of the parameters, resorting once again to the auxiliary classes. Excerpts of this class are shown in the following listing:

```
package Chat;

public class _st_ChatClient
  extends org.omg.CORBA.portable.ObjectImpl
  implements Chat.ChatClient {
 ...

  public void receiveMessage(Chat.Message message) {
    try {
      org.omg.CORBA.portable.OutputStream _output =
        this._request("receiveMessage", true);
      Chat.MessageHelper.write(_output, message);
     org.omg.CORBA.portable.InputStream _input = this._invoke(_output, null);
    } catch(org.omg.CORBA.TRANSIENT _exception) {
      receiveMessage(message);
    }
  }
}
```

For the opposite side, the server, a skeleton is created which is stored in the file _XXXImplBase.java. This skeleton accepts the call, unpacks the parameters, and forwards it to the actual implementation. To make this clearer, the next piece of code shows the point of the ChatServer skeleton, where a call of the login() method is forwarded.

```
package Chat;

abstract public class _ChatServerImplBase
  extends org.omg.CORBA.portable.Skeleton
  implements Chat.ChatServer {
 ...
 public static boolean _execute(Chat.ChatServer _self,
  int _method_id, org.omg.CORBA.portable.InputStream _input,
  org.omg.CORBA.portable.OutputStream _output) {
   switch(_method_id) {
   case 0: {
     try {
       java.lang.String name;
       name = _input.read_string();
       Chat.ChatClient chatter;
       chatter = Chat.ChatClientHelper.read(_input);
       _self.login(name,chatter);
     }
     catch(Chat.Reject _exception) {
       Chat.RejectHelper.write(_output, _exception);
       return true;
     }
     return false;
   }
   case 1: {
     ...
   }
   throw new org.omg.CORBA.MARSHAL();
  }
}
```

The files _example_ChatClient.java and _example_ChatServer.java are without doubt the most important files for developers.

They contain a code skeleton out of which the implementation of client and server can be developed. Before we discuss these files and their contents in more detail, we will first present the mapping function from IDL to Java.

5.7 IDL–Java mapping

Since the interfaces of a CORBA system are specified in IDL, this must be mapped to a Java interface (or another language). For each IDL element, such as module, interface and attribute, it must be exactly determined how this element is going to be implemented in Java. Only then, cross-compatibility between a C++ application and a Java program or between different ORBs is possible. Therefore, such mappings from IDL to the implementation language are standardized by the OMG.

For Java too there exists a mapping standard, which will now be briefly introduced. On the syntax side, the IDL is rather strongly orientated towards C++, but since Java as well shows a certain similarity with C++, the mapping from IDL to Java is not too complicated. Thus, for example, the basic types, such as boolean, char, float, and so on, match in the two languages and can be directly mapped onto each other. But already the simple data types present certain smaller problems the developer must well know to avoid difficulties. Thus, for example, IDL includes both signed integer types (short, long, and long long, stored in 16, 32, and 64 bits respectively) and unsigned integer types (unsigned short, unsigned long, and unsigned long long). In Java, instead, all integer types are always signed. Unsigned, 16 bits cover a value range from 0 to 65,535, whereas with the sign, the value range reaches from -32,768 to 32,767. Now, both the signed (for example short) and the unsigned (for example unsigned short) IDL types are mapped onto the same signed data types in Java (for example short). This can lead to errors in the interpretation of the value. If, for example, a parameter is passed as IDL unsigned short and has a value greater than 32,767, it is interpreted in Java as a negative value. Therefore, one should do without unsigned types already in the IDL specification, or intercept such cases in the

Problems of mapping

implementation. A similar problem occurs in the conversion of characters (char). In Java, characters are coded in UNICODE, using 16 bits, while in IDL, the char type is only represented with 8 bits. Therefore, an additional IDL 16-bit type was introduced, named wchar. No such problems occur, however, with floating point numbers, because the same standard is used in both cases.

Complex data structures

For complex data types, IDL provides expressive mechanisms of good old C tradition, such as typedef, struct, and union, which are not needed in an object-oriented language because they are defined through appropriate classes. However, since the mechanisms are present in IDL, they must be properly mapped. Typedefs in IDL are simply ignored in Java, so that, for example, the string type continues to be substituted for a typedef string Name; defined in IDL. The enumeration type enum also does not exist in Java and must be simulated via the creation of constants. For structs and unions, classes are created that provide the corresponding functionality.

Thus, for example, the IDL for the ChatService defines a structure for a message which contains two strings, one for the name of the sender and one for the message itself.

```
struct Message {
    Name name;
    string message;
};
```

Out of this, the IDL compiler creates the classes Message, MessageHelper, and MessageHolder. Message represents the class which replaces the IDL's struct, and wherever the struct is used in the IDL definition, this class must be used in Java. The following listing shows the generated Message class.

```
package Chat;

final public class Message {
  public java.lang.String name;
  public java.lang.String message;

  public Message() { }
```

```
  public Message(java.lang.String name,java.lang.String message) {
    this.name = name;
    this.message = message;
  }

  public java.lang.String toString() {
    org.omg.CORBA.Any any = org.omg.CORBA.ORB.init().create_any();
    Chat.MessageHelper.insert(any, this);
    return any.toString();
  }
}
```

Attributes

Operations and parameters

Operations and attributes in IDL are mapped onto appropriate methods in Java. For attributes, read methods and, if they are not declared as readonly, write methods are created which allow access to an attribute of a class. In the case of operations, the parameters too must be adequately handled. In a local program, parameters are passed as references to objects (or as values with basic types). In remote calls this is not possible, so they are usually passed as copies. For operations with only in parameters, things are simple: the copy is read by the called method, but not changed, so that no further measures need to be taken. With out and inout parameters, modified values must be copied back into the original address space. For this purpose, *Holder* classes are created which in remote method calls are passed and also returned as parameters, so that the caller can read the changes in these Holder objects. Holder classes are always structured in the same way: they have a constructor used for inserting the object and a value out of which the object can be fetched back, plus methods for serializing and deserializing. The type information is held in a TypeCode, which can also be queried.

```
final public class MessageHolder implements
                                    org.omg.CORBA.portable.Streamable {
  public Chat.Message value;
  public MessageHolder() {
  }
```

```
  public MessageHolder(Chat.Message value) {
    this.value = value;
  }
  public void _read(org.omg.CORBA.portable.InputStream input) {
    value = MessageHelper.read(input);
  }
  public void _write(org.omg.CORBA.portable.OutputStream output) {
    MessageHelper.write(output, value);
  }
  public org.omg.CORBA.TypeCode _type() {
    return MessageHelper.type();
  }
}
```

These two classes, Message and MessageHolder, need the MessageHelper class which has equally been generated and which is, in particular, responsible for the conversion of the parameters into a linear data stream (*marshalling*) and their reconversion. Besides a variety of other methods, this class also contains methods required for type restriction and name binding. The following listing shows only some excerpts of the MessageHelper class.

```
abstract public class MessageHelper {
   public static void write(org.omg.CORBA.portable.OutputStream _output,
     Chat.Message value) {
       _output.write_string(value.name);
       _output.write_string(value.message);
   }
   public static void insert(org.omg.CORBA.Any any, Chat.Message value) {
    org.omg.CORBA.portable.OutputStream output = any.create_output_stream();
      write(output, value);
      any.read_value(output.create_input_stream(), type());
  }
}
```

IDL interfaces are mapped onto Java interfaces, which can subsequently be implemented by means of appropriate classes. However, because of this indirection, inheritance becomes much more flexible: in IDL, multiple inheritance is allowed, which in Java applies only to interfaces, but not to classes. The modular structure in IDL is projected onto the corresponding Java packages, which are stored in Java's usual directory structure.

Thus, out of the definition of the ChatClient, the idl2java compiler creates the following interface, in which, for example, the generated Message class too appears again.

```
package Chat;

public interface ChatClient extends org.omg.CORBA.Object {
  public void receiveEnter(java.lang.String name, Chat.ChatClient chatter);

  public void receiveExit(java.lang.String name);

  public void receiveMessage(Chat.Message message);
}
```

The generated interface of the ChatServer looks as follows:

```
package Chat;
public interface ChatServer extends org.omg.CORBA.Object {
  final public static short MaxClients = (short) 20;
  public short numOfClients();

  public void login(java.lang.String name, Chat.ChatClient chatter)
    throws Chat.Reject;

  public void logout(java.lang.String name);

  public void send(Chat.Message message);
}
```

However, these are still only interfaces and not classes that include an implementation. The steps that lead up to the implementation will be presented in the following section, first with the aid of a very small and simple example, and subsequently with the chat interface shown above.

5.8 A simple example

Let us take a really simple IDL and walk through the subsequent steps. The IDL we are going to use is again the well-known example of the ball and the bat. The server (that is, the ball) is described by the following IDL:

```
module BatBall {
  interface Ball {
     void hit(in string by);
  };
};
```

Out of this description, an IDL compiler (idl2java BatBall.idl) generates the necessary Java files whose exact meaning will be explained in the next section. The most important file generated for the present is the program skeleton, created by VisiBroker as _example_Ball.java. We rename it into BallServer and implement it. The initialization of the ORB, which is carried out here in the main() method, will also be discussed in more detail in the next section. Here, we will only point out one peculiarity of VisiBroker. VisiBroker includes a simple name service which resembles that of RMI. Thus, objects can be registered with the ORB with a name and can also be retrieved via this name, which represents a great improvement on the usual way, but does not correspond to the standard. Our service is registered under the name "Ball", which the constructor automatically takes over. A possible implementation might look as follows:

```
package BatBall;
import org.omg.CORBA.*;
```

```
public class BallServer extends BatBall._BallImplBase {
  public BallServer( String bind_name ) {
    super( bind_name );
  }

  public void hit(java.lang.String by) {
    System.out.println("Ball has been hit by" + by);
  }

  public static void main(String args[]) {
    try {
      ORB orb = ORB.init();
      BOA boa = orb.BOA_init();
      BallServer ball = new BallServer("Ball");
      orb.connect(ball);
      boa.obj_is_ready(ball);
      boa.impl_is_ready();
    } catch (Exception e) { e.printStackTrace(); }
  }
}
```

Subsequently, a client can be written which binds itself to the above server object and calls it. Here too the ORB is initialized, which will only be explained in the next section.

```
package BatBall;
import org.omg.CORBA.*;
public class Bat {
  public static void main(String[] args) {
    ORB orb = ORB.init();
    Ball ball = BallHelper.bind(orb,"Ball");
    ball.hit("Marko");
    System.out.println("I hit the ball");
  }
}
```

Now the individual parts of the program can be compiled and started. For this purpose, the VisiBroker provides its own compiler and its own execution environment which (instead of `javac` and `java`) are called `vbjc` and `vbj`.

```
sun> vbjc -d . BallServer.java
sun> vbj BatBall.BallServer

lin> vbjc -d . Bat.java
lin> vbj BatBall.Bat

sun| I hit the ball

lin| Ball has been hit by Marko
```

5.9 A chat system with CORBA

Now we will turn to an extensive example. The IDL definition of the "Chat" example has already been presented earlier in this chapter. Now, the complete implementation will be shown. Here too, the IDL compiler generates a pattern or code skeleton, which can be renamed and modified, and which can thus serve as a basis for the actual implementation. The pattern for the client is generated in VisiBroker as _example_ChatClient.java and has been renamed MyChatClient for further elaboration.

```
package Chat;
import java.util.Vector;
import java.io.*;
import java.awt.event.*

public class MyChatClient extends Chat._ChatClientImplBase {

  ChatFrame gui;
  String name;
  Chat.ChatServer server = null;

  public MyChatClient(String _name, Chat.ChatServer _server) {
    super(_name);
    name = _name;
    server = _server;
    gui = new ChatFrame("Chat mit CORBA");
```

```
    // When Enter is pressed in the input field ...
    gui.input.addKeyListener (
      new KeyAdapter() {
        public void keyPressed(KeyEvent e) {
          if (e.getKeyCode()==KeyEvent.VK_ENTER) {
            sendTextToChat(gui.input.getText());
            gui.input.setText("");
          }
        }
      }
    );

    // When the chat window is closed ...
    gui.addWindowListener(
      new WindowAdapter() {
        public void windowClosing(WindowEvent e) {
          server.logout(name);
          System.exit(0);
        }
      }
    );
    try {
      server.login(name, this);
    } catch (Exception e) {  e.printStackTrace(); }
  }

  public void sendTextToChat(String message) {
    server.send(new Chat.Message(name,message));
  }

  public void receiveEnter(java.lang.String name, Chat.ChatClient chatter) {
    gui.output.append(name+" entered \n");
  }

  public void receiveExit(java.lang.String name) {
    gui.output.append(name+" left \n");
  }
```

```
  public void receiveMessage(Chat.Message message) {
    gui.output.append(message.name+": "+message.message+"\n");
  }
}
```

Once the individual parts have been generated out of the IDL, the implementation is no longer difficult. Programming is, however, greatly simplified if the IDL definition itself is already set up with a view to the best possible conformity with Java. Thus one should, if possible, do without using inout and out parameters or structs, and so on. This is obviously not always possible in a CORBA context, where the original idea is to develop the IDL in a language-independent way.

Finally, we will show the implementation of the chat server. It should be noted that the server inherits from the skeleton class Chat._ChatServerImplBase, which is in turn derived from the ChatServer interface. In this way, the class implements the original interface as well as the functionality of CORBA.

```
package Chat;
import java.util.*;

public class MyChatServer extends Chat._ChatServerImplBase {

  Hashtable chatters = new Hashtable();

  public MyChatServer(java.lang.String name) {
    super(name);
  }

  public synchronized void login(java.lang.String name, Chat.ChatClient newClient)
        throws Chat.Reject {
    Enumeration enum = chatters.elements();
    chatters.put(name, newClient);
    Chat.ChatClient client = null;
```

```
    while (enum.hasMoreElements()) {
      client = (Chat.ChatClient) enum.nextElement();
      client.receiveEnter(name, newClient);
    }
  }

  public synchronized void logout(java.lang.String name) {
    chatters.remove(name);
    Enumeration enum = chatters.elements();
    while (enum.hasMoreElements()) {
      ((MyChatClient)
        enum.nextElement()).receiveExit(name);
    }
  }

  public synchronized void send(Chat.Message message) {
    Enumeration enum = chatters.elements();
    while (enum.hasMoreElements()) {
      ((Chat.ChatClient)
        enum.nextElement()).receiveMessage(message);
    }
  }

  public short numOfClients() {
    return (short) chatters.size();
  }
}
```

5.10 Starting a server

In order to start a ChatServer in such a way that it can be addressed via CORBA, several steps are required which are more or less the same for each service and which are frequently included in the main() method of a service. Because of the generic nature of these steps, we will introduce a dedicated class which only contains an appropriate main() method (schematically shown in Figure 5.7).

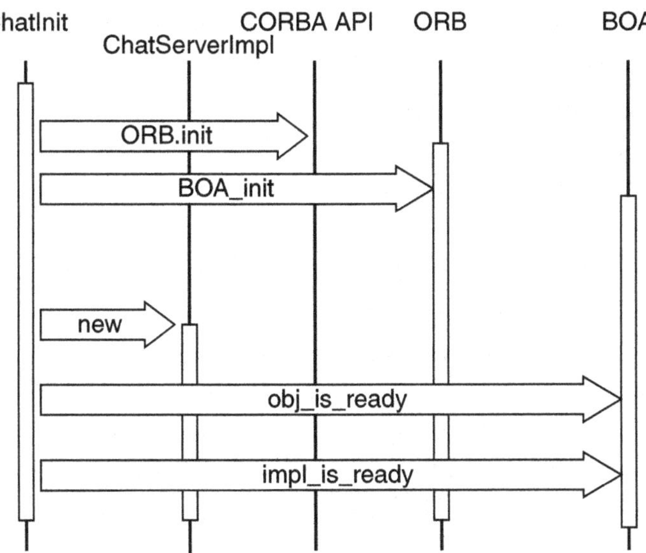

First of all, a reference to the ORB is needed. For this purpose, the static method ORB.init() is called, which starts and initializes the ORB, if necessary, and returns such a reference. Also the object adapter, which is responsible for the activation of object instances, must be initialized. In the standardization, up to now, only a so-called Basic Object Adapter (BOA) was required which is, however, not fully specified and therefore implemented in rather different ways. This shall be replaced by a Portable Object Adapter (POA). It is also possible to start a server completely without an object adapter, but then it can no longer be referenced after termination of the main program.

Subsequently, an instance of the ChatServer is created and registered with the ORB. When a BOA is used, the object must in addition be registered with the BOA through a call of obj_is_ready(). With the call of impl_is_ready(), the BOA finally begins to wait for calls for this object. Then a reference to this object must be made known, via which ChatClients can call this service. This can happen in various ways, for example by registering with a name service. For simplicity's sake, in our example the reference will only be output in a textual form, which can then be specified at the start of the client.

```
import org.omg.CORBA.*;
import Chat.*;
public class StartChatServer {

  public static void main(String args[]){
    try {
      ORB orb = ORB.init();
      BOA boa = orb.BOA_init();
      MyChatServer server = new MyChatServer();
      orb.connect(server);
      System.out.println(orb.object_to_string(server));
      boa.obj_is_ready(server);
      boa.impl_is_ready();
    } catch (Exception e) { e.printStackTrace(); }
  }
}
```

Then the server is started and, from that moment on, is at the client's disposal.

```
sun> java StartChatServer
sun| IOR:000000000000001849444c3a436861742f436861745365
727665723a312e3000000000000100000000000000004c000100000000
000f3133342e3130302e31312e3137350000405b00000000002c00
504d43000000001000000001849444c3a436861742f43686174536572
7665723a312e3000000000000019740f141
```

5.11 Starting a client

Now we have reached the point where it is possible to start a client that can register with the ChatServer and participate in a chat. Here too, we will show a class which is only responsible for starting the client and which contains only a main() method.

```
import org.omg.CORBA.*;
import Chat.*;

public class StartChatClient {

  public static void main(String args[]) {
    try {
      ORB orb = ORB.init();
      BOA boa = orb.BOA_init();
      org.omg.CORBA.Object serverObj = orb.string_to_object(args[1]);
      Chat.ChatServer server = ChatServerHelper.narrow(serverObj);
      MyChatClient client = new MyChatClient(args[0], server);
      orb.connect(client);
      boa.obj_is_ready(client);
      boa.impl_is_ready();
    } catch (Exception e) {
      e.printStackTrace();
    }
  }
}
```

The client can now be started.

```
lin> java StartChatClient marko IOR:000000000000001849444c3
a436861742f436861745365727665723a312e300000000001000000
000000004c000100000000000f3133342e3130302e31312e3137350
000405b00000000002c00504d4300000001000000 1849444c3a4368
61742f436861745365727665723a312e3000000000019740f141
```

5.12 References

Since CORBA is a standard and not a product, a wide range of documents on CORBA and the OMA are publicly available on the Web from the OMG. However, as usual for standards, they are rather dry reading. Obviously there are also quite a number of books in which CORBA is not defined, but explained. A very good book is [Siegel 1996] which will shortly see the publication of a second, updated edition. This book includes an overview of different languages and of architecture in general. Several books are dedicated especially to CORBA in connection with Java. A good, easy-to-read book for beginners is [Orfali and Harkey 1997]. For the ambitious reader, we rather recommend [Vogel and Duddy 1998]. The most up-to-date book is [Redlich 1999b], which also discussed the CORBA 3.0 standard.

An overview on further information, sources, and products can be found in [Links 1999]. The two most widely employed products, Orbix and VisiBroker, come from [Technologies 1999] and [Inprise 1999]. An ORB which is freely available, even together with the source code, is called MICO and is described in [Puder and Römer 1998]. More advanced concepts for application and management are discussed in [Linhoff-Popien 1998].

6 Voyager

A David has set out to spread fear amongst the Goliaths in the field of distributed systems. A small Texas company has brought forth a handful of programmers who with great ambition and involvement are developing an extension for Java that does surprising things for distributed processing. The name of this company is ObjectSpace; their product is Voyager.

Even prior to Voyager, ObjectSpace had given rise to much comment in the Java area through a collection of classes for standard data structures and algorithms, the Java Generic Library or JGL (pronounced 'juggle'). JGL is freely available and represents a quasi standard in this field. Even though we are not going to discuss JGL any further, it is certainly worth while to take a deeper look into this library [ObjectSpace 1998a].

The far more interesting product in the context of this book, however, is Voyager. This is a completely Java-compatible runtime environment and library which aims at an exhaustive solution for many areas and problems of distributed programming. Subjects dealt with include object migration, distributed garbage collection, integration of CORBA and DCOM, autonomous mobile objects (which are usually – and also in the further course of this book – called mobile agents) and distributed persistence. This list is not complete and grows with each new version of Voyager. In this chapter, we will present the fundamental techniques of Voyager. However, Voyager offers solutions to so many aspects, that it did not seem adequate to treat them all in one chapter. Therefore, Voyager will continue to appear in several other chapters in the appropriate context.

In Summer '97, Voyager was presented in a first version, which was already greatly acclaimed by the specialists. In this version, a compiler (the vcc) was used to create "virtual classes" of a Java class which then, similar to proxies or stubs, could represent a remote object on a local computer and forward calls. As opposed to proxies, however, the virtual class was dealt with explicitly, so that remote object handling was directly expressed in the type system and could be checked by the compiler. This version already included intelligent messengers, mobility of objects, mobile agents, and persistence.

Since November '98, version 2 has been available, and since May '99 version 3, which further extends the possibilities of Voyager and integrates additional techniques, such as RMI, CORBA, and DCOM. The runtime environment of these versions is by now capable of generating a proxy for an object at runtime, so that compilers such as the already mentioned vcc or rmic are no longer required. In particular, this version offers the following features:

Basic techniques:

- Remote objects. For any Java class, a *remote object* can be generated at runtime out of a local object. To do this, no files need to be modified, and no additional compiler is required. Remote objects are represented by so-called proxies. The normal object and the remote proxy are both derived from a common interface.

- Remote referencing. Remote objects can be referenced transparently. References to remote objects are of the type of the common interface. Thus remote objects can be accessed in the same way as local ones.

- Remote generation. Objects can be generated not only on the local computer, but also on a remote computer.

- Distributed garbage collection. Objects are only deleted from memory when neither local nor remote references to the object exist.

- Exception handling. Exceptions thrown by a remote object are not lost, but forwarded to the local computer.

- Name service. Objects on a remote computer can be made known and accessed through a name. This is very helpful for initiating a distributed application.

Supplemental techniques:

- Object migration. Java allows mobility of code, so that applets can be downloaded via the Internet. But Java alone does not allow the migration of objects which is, however, very interesting for distributed programming. This is only made possible by Voyager.

- Mobile agents. Furthermore, such mobile objects can be autonomous, that is, migrate on their own. With this, Voyager provides a platform for mobile agents, a new programming paradigm, which is currently being ardently discussed.

- Applet-to-applet communication. Strictly speaking, Java allows an applet to contact only its original server. With Voyager, it is possible to circumvent this by setting up a hub on the server which transparently allows communication between applets, even on different computers.

- Group communication. With Voyager, both multicast and event-driven publish-subscribe are possible.

- Activation. Objects which are no longer present in local memory, but in a database, but which are still remotely referenced, can be automatically reactivated and loaded into memory.

- Database-independent distributed persistence. Voyager provides its own simple way to keep data persistent, thus responding to the needs of distributed systems, for example, by activation. This concept is put into practice by means of VoyagerDB.

Integrative techniques:

- Object Request Broker. Voyager includes its own ORB which is used to integrate other distributed communication mechanisms.

- CORBA. Via Voyager, Java objects can be directly addressed by another CORBA application.

- DCOM. Even Microsoft's Distributed Component Object Model will be integrated into Voyager. So far, this has only been announced, but it should work as seamlessly and simply as it did for the successful CORBA integration.

- RMI. In order to harmonize the Java techniques amongst each other, RMI has been integrated as well.

6.1 The Voyager runtime environment

Starting and terminating Voyager

In contrast to sockets or iBus, Voyager is not only a library, but also includes a runtime environment required for the execution of Voyager programs. This runtime environment must be started at the beginning of a Voyager program and should be terminated as well. It is started via the Voyager class which provides the static methods startup() for the creation and shutdown() for the termination of the runtime environment, plus several methods to inform other classes of these events. For each program, this runtime environment can and must be started exactly once. If it has already been started, the corresponding StartupException is triggered. Thus the shortest possible Voyager program looks more or less like this:

```
import com.objectspace.voyager.*;

public class ShortestVoyagerProg {

  public static void main( String[] args ) {
    try {
      Voyager.startup(); // start as client
```

```
    } catch( StartupException exception ) {
     System.err.println("Voyager is already running");
    }
    Voyager.shutdown();
  }
}
```

Features of the runtime environment

In this runtime environment it is now possible to make use of the various features of Voyager. Thus, for example, such a program could appear as a client of other Voyager programs and call these. However, in order to be able to be contacted by others, a well-defined entry point for a communication must be present. Since the above program still lacks it, it is merely a client. To be able to act as a server as well, the runtime environment or objects contained in it must be addressable via a URL. In the simplest case, this consists of the computer name and a port number. To assign the server a specific port number, this is passed through the `startup()` method.

```
Voyager.startup("8000");
```

Now this Voyager runtime environment can be addressed via a URL; if, for example, the program was executed on the `sun` machine, this would be `//sun.informatik.uni-hamburg.de:8000`. When a Voyager runtime environment is to appear only as a server, without a program running in it, it can be started from the command line by calling the `voyager` program and specifying a port number as the argument:

```
sun> voyager 8000
sun| voyager core technology 2.0, copyright objectspace 1997, 1998
```

Source code downloading

The runtime environment is also responsible for the downloading of source code via the network from other computers, when needed. This is important for remote generation and migration of objects. If the code for a class is not contained in the local search path (CLASSPATH), Voyager tries to download it from other computers. For reasons of security, however, this is only allowed after explicit authorization by the programmer or the administrator. In a program, the command VoyagerClassLoader.addResourceLoader(URL) must be called for this purpose. When Voyager is started from the command line, the option -c URL must be used to specify from where class code may be downloaded. The URL can either belong to a directory or to an HTTP server, which has the classes available in a similar way as with applets.

```
sun> voyager 8000 -c file:///usr/local/www/classes/
lin> voyager 7000 -c http://www.informatik.uni-hamburg.de/classes/
```

Integrated HTTP server

In the runtime environment itself, too, an HTTP server is present which can carry out these tasks. This must, however, be activated. From the command line, this is achieved by the option -r, while in the program, the ClassManager.enableResourceServer() command can be called. Then, all classes that are available to the runtime environment can also be requested by remote runtime environments.

```
sun> voyager 8000 -r
win> voyager 9000 -c http://sun.informatik.uni-hamburg.de:8000/
```

6.2 Remote objects

Once the runtime environment has been started, Voyager can be used to access objects on remote computers (or other virtual machines on the same computer). Similarly to RMI or CORBA, remote objects are represented by local placeholders, called proxies in Voyager. As opposed to RMI and CORBA, these are, however, not generated by a compiler at compile time, but at runtime. Thus no additional compiler is needed. To be able to create these proxies, the Voyager runtime environment requires the description of the interface of an object in an interface.

Proxy

Let us take the same example used with RMI: a bat hits a (remote) ball. Thus the bat needs a proxy object of the ball. The class definition of the ball initially looks as follows:

```
public class Ball {

  public void hit() {
    System.out.println("Ball has been hit")
  }
}
```

Interfaces

The interface belonging to this class contains all public methods and attributes, but not the constructors or the methods with restricted visibility. The name of the interface is usually composed out of the name of the class and a prefixed "I" for interface. This is, however, only a convention and not mandatory.

```
public interface IBall {

  public void hit();
}
```

The class itself should implement this interface and be modified accordingly. Although this is not strictly necessary because the interface is chiefly used for the generation of proxies, it would nevertheless be good programming style.

```
public class Ball implements IBall{ ...
```

Handling of existing classes

For some classes it may not be possible to carry out this modification, for example, classes which are present only in compiled form or which are to be integrated at a later stage. For such cases, Voyager provides a tool that automatically performs the creation of an appropriate interface. This tool, called igen, can be applied both to source code and compiled code and generates an interface in Java. The original class is not modified, which actually makes it type-incompatible with this interface. Therefore, this tool should be exclusively used for classes to which one has no access oneself.

Voyager is then capable of generating a proxy at runtime, which is type-compatible with this interface. There are several methods to obtain this proxy:

- Local generation for a known object. From a local reference to an object, a proxy can be created by calling the static method Proxy.of(Object obj).

- Use of a name service. Voyager provides a name service where existing objects can be registered with their names. Other programs can then obtain a proxy for this object by calling Namespace.lookup(String name).

- Remote generation. An object can be created on a remote computer running a server by calling Factory.create(String classname, String url). The result is a proxy for this object.

These three techniques will now be explained with the aid of small examples. The simplest method is the first one. A proxy for a locally known object, for example an object of the Ball class, can be generated with the following lines.

Creating a proxy

```
Ball ball = new Ball();
IBall iball = (IBall)Proxy.of(ball);
```

The return value of the Proxy.of() method is the dynamically generated Proxy, whose type must be restricted to the corresponding interface (*casting*). This proxy could now be passed to other remote objects, but this presumes that other remote objects are already known. So, what do we do at the very beginning, to introduce remote objects to each other when an application is being started up?

Frequently, objects which exist on one of the computers on a network need to be made accessible to other programs and be available to them as servers; a typical case in a client/server architecture. For this purpose, Voyager provides a name service which can be accessed via the Namespace class. The bind() method is used to assign an object a name.

Name service

```
Namespace.bind("8000/Ball",iball);
```

When another program knows both computer and port, together with this name, it can access this object. Let us assume the object was created and registered on the sun machine. The lookup() method then provides a proxy for this object. Obviously, the proxy must be cast onto the correct type, namely the type of the common interface IBall, with which the proxy of the object is compatible.

```
IBall ball = (IBall) Namespace.lookup("//sun:8000/Ball");
```

In the following example, a BallMachine is to create a Ball on the sun computer and register it with the name service.

```
import com.objectspace.voyager.*;

public class BallMachine {

  public static void main(String[] args) {
    try {
      Voyager.startup("8000"); // start as server
      Ball ball = new Ball();
      IBall iball = (IBall)Proxy.of(ball);
      Namespace.bind("8000/Ball",iball);
    } catch( Exception exception ) {
      System.err.println( exception );
    }
  }
}
```

Another program, Bat, is to fetch a reference to this Ball object via its name and then play this Ball.

```
import com.objectspace.voyager.*;

public class Bat {

  public void play(IBall ball) {
    ball.hit();
  }

  public static void main(String[] args) {
    try {
      Voyager.startup(); // start as client
      Bat bat = new Bat();
      IBall ball = (IBall) Namespace.lookup("//sun:8000/Ball");
```

```
            bat.play(ball);
        } catch( Exception exception ) {
            System.err.println( exception );
        }
        Voyager.shutdown();
    }
}
```

The two programs can now be started on two different computers, get acquainted via the name service, and communicate:

sun> java BallMachine

lin> java Bat

sun| Ball has been hit

Remote generation

The third possibility of obtaining a proxy for a remote object is to generate the object itself remotely. Then, an application can be started on one computer and distribute itself onto other computers. The only precondition is that Voyager runtime environments are running as servers on the remote computers. To use an object remotely, the Factory class is employed. It has a static method, create(), which is passed the name of the required class and a URL of the target computer, each as a String. The result is a proxy for the newly created object.

```
IBall ball = (IBall) Factory.create("Ball","sun:8000");
```

With this, the above example can be modified in such a way that it can be started from one computer. A BallMachine is then no longer needed. Also the name service can be done without.

```
import com.objectspace.voyager.*;

public class Bat {

    public void play(IBall ball) {
        ball.hit();
    }
```

```
  public static void main(String[] args) {
    try {
      Voyager.startup();
      Bat bat = new Bat();
      IBall ball = (IBall) Factory.create("Ball","sun:8000");
      bat.play(ball);
    } catch( Exception exception ) {
        System.err.println( exception );
    }
    Voyager.shutdown();
  }
}
```

This program can now be started from one computer, but run distributed on two different computers. On the remote computer, however, the Voyager server must be started. From the second computer, an object is created on the first one and then called remotely.

```
sun> voyager 8000
sun| voyager core technology 2.0, copyright objectspace 1997, 1998
lin> java Bat

sun| Ball has been hit
```

In remote generation it is also possible to use constructors with arguments. The parameters are passed by wrapping them in an Object array and specifying them as an additional argument for the create call. Let us assume that the Ball had a constructor with a weight or a size as its argument. Then the constructor would be called as follows:

```
Object[] arguments= new Object[]{new Integer(5)};
IBall ball = (IBall) Factory.create("Ball",arguments,"8000");
```

6.3 Migration of objects

The techniques for distributed programming shown up to now allow communication between objects on remote computers.

However, a very important aspect of distributed programming is the migration of objects. An object shall be able to be shifted from one computer to another, taking all its information contents with it. This should preferably be possible at any point of time, even if an operation is currently being performed on this object. The entire state of affairs and all references to other objects must be maintained.

Migration maintains identity

This is not possible with the techniques shown up to now. Although approaches such as iBus, RMI, or CORBA allow objects to be copied and – thanks to Java – the code of a copied object can be downloaded, the object loses its identity. Objects which reference the original still hold only a reference to the original even after copying and have no information at all about the copy. The original and the copy are different objects. They are used independently of each other, and their internal states drift apart. A consistent view of the system can only be obtained with great effort. The attempt of simulating migration via copying succeeds only at a very high cost, as references to the original are no longer valid after copying or must be converted one by one.

A copy has a different identity

Migration of objects is of essential importance. It is technically difficult and has been implemented until now only in very few systems. An example of such a system is Emerald [Black *et al.* 1987]; however, the code is not migratable, so that objects can only migrate to computers on which the compiled class code already exists. In Java, instead, code migration is a fundamental element of the language. Only this allows applets to be downloaded and started via the Internet. But migration of objects is currently not yet possible in Java. However, Java provides a good basis for such a mechanism, and with Voyager, a solution is now available.

Introducing migration into Java

Migration is important, if not required, for the following fields of application:

- Minimizing time consumption. Access to a remote object via a network is significantly more time-consuming than local access. This is a fact which will not change even in the future. The processing speed of computers increases faster than the transmission speed via a network. This means that in the case of several (a sufficient number of) accesses, migration of an object is less expensive than remote communication. Obviously, it has to be carefully considered which objects are to be migrated, how voluminous the objects to be migrated are, and whether migration does not take more time in the first place than the remote calls.

- Load balancing. In order to distribute the load of computers equally, for example in a computer network or a cluster, individual programs are terminated on one computer and restarted on another. Often this requires a complete reconfiguration of the system. With object migration, it becomes possible to shift objects simply from an overloaded to a less loaded computer.

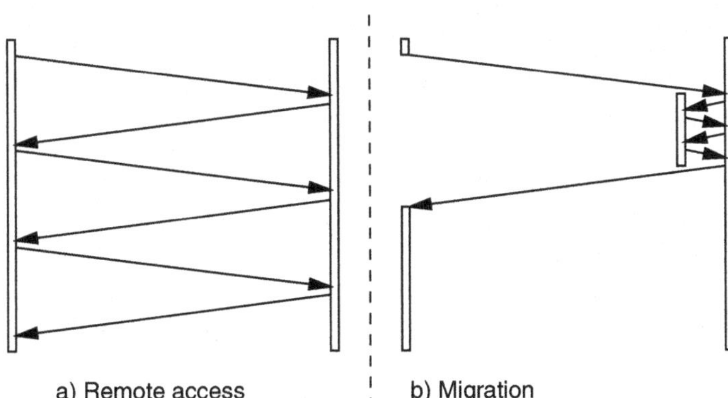

Figure 6.1 *Difference between remote and local access.*

- Change of ownership or responsibility. Frequently, several companies or departments are involved in the processing of an object. This means that during the life cycle of an object, the ownership of or the responsibility for an object may change. Then it should, however, also be possible to migrate objects into the appropriate area of responsibility. A design department can, for example, create a CAD drawing which is subsequently needed in stock keeping and then sold to the production department. As long as the design is worked upon, the CAD object should be stored on the server of the design department. Once terminated, it should migrate to the production computer. Nevertheless, both the design department and the stock keeping people should continue to have access to this object.

- Mobile devices. An essential limitation of mobile devices against computers that are permanently connected to a network is that they are not continuously on-line, but rather sporadically. The cost for a connection to the network is substantially higher, and the bandwidth is lower. Analogously, this also applies to home PCs which are only occasionally and for a short time connected via modem to the Internet or a company network. For such devices, it is an advantage when objects to be processed do not have to be referenced remotely, but can be migrated to the device. Subsequently, the device can go off-line and the object can be processed. At a suitable later point in time, the processed or newly created object can then be migrated back.

Voyager allows migration

Voyager allows the migration of objects, for practically arbitrary objects and, moreover, in a rather easy way for the programmer. With Voyager, the capabilities of objects can be dynamically extended at runtime. It is possible to create so-called facets from an object, which can then implement additional methods for the object.

Mobility of objects is one application for this kind of dynamic extension. Mobility.of()is used to create a facet from an object a which implements an interface IMobility and thus makes the moveTo()method available in two variations. In the first one, the method can be passed a URL. Then the corresponding object moves to the computer specified by the URL, where a Voyager runtime environment must be running. In the second variation, a reference to a remote object, a proxy, is passed, and the addressed object moves to the same computer on which the remote object is located.

```
try {
  IMobility mobileObj=Mobility.of(a);
  mobileObj.moveTo("win.informatik.uni-hamburg.de:8000");
} catch (MobilityException e) {
  System.out.println(e);
}
```

From the programmer's point of view, references to a migrating object are maintained. Behind the scenes, Voyager takes care that a call sent to such an object is forwarded to the current location of the object. For this purpose, the Voyager runtime environment remembers where migrating objects have been moved. When, subsequently, an attempt is made to access them, the runtime environment creates an internal exception which contains the new location. The proxy that has sent the call intercepts this message, reads the new location, and resends the call. This mechanism works even when an object is moved several times.

Handling current calls

Voyager does not interrupt a method call that is currently being executed, but waits until it has been terminated, before an object is moved. However, newly arriving method calls are held until the migration has been carried out, so that subsequently, these calls can be forwarded to the new location. This is, however, only possible for methods that are marked as synchronized. Therefore, preferably all methods of an object to be moved should be synchronized. Furthermore, all objects to be migrated must implement the Serializable interface, since internally Java's serialization mechanism is employed for the migration.

Thus the Ball class should be adapted as follows in order to be migratable:

```
import java.io.*;

public class Ball implements IBall, Serializable {

  synchronized public void hit() {
       System.out.println("Ball has been hit");
  }
}
```

An application can now move an object of the Ball class. In the following example, a ball and a bat are created on the sun computer. When the bat hits the ball, the ball is moved to another computer. For this purpose, the computers lin and mac are available, which must both be running a Voyager runtime environment.

```
import com.objectspace.voyager.*;
import com.objectspace.voyager.mobility.*;

public class Bat {

  public void play(IBall ball, String url) {
    try {
      ball.hit()
      Mobility.of(ball).moveTo(url);
    } catch (MobilityException e) {
      System.out.println(e);
    }
  }

  public static void main(String[] args) {
    try {
      Voyager.startup("7000");
      ClassManager.enableResourceServer();
      Bat bat = new Bat();
      IBall ball = (IBall) Proxy.of(new Ball());
      bat.play(ball,"//lin:8000");
      bat.play(ball,"//mac:9000");
      bat.play(ball,"//sun:7000");
    } catch( Exception exception ) {
        System.err.println( exception );
    }
    Voyager.shutdown();
  }
}
```

When this program is executed, the following messages are displayed. Please note that the reference to the ball does not change, but that the proxy always finds the ball on the correct computer.

```
lin> voyager 8000 -c http://sun:7000

mac> voyager 9000 -c http://sun:7000

sun> java Bat
sun| Ball has been hit

lin| Ball has been hit

mac| Ball has been hit
```

Measures for migration

Usually, the migration is completely transparent to the migrated object. It is not even told that it has been moved. In some cases, however, it can be very useful if it gets to know this, so it can mop up behind itself or take specific measures at its new location. A possible example could be that the object is stored in a local database and, in case it migrates, should also migrate from one database to another. This case too is covered in Voyager. When an object to be migrated additionally implements the IMobile interface, Voyager calls the methods preDeparture(), preArrival(), postArrival(), and postDeparture() in the appropriate order. The preDeparture()method is passed both origin and target as String. The migration itself is completed with the call of postArrival(), however, with postDeparture() there is still the possibility to call the meanwhile obsolete copy on the source computer, to mop up. A corresponding extension of Ball might thus look as follows:

```
import java.io.*;
import com.objectspace.voyager.mobility.*;

public class Ball implements IBall, IMobile, Serializable {

  synchronized public void hit() {
    System.out.println("Ball has been hit");
  }

  public void preDeparture(String source, String dest) {
    System.out.println("Ball about to move from "+source+" to "+dest);
  }
```

```
  public void preArrival() {}

  public void postArrival() {
    System.out.println("Move was successful");
  }

  public void postDeparture() {}
}
```

During a migration of a ball object from sun to lin, the following sequence is displayed.

```
sun| Ball has been hit
sun| Ball about to move from tcp://sun:7000 to tcp://lin:8000

lin| Move was successfull
```

Thus, Voyager makes it possible to move simple objects in an easy way. But what about object structures that are somewhat more complex? What happens with objects pointed to by the migrating object? Are they migrated too, or copied, or not moved at all? This is a general problem of migration. On the one hand, the migrated object must be able at its new location to continue accessing all objects it could access before; on the other hand, these objects may also still be needed at the old location. When the object is copied, instead, it exists twice, and changes to one copy are not made to the other copy as well. Another alternative is to reference the objects via proxies. Proxies can be copied without problems and always forward calls to their original. However, this has the disadvantage that remote calls are substantially more expensive in terms of time consumption.

Problems of migration

Let us look, for example, at the scenario in Figure 6.2: an object a of type A references an object b of type B, plus an object of type C via a proxy which also implements the interface IC and will be called c. The actual object is located on the lin computer. Furthermore, the same objects are referenced by an object d. Now the object a is to be moved from the sun computer to the win computer.

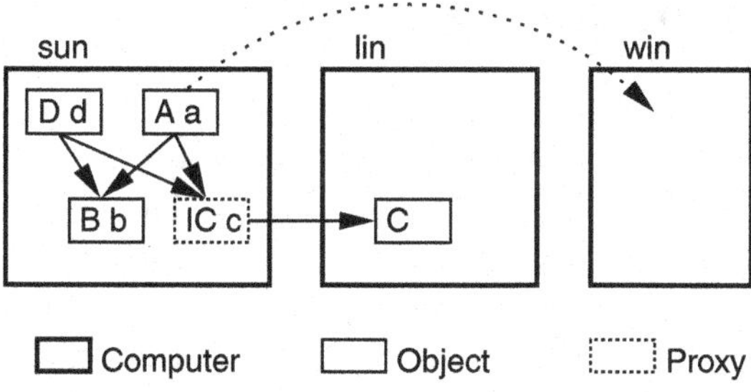

Figure 6.2
An object structure: object a is to be moved.

After the moveTo() command, object a is moved to the win computer. There too, all references must be valid, in other words, the referential integrity must be maintained. Since object d as well contains references to b and c, these must not simply be moved away, but copied. The consequence for object b is that it now occurs in two versions and a and d may, under certain circumstances, end up with different views to this object. No consistency can be guaranteed. For object c, instead, this only means that there is a new proxy for the original. By incrementing the reference counter, the internal mechanism of Voyager ensures that this reference too is taken into consideration during garbage collection. The resulting scenario is shown in Figure 6.3.

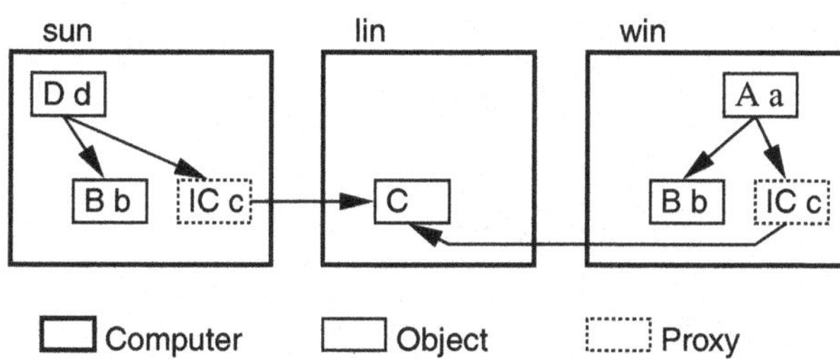

Figure 6.3
After the migration of a.

A further problem is obviously constituted by local references to objects to be migrated, such as object a in the above example. These lose their validity when the object is moved. For this reason, objects that are to be moved should exclusively be referenced via proxies.

6.4 Remote calls

In a non-distributed system, method calls are usually synchronous, that is, the call blocks until the method has been executed and, where applicable, a result has been returned. Then the next command is processed. In distributed systems, however, runtimes of messages are so long that it makes sense not to let the call block, but to process the next command immediately and to "fetch" the result only at a later, more appropriate point in time. This behavior is called asynchronous.

This distinction is not relevant for non-distributed systems, such as normal Java programs, but it is for distributed systems. Distributed systems must react in a much more flexible way to different runtimes and delays. In Java alone, an asynchronous call can be simulated by the creation of a new thread, but this means a lot of programming effort and additional complexity.

The Future concept

Voyager offers a simpler alternative: asynchronous messages are implemented by means of the *Future* concept.

To issue an asynchronous call, the static method invoke() of the Future class is called. This call immediately returns a result which is, however, initially only a placeholder and not the result itself. This can only be read at a later stage instead of the placeholder. The invoke() method must be passed the intended method call subdivided into its individual components. A normal method call consists of the target of the call (the object on which the method is to be executed), the method name, and the call parameters. It may have, for example, the following form:

```
object.method(param1, param2);
```

The invoke()method can be passed the target as a reference, whereas the method name must be specified as a String. The parameters cannot simply be listed, but must be encapsulated in an object array. Simple types, such as int or bool must be converted into their object counterparts (Integer, Boolean). Thus, an asynchronous call will look as follows:

```
Future.invoke(object, "method", new Object[] {param1,param2});
```

This call returns a result of Result type. The isAvailable() method of this class indicates whether the real result has already arrived. The methods readInt(), readByte() etc. and readObject() can then be used to read the result. When these methods are called while the result has not yet arrived, they block until it arrived. If the call has triggered an exception, this is indicated by the isException() method.

Let us look at a brief example. A Timer object is to simulate an slightly higher time consumption for the transmission of a message. The timer blocks for a specified time (indicated in milliseconds), and then returns a result, in this case a simple 'one'.

```
public class Timer implements ITimer {

  public int alarm(int milliseconds) {
    try {
      Thread.sleep(milliseconds);
      System.out.println("ALARM");
    } catch (Exception e) {}
    return 1;
  }
}
```

In a synchronous call, a calling object would have to wait until the result is returned. The alternative of the asynchronous call allows something sensible to be done, instead.

```
import com.objectspace.voyager.*;
import com.objectspace.voyager.message.*;
public class TimerClient {

  public static void main(String args[]) {
    try {
      Voyager.startup();
      ITimer timer = (ITimer) Factory.create("Timer","//sun:8000");
      Result result = Future.invoke(
        timer,"alarm", new Object[]{new Integer(2000)});
```

```
        if (!result.isAvailable()){
          System.out.println("Waiting for result, doing something else");
        }
        int res = result.readInt();
        System.out.println("Result returned");
      } catch (Exception e) {
        System.out.println(e);
      }
    }
}
```

During execution of this program it becomes evident that the application is capable of doing something else while it waits for the result. In this case, only a string is displayed (Waiting for result, doing something else), but in practical applications, waiting times can thus be employed in a useful way.

```
sun> voyager 8000
```

```
lin> java TimerClient
lin| Waiting for result, doing something else
```

```
sun| ALARM
```

```
lin| Result returned
```

One-way calls

When only a method is to be triggered on a remote computer, but the result is not relevant or the method does in any case not yield a result, Voyager also offers the possibility of issuing a "one-way" call. There is, however, no feedback as to whether the call has arrived, initiated or terminated successfully, or been aborted with an error. Therefore, this kind of call is also known as "fire-and-forget". As in the asynchronous case, the call is generated via the invoke() method, here however of the OneWay class. There is also a corresponding Sync class with the invoke()method. This, however, corresponds to the standard behavior and will therefore be needed only in very rare cases.

A much more useful feature is a variation of the invoke() method, which allows for three additional parameters. The first of these, a Boolean switch, specifies whether a result object is transmitted as a copy or a proxy for the original object is returned. With the second parameter, a time limit can be set for the blocking of the readXxx() method so that, for example, it becomes possible to react to the non-arrival of a message. As a third parameter, a reference to an EventListener can be passed, which is informed of the termination of the method call via a callback. Thus the result must neither be waited for (readXxx()) nor polled (isAvailable()), but can arrive as an event.

6.5 Group communication

In the previous sections, remote objects were created, moved, and called. The following section will show how several distributed objects can be called at the same time. For this purpose, Voyager provides two mechanisms, one multicast and one publish/subscribe mechanism. Both are based on a concept called Voyager Space. A space is an object space which can be spread across a distributed system and in which the most varied objects can "exist". All objects of a specific type that populate this space can be called simultaneously.

Voyager Space

A space is composed of individual containers, called subspaces. A space is exclusively perceived through these subspaces and constitutes itself by connecting the subspaces to each other. A subspace can be created with

```
Subspace localSubspace = new Subspace();
```

Subsequently, it can be connected to other, even remote subspaces. Information on other subspaces can be gathered via the usual mechanisms of Voyager, such as the transmission of a proxy to a subspace or a name entry in the Namespace of a computer. Subspaces are connected by means of the connect() method, which does not only establish a unidirectional, but a bidirectional connection.

Connecting subspaces

```
ISubspace remoteSubspace = (ISubspace) Namespace.lookup("//sun:9000/Subspace");
localSubspace.connect(remoteSubspace);
```

With the connection of subspaces, a non-directional graph, that is, a mesh of subspaces is built up. All subspaces reachable inside this graph constitute the space. Subspaces can also be connected to several other subspaces and be reachable via several paths, as shown in Figure 6.4.

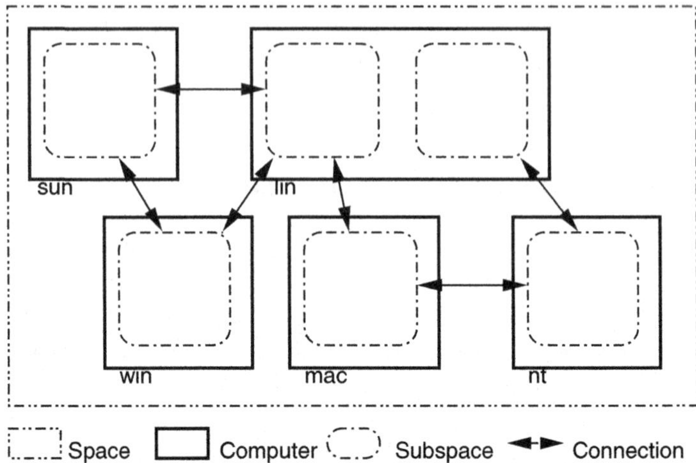

Figure 6.4 *A space is constituted by subspaces.*

Inside a subspace, objects can exist. They are added to a subspace by means of the add() method.

```
localSubspace.add(client);
```

Messages are forwarded by a subspace along the connections with all its neighbors, which in turn forward them, and so on, until the entire space is permeated with this message. Voyager ensures that a message is accepted exactly once by each subspace. Inside the subspace, the messages are forwarded to all objects to which the message is destined (see Figure 6.5).

Distributing messages in a space

There are two alternatives to distribute a message in a space. In the first one, similarly to an asynchronous call, an invoke() method of the Multicast class is called. As its arguments, this contains the method name, the parameters in form of an object array, and the class type.

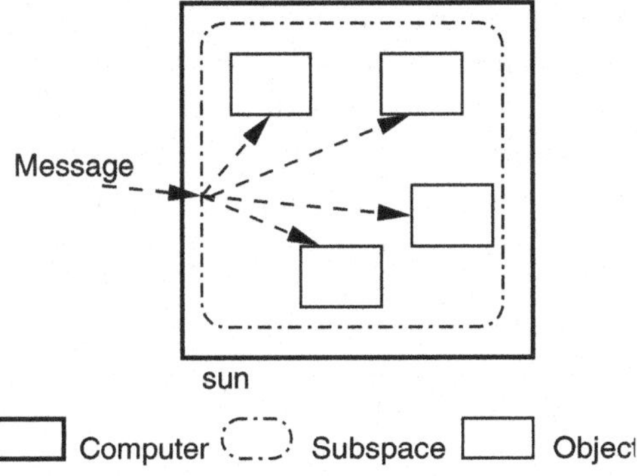

Figure 6.5
Messages are distributed in the subspace.

```
Object[] parameter = new Object[]{param}
Multicast.invoke(subspace,"methodName",parameter,"ClassName");
```

In the second alternative, similarly to a remote call via proxies, a special multicast-capable proxy, that is, a MulticastProxy, is created. It is, however, not generated for an instance, but for a class. On this proxy, all methods provided by the corresponding class can be called, and the call is sent to all corresponding instances in the space. Parameters are passed as usual.

```
IClassName mcastProxy = localSubspace.getMulticastProxy("ClassName");
mcastProxy.methodName(param);
```

6.5.1 A chat system with Voyager Space

As with all previous multicast techniques, the following example will present yet another chat system. We will be using the same graphical interface of the ChatFrame class, whose code can be found in Appendix A. In the program listed below, no server is needed, and all clients are symmetric. The first ChatClient registers its Subspace under the name of "ChatSubspace" with the name service of the Voyager runtime environment on its computer. The second client receives the URL for this name and can therefore connect to the first one. This client too registers with the name service. All additional clients can connect to any existing client, so that an arbitrarily structured mesh of connections can develop (in the implementation listed below, only one connection each is realized, but it can be easily extended to multiple connections).

```
public class ChatClient implements IChatClient{

  ChatFrame gui;
  ISubspace subspace;

  public ChatClient(ISubspace subspace) {
    gui = new ChatFrame("Chat with Voyager Space Multicast");
    this.subspace = subspace;

    // when Enter is pressed in the input field...
    gui.input.addKeyListener(
      new KeyAdapter() {
        public void keyPressed(KeyEvent e) {
          if (e.getKeyCode() == KeyEvent.VK_ENTER) {
            sendTextToChat(gui.input.getText());
            gui.input.setText("");
          }
        }
      }
    );
  }

  public void sendTextToChat(String str) {
    Multicast.invoke(subspace,"receiveFromChat",new
Object[]{str},"ChatClient");
  }

  public void receiveFromChat(String str) {
    gui.output.append(str+"\n");
  }
```

```
  public static void main(String[] args) {
    try {
      Voyager.startup(args[0]);
      Subspace localSubspace = new Subspace();
      Namespace.bind("ChatSubspace",localSubspace);
      ChatClient client = new ChatClient(localSubspace);
      localSubspace.add(client);
      if (args.length>1) {
        ISubspace remoteSubspace = (ISubspace) Namespace.lookup(args[1]);
        localSubspace.connect(remoteSubspace);
        IChatClient mcastProxy = (IChatClient)
          localSubspace.getMulticastProxy("IChatClient");
        mcastProxy.receive("New Client connected");
      }
    } catch (Exception e) {
      System.out.println(e);
    }
  }
}
```

This program is called with the specification of the port number on which the runtime environment is to be started and, if the program is to be connected to an existing chat, with a URL of a registered chat subspace.

```
sun> java ChatClient 9000
```

```
lin> java ChatClient 8000 //sun:9000/ChatSubspace
```

6.6 References

Voyager is so recent that is has hardly been discussed in the literature. [Griffel 1998] mentions Voyager in connection with component technology, but unfortunately only refers to version 1. [Nelson 1998] deals extensively with the mobility of objects and, amongst others, also discusses Voyager. In scientific contributions to conferences and workshops, however, the subject of object migration is given much space, for example at the

ECOOP [Jul 1998] or the OOPSLA [OOPSLA 1998]. A workshop dedicated to mobile object systems took place in 1996 (MOS'96) and is documented in [Vitek and Tschudin 1997].

The documentation made available by ObjectSpace themselves [ObjectSpace 1998b] is good, but very concise. However, it includes a whole series of examples which demonstrate many of Voyager's features. As the Voyager package itself, the documentation too can be downloaded from www.objectspace.com. ObjectSpace also maintain a mailing list (voyager-interest@developer.objectspace.com), which usually provides users with help on their particular problems very quickly. An archive of this mailing list is available under www.distributedobjects.com/portfolio/archives/voyager/index.html.

7 Mobile agents

An ardently discussed new programming paradigm is that of agents. In this context, unlike the agents we know from gothic novels and the silver screen, the term does not hide anything secret or dangerous. It is not a new kind of computer virus or other hacker tool, but a serious metaphor used in the area of programming.

Software agents

In this book, the term agent will be initially limited to software agents. However, one could also think of hardware agents (for example robots). Both are different from human agents (such as agents of artists or a travel agency). Software agents are programs which, in a certain way, represent users and can act on their behalf.

Software agents can be further classified by their application area, their degree of intelligence, and their degree of mobility. Since we are generally talking about the programming concept and not about actual fields of application, the classification by application areas will not be taken into account. Moreover, mobile agents are of much greater interest in the context of this book than stationary ones. The term "intelligent agent", however, is still controversial.

Intelligent agents

Intelligent agents are developed and used in the field of Artificial Intelligence and have the capabilities of learning, adapting to environments, developing action plans, and so on. They have been a subject of artificial intelligence research for about 30 years. They are, however, acquiring a new significance through the aspect of mobility and the resulting possibilities for the Internet.

Some authors [Brenner *et al.* 1998] argue that agents must always possess a certain degree of intelligence because otherwise they could not be autonomous, and use the term "intelligent agent" as a generic term for software agents. In this book, we do not share this view, since software agents do not have to be more or less intelligent than any other common program. Intelligence and mobility are instead regarded as orthogonal concepts which exist independently from each other, but can be combined with one another. The following pages will chiefly deal with the mobility of agents. Furthermore, we will limit the discussion to the area of object-oriented programming which, due to the concept of mobility, practically corresponds to a limitation to Java.

Mobile agents

A mobile agent is an object or a program which can move from computer to computer and can do so, as opposed to mobile objects, in an autonomous way. This means that a mobile agent can decide by itself when and where it wants to migrate and what it will then execute. This decision can be made in an "intelligent" way, for example by having learned through experience where the best information can be found on a specific subject. It may, however, also proceed in a purely algorithmic way by following a programmed list or a series of links.

Significance of mobile agents

Opinions on the significance of mobile agents differ widely. Optimistic views foresee a complete penetration of the Internet, both in the business and the private sector. More pessimistic views, instead, give mobile agents hardly a chance – they could as well be replaced by other techniques such as remote communication and represent a much higher risk potential than their alternatives. The only unanimously accepted fact is that the development in this field is only at its very beginning and that many novelties are still to be expected. Activities in this area of research are growing very dynamically. Enterprises too are investing in the development of such sytems. However, whether agents will succeed in the end or not, is not yet foreseeable.

Possible areas of application

But certainly the idea of giving an agent a task which it then tries to solve on its own and in a mobile way, is very tempting. There are lots of applications waiting for this kind of programming. A few examples follow:

Distributed information gathering. Search engines such as AltaVista or HotBot load huge amounts of data from the Internet, process them, and generate indices. Instead, a mobile agent could visit the individual servers, view the information on offer, return to the database of the search engine, and insert the knowledge it has gathered.

Stock exchange monitor. In stock exchanges, a huge quantity of information is generated. Of this, however, only a small part is of interest for an investor, who might be only interested in the values of specific stocks or in changes of a specific nature. Instead of loading and processing the whole information, an agent can, for example on the computer of the stock exchange itself, monitor the values and report precisely those events that are of interest.

Electronic price comparison. In a given infrastructure, an agent can search for all manufacturers of a product and determine the cheapest supplier. The agent could even take additional knowedge into account, such as payment method or physical location and resulting costs and savings such as discounts or transport expenses. Thus, one could for example look for a reasonably economical hotel in the vicinity of a specific venue.

Added value services. When not only one product is required, but a combination of products, that is, the value is only determined by the combination, we talk about a value added service. This can, for example, be a combination of bus, train, and air travel, or the booking of opera tickets, a hotel room, and a table in a restaurant. Agents are very much suited to this kind of task. They can visit the different suppliers, combine the offers, and find a suitable solution.

Just-in-time production. More and more frequently, modern production plants work with a minimum of stock. Instead, production material must be delivered just in time. A mobile agent could monitor the stocked quantities of such materials and organize supplies when a given threshold value is undershot.

Advantages of mobile agents

Mobile agents offer a series of advantages over previous programming paradigms such as the currently prevailing client/server paradigm. The most important advantages are:

- Mobile agents can help reduce the network load. Although mobile agents, which travel together with their state and their code (or part of it), are quite voluminous, the transmission of raw data can already be more expensive than the transmission of the agent. A much more important aspect is, however, that mobile agents turn many remote accesses into many local accesses plus one migration, as shown in Figure 7.1.

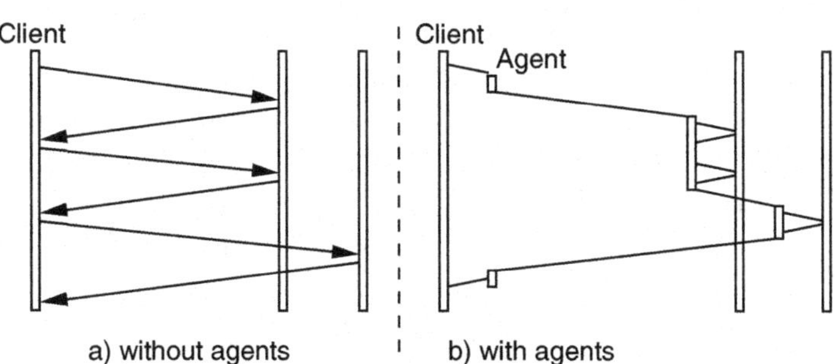

Figure 7.1 *Network load reduction through agents.*

- While the agent is working inside the network, the mandator can go off-line and fetch the result during the next on-line connection.

- Mobile agents represent a possibility of remote programming. With remote method calls, such as in RMI, the remote method must already exist and be made available at the remote location. A mobile agent, instead, can be programmed by its mandator, sent out, called back, reprogrammed, and sent out again. Thus the mandator can satisfy its own requirements with much greater precision, and react to new demands with more flexibility.

However, the employment of mobile agents also creates problems which currently represent a big challenge for research. How far these problems can be remedied in the coming years is not yet clear. These are the most serious problems:

Problems with mobile agents

- Complexity. Mobile agents are not intelligent by nature. Their intelligence must first be implemented by a programmer. This gives rise to high development costs and complex programming tasks.
- Infrastructure. Agents can only migrate to places where they are welcome and find an infrastructure from which they can benefit. Until now, such infrastructures exist only in exceptional cases. A wide-scale diffusion can only be expected if the benefit outweighs the costs for the provider of such an infrastructure.
- Security. Another very important problem is that of security. This obviously also applies to other solutions, but with mobile agents, additional dangers arise. Mobile agents carry information. This is usually condensed or personalized and thus of value for third parties. The information may regard hobbies, habits, or the financial situation. Some agents will even carry electronic currency. This information is a lot easier to access than, for example, a client which runs behind a firewall and uses only remote communication. Such information can be stolen, falsified or manipulated. Mobile agents also carry the code that must be interpreted on a remote machine. Moreover, the agent cannot rely on the fact that it will really encounter the execution environment it expects, and not a modified one. Agents are particularly difficult to protect against an attack of a malicious environment. However, agents too represent a potential danger for the environment, the so-called engine. The additional points of attack that appear on top of the usual security problems are shown in Figure 7.2.

Different agent systems

The history of mobile agents is not very long and begins in the early 90s. The first commercially available system was Telescript by General Magic. The developers of Telescript can claim

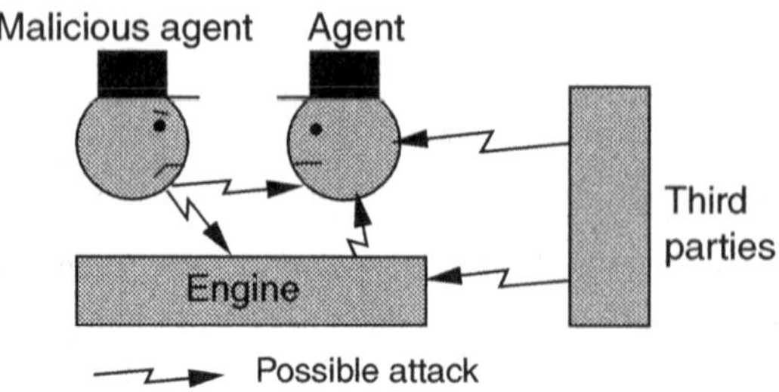

Figure 7.2 Dangers in agent systems.

the honor of having invented the concept of mobile agents; however, most unfortunately, the system was economically not successful – a fate shared by many pioneers. Telescript was an independent language which has not survived the enormous success of Java. Most of the currently available systems are now based an Java. General Magic too are now offering a second generation product based on Java, called Odyssey. Nevertheless, Telescript has attracted a lot of attention and has had great influence on the development. There is still a lot to be expected from General Magic.

One of the most well-known agent systems are the aglets developed by IBM Japan. They are freely available. The fact that their developers, Danny B. Lange and Mitsuru Oshima, have published a book [Lange and Oshima 1998] specially dedicated to their system, makes it the best documented system around.

Another faction is that of the Tcl-based agent systems, such as Agent Tcl or Ara. In other languages as well experiments are made with mobile agents, mainly in interpreted languages such as Perl, Python, or Scheme. The greatest significance, however, must clearly be attributed to Java-based systems, two of which, aglets and Voyager agents, will be discussed in more detail.

7.1 Aglets

Danny B. Lange's aglet system presents itself as a light-weight agent system, which provides the features of agents in a relatively simple, but sufficiently complete manner. It has been developed at IBM Japan and is available free of charge. It is a simple and illustrative system which is very well suited for getting acquainted with agents and agent technologies.

The word aglet is composed out of the words agent and applet. The intention is to hint at a certain similarity between applets and aglets. Applets can only be executed in a specific context and, compared to normal applications, are subject to restrictions that guarantee the security of the execution environment, usually a browser. The execution environment for aglets is called *context* and is an independent application which must be running before an agent can move there. An aglet is created, exists, works, sleeps, and dies in such a context. Aglets are also capable of traveling from one context to another.

Aglet context

In the aglet system, each agent description is derived from the Aglet class. Thus each agent automatically inherits a series of cpabilities and characteristics, and each agent has a uniform interface. The Aglet class also defines several methods which are to be overridden in the creation of a user-defined agent and which then constitute the characteristics of that special agent. In the following lines, the most important methods are described in the order in which they are called during the life cycle of an agent.

Life cycle of aglets

In the creation of a new agent, the onCreation() method is called, in which the agent can initialize itself. Once an agent has been brought to life and has been initialized, its run() method is called. In this method it can be specified what the task of the agent is and how it is supposed to perform this task. This method is executed every time the agent enters a new context or is activated. When a message arrives for the agent, the handleMessage() method is processed in which the agent can react to this message. Before an agent is destroyed, it is given the possibility to clean up behind itself and thus kind of prepare its own death by means of a call to onDisposing(). Thus, an agent typically has the following form:

```
import com.ibm.aglet.*;

public class MyAgent extends Aglet {

  public void onCreation(Object o) {
    // initialize agent
  }

  public run() {
    // define activity
  }

  public boolean handleMessage(Message message) {
    // react to messages
  }

  public void onDisposing() {
    // prepare for dying
  }
}
```

Agents can be created in two ways: either afresh, as instances of their class, or as a copies of other agents, so-called *clones*. In the second case, the copied agent receives its own identity and a corresponding identifier, but it contains the same state as its original.

Creation of agents is one of the tasks of the execution environment, the context. An agent can be created either from within the graphical user interface or by another program. For this, a reference to the execution environment is needed, which can be obtained through an agent via the getAgletContext() method. Then, the createAglet() method can be used to create a new agent. It must be specified where the code for this new agent can be found (the *CodeBase*), what the agent's class is called, and, if needed, an arbitrary object can be passed as a parameter. This parameter can be read and used by the new agent through its onCreation() method. Other agents can only access an agent via a proxy. On the one hand, this has the purpose of representing remote agents locally through a placeholder; on the other hand, it has a security aspect: in Java it is not possible to allow some objects, for example the context, to have access to public methods and to deny this access to other objects, for example foreign agents. Through this mechanism, public methods of agents can be better protected against unauthorized access. Thus the result of the creation is a proxy of an agent.

```
AgletContext context = getAgletContext();
AgletProxy myAglet;
myAglet = context.createAglet(getCodeBase(), "MyAgent", null);
```

The agent begins its work by following its run() method. It can double itself by means of the clone() method, migrate to another context with the dispatch()method, or call another agent with retract(). Finally, it can destroy itself with the dispose() method after it has done its work. It can also pause, make itself persistent in a database or a file, and wait for reactivation. Via the proxy, many of these methods are also remotely accessible, so that an agent can, for example, create a subagent and remote-control it. This life cycle of an agent is shown in Figure 7.3.

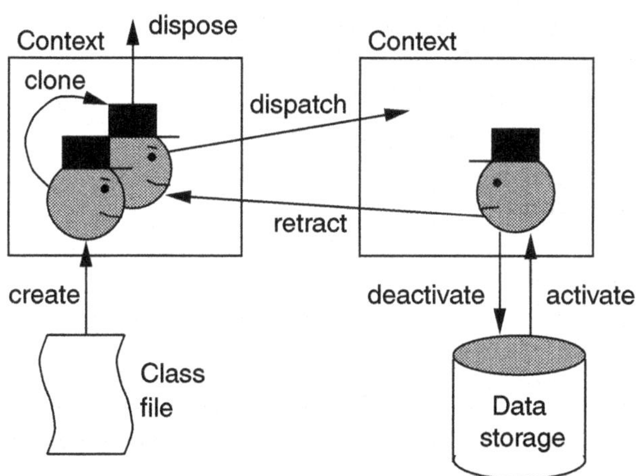

Figure 7.3 *The life cycle of aglets.*

Communication between agents

Agents can communicate with each other by exchanging messages. One agent creates a message of Message type and sends it to another agent. The message bears a label (*kind*) of String type, through which the different message types can be distinguished, and has a content which may be of any type, such as an integer, a Boolean value, and so on, or an object of arbitrary type. With a call of the sendMessage() method of an agent proxy, this message can then be sent to another agent.

```
Message message = new Message("Greeting", "Hello Agent");
myAglet.sendMessage(message);
```

When a message is sent to an agent, its handleMessage()method is called so that the agent receives the message. Form the label, it recognizes the message type and can react accordingly. Whether the message is of a specific kind can be determined by calling message.sameKind(). The handleMessage() method usually shows a cascade of if-instructions of such sameKind() checks. However, in this way an agent can only react to messages with known labels.

The receiver can extract the arguments from the message and process them with a call to getArgs(). It can also send a direct reply to this message, by simply calling the sendReply() method of the Message.

```
public boolean handleMessage(Message message) {
  if (message.sameKind("Greeting")) {
    String str = (String) message.getArg();
    System.out.println(str);
    String reply = System.in.read();
    message.sendReply(reply);
    return true;
  } else
    return false;
  }
}
```

Obviously, the sender must be appropriately prepared for an answer to be able to read it. Thus the above message sending procedure could be extended, for example, in the following way:

```
String reply = (String) myAglet.sendMessage(message);
```

By default, such calls are synchronous, that is, the sendMessage() message call blocks until an answer arrives. There is, however, also an asynchronous call available, which is issued by the sendFutureMessage()method and returns a FutureReply object which can be polled or waited for. It is even possible to use multicast messages with publish/subscribe semantics.

7.1.1 A chat system with aglets

The agent technology too will be demonstrated with the aid of the "Chat" example. In the implementations of the previous techniques, independent programs were started on each computer, which were then connected and amalgamated into one application through communication mechanisms such as sockets, RMI, or CORBA. This is not what we want to do here (although it would obviously be possible as well). Instead, a chat is to be started on one computer where two agents will be generated, one of which remains on the local computer and the other is sent to a communication partner. Thus the application is started on one computer and then distributed.

The following implementation initially creates a single ChatAgent with the habitual ChatFrame interface, which is listed in Appendix A. To create a new agent and send it to another computer or to another execution environment on the same computer, the address of the remote environment is entered as a URL in the input line. This can obviously also be the local address. The protocol the agents use to communicate is called ATP (Aglet Transfer Protocol), so that the URL begins with atp://. The client recognizes this input and reacts accordingly. The default port number for aglets is 4434; however, the execution environment can be started with any free port number. A typical example would be atp://sun.informatik.uni-hamburg.de:4434/. When an execution environment with the corresponding port number is running on the target computer, a newly created agent migrates there and starts its graphical user interface. Subsequently, users can enter messages in the chat and talk to each other. The agents send messages of

Message type back and forth and react accordingly. Upon termination of the program, a **Message("bye")** is sent, and the agent dies.

In the following implementation, only two communication partners at a time can "chat" with each other. However, the implementation can be easily extended to enable several chat partners to be managed. The aglet system also provides a multicast which, however, will not be discussed at this point.

```
import com.ibm.aglet.*;
import com.ibm.aglet.event.*;
import java.io.*;
import java.net.URL;
import java.awt.event.*;

public class ChatAgent extends Aglet {

  String name = "Unknown";
  ChatFrame gui = null;
  AgletProxy chatPartner = null;

  public void onCreation(Object o) {
    chatPartner = (AgletProxy) o;
    try {
      name = (String) getAgletContext().getProperty("aglets.user.name",
                                                    "Unknown");
    } catch (Exception ex) {
      ex.printStackTrace();
    }
  }

  public void run(){
    gui = new ChatFrame("Chat with aglets");

    // When Enter is pressed in the input field ...
    gui.input.addKeyListener (
      new KeyAdapter() {
```

```
        public void keyPressed(KeyEvent e) {
          if (e.getKeyCode()==KeyEvent.VK_ENTER) {
            String msg = gui.input.getText();
            if (msg.startsWith("atp://")) {
              dispatchNewPartner(msg);
            } else {
              sendTextToChat(gui.input.getText());
              gui.output.append(gui.input.getText()+"\n");
              gui.input.setText("");
            }
          }
        }
      }
    );

    // When the chat window is closed ...
    gui.addWindowListener(
      new WindowAdapter() {
        public void windowClosing(WindowEvent e) {
          dispose();
        }
      }
    );
  }

  public void onDisposing() {
    try {
      if (chatPartner != null) {
        chatPartner.sendMessage(new Message("bye"));
      }
    } catch (Exception ex) {
      ex.printStackTrace();
    }
    gui.dispose();
    gui = null;
  }
```

```
public boolean handleMessage(Message message) {
  if (message.sameKind("text")) {
    String str = (String) message.getArg();
    gui.output.append(str+"\n");
    return true;
  } else if (message.sameKind("bye")) {
    gui.output.append("Bye Bye..");
    try {
      Thread.currentThread().sleep(3000);
    } catch (Exception ex) {}
    message.sendReply();
    chatPartner = null;
    dispose();
  }
  return false;
}

private void sendTextToChat(String text) {
  try {
    chatPartner.sendMessage(new Message("text", name + " : " + text));
  } catch (Exception ex){ System.out.println(ex); }
}

private void dispatchNewPartner(String destination) {
  try {
    if (chatPartner != null) {
      chatPartner.sendMessage(new Message("bye"));
    }
    AgletContext context = getAgletContext();
    chatPartner = context.createAglet(null, "ChatAgent", getProxy());
    chatPartner.dispatch(new URL(destination));
  } catch (Exception ex) {
    ex.printStackTrace();
  }
}
}
```

This program can be compiled with any Java compiler. To be able to start it, the execution environment must be started first with agletsd. This creates a graphical user interface for the management of agents, their creation, migration, destruction, and monitoring. It is shown in Figure 7.4.

Starting the example

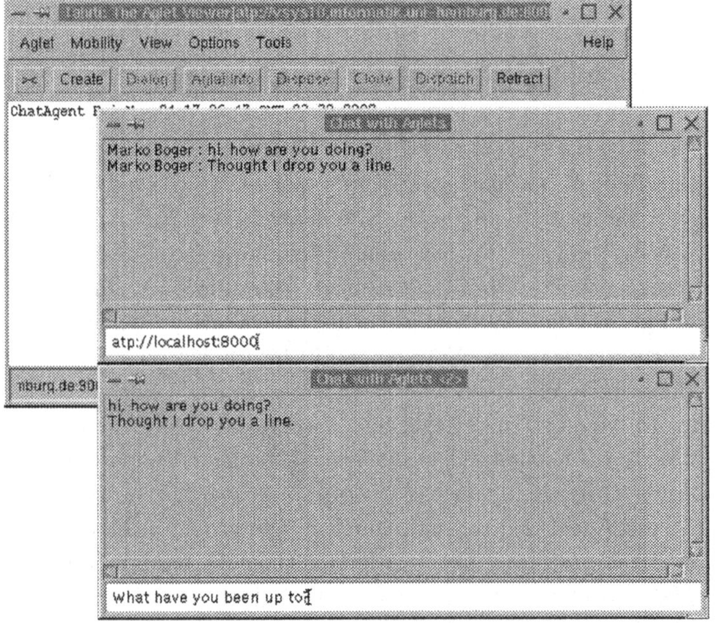

Figure 7.4
Aglet chat and Tahiti aglet environment.

Since, however, books are not a very suitable medium for the demonstration of graphical interfaces, the application will be controlled via its command line version. The graphical interface can be controlled by equivalent commands and specifications.

After two execution environments – as shown above – have been started, the createcommand can be used to create a chat agent. First, the address of the desired communication partner is specified in the ChatAgent, here atp://sun.informatik.uni-hamburg.de:9000/. Then, arbitrary messages can be sent.

```
lin> javac ChatAgent.java

sun> agletsd -port 9000
```

```
lin> agletsd command line
lin| [IBM Aglets Class Library 1.03 Revision: 8]
lin| [Creating com.ibm.aglets.tahiti.CommandLine]
lin> create file:///Buch/Code/Agents/Aglets/chat/ ChatAgent
```

7.2 Mobile agents in Voyager

The Voyager system presented in Chapter 6 also supports the paradigm of mobile agents. In contrast to the aglets, however, the concept of the mobile agent in Voyager is only one of many concepts for distributed programming. Therefore, although aglets are probably a nicer system for studying agents and getting familiar with their use, for practical application in distributed systems, Voyager might be the superior and more comprehensive product.

Agents as facets of an object

In Voyager, mobile agents are created by means of the already mentioned facets, which can be generated out of any object. An agent facet of an object is created by means of the call Agent.of() through which it also provides the methods of the IAgent interface which can then be used in addition to the previous properties of an object. Thus, in contrast to other approaches, in Voyager the set of possible objects is not restricted to user-defined objects derived from a class or an interface, but in principle each and every object can become a mobile agent. In most cases, however, a class that is to be used as a mobile agent is written specially for that purpose. Usually, such classes create this facet of themselves by means of Agent.of(this).

Characteristics of a Voyager agent

The most important difference between a mobile object and a mobile agent in Voyager is the property of autonomy. This means, on the one hand, that the agent can move by itself, on the other hand, that an autonomous mobile agent is not subject to garbage collection. Thus it is not destroyed when it is no longer pointed to, but can continue to live autonomously and become active itself. This property can be toggled on and off with setAutonomous().

Furthermore, a mobile agent can also move itself, which, similarly to mobile objects, it can initiate with the moveTo() method, which is made available here by the IAgent interface. This method can be passed a remote object or a URL, that is, the location to which the agent is to move. In addition, it can be specified which method of the agent is to be called at the target location and, if needed, the parameters of this method can be passed. Once the agent has moved to an object, the agent is also passed a reference to this object so it can contact the object.

These are all of the additional methods Voyager provides for agents. However, given that the entire framework for Voyager is available as well, this is largely sufficient.

7.2.1 A chat system with Voyager agents

Obviously, the agents in Voyager will also be demonstrated with the aid of a chat example. The fact that Voyager's agent system fits so neatly into the common framework of Voyager and into the concepts of normal object-oriented programming lets this implementation look much more similar to the previous ones than the implementation with aglets. The difference compared to an implementation without agent technology is very small. The most significant feature is that when the agent is moved onto a different computer, the moveTo() command allows a callback function to be specified which the agent executes automatically upon arrival. To make this additional functionality available, the Agent.of() call is used to create an agent facet of the actual object.

```
import com.objectspace.voyager.*;
import com.objectspace.voyager.agent.*;
import java.io.*;
import java.awt.event.*;

public class ChatAgent implements IChatAgent, Serializable {

  ChatFrame gui = null;
  IChatAgent chatPartner = null;
```

```
public ChatAgent(IChatAgent partner) {
    chatPartner = partner;
}

public void startup(){
   gui = new ChatFrame("Chat with Voyager agents");

   // When Enter is pressed in the input field ...
   gui.input.addKeyListener (
      new KeyAdapter() {
         public void keyPressed(KeyEvent e) {
            if (e.getKeyCode()==KeyEvent.VK_ENTER) {
               String msg = gui.input.getText();
               if (msg.startsWith("//")) {
                  newPartner(msg);
               } else {
                  sendTextToChat(gui.input.getText());
                  gui.output.append(gui.input.getText()+"\n");
                  gui.input.setText("");
               }
            }
         }
      }
   );

   // When the chat window is closed ...
   gui.addWindowListener(
      new WindowAdapter() {
         public void windowClosing(WindowEvent e) {
            chatPartner.bye();
            chatPartner = null;
            gui.dispose();
         }
      }
   );
}

public void bye() {
   gui.output.append("Bye Bye..");
```

```
    try {
      Thread.currentThread().sleep(3000);
    } catch (Exception ex) {}
    gui.dispose();
    chatPartner = null;
  }

public void receive(String message) {
  gui.output.append(message+"\n");
}

 private void sendTextToChat(String message) {
    try {
      chatPartner.receive(message);
    } catch (Exception ex) {
      ex.printStackTrace();
    }
 }

 private void newPartner(String destination) {
    try {
      if (chatPartner != null) {
        chatPartner.bye();
      }
      IChatAgent me = (IChatAgent) Proxy.of(this);
       chatPartner = (IChatAgent) Proxy.of(new ChatAgent(me));
      IAgent chatAgent = Agent.of(chatPartner);
      chatAgent.moveTo(destination,"startup");
    } catch (Exception ex) {
      ex.printStackTrace();
    }
 }

 public static void main(String[] args) {
    try {
      Voyager.startup("8000");
      ClassManager.enableResourceServer();
```

```
        ChatAgent agent = new ChatAgent(null);
        agent.startup();
      } catch (Exception e) {
        e.printStackTrace();
      }
    }
  }
```

At start-up, the same interface appears as with the aglets and all other chat examples. An additional chat partner can be created by entering a URL of a Voyager daemon in the input window, for example, //sun:9000.

```
sun> voyager 9000 -c http://lin:8000
```

```
lin> java ChatAgent
```

7.3 References

The term "agent" is quite frequently used in the literature; however, it mostly refers to intelligent agents in Artificial Intelligence. A rather wide range of books is available on the sunject. However, good books on mobile agents are only now beginning to appear.

A good introduction to the field and its concepts is given by [Caglayan and Harrison 1997], [Knapik and Johnson 1998], and [Brenner *et al.* 1998]. A more practically oriented book which gives an exemplary overview of some existing agent systems (Telescript, Agent Tcl, Ara, Aglets) is [Cockayne and Zyda 1998]. A highly recommendable book is the one published by the chief developers of the aglet concept, [Lange and Oshima 1998], which is, however, also restricted to this specific subject. Danny B. Lange is now working with the team of General Magic [Magic 1998], who, with Telescript, had developed one of the first systems and are now working on Odyssey. The aglet system can be downloaded via the URL http://www.trl.ibm.co.jp/aglets, the Voyager system via http://www.objectspace.com/.

Current research trends can be found in the publications of the Mobile Agents Workshop, which until now has taken place twice: [Rothermel and Popescu-Zeletin 1997] and [Rothermel and Hohl 1998].

8 JDBC

Databases are part of nearly every major software system. Since the quantities of data are nearly always too large to be permanently kept in the main memory of a computer, and because individual computers are switched off (or crash) from time to time, this data must be stored in a storage system. This may simply be a file system, but if this data is to be accessed more than once at various points in time, it is usually more efficient to store the data in databases. Also (and in particular) distributed applications are often connected with persistent data storage. Here, their function often exceeds that of simple storage of data: databases are also well suited for the connection of different applications and hardware systems. Since databases have a long history of use and many older systems manage their data in this way, they also represent a possibility of connection between new and old systems. Databases also offer the possibility of remote access and thus remote data communication. Remote database access is probably the most widely used mechanism for distributed communication. Therefore, the next chapters of this book are dedicated to the subject of persistence.

Databases in distributed systems

Among existing database technologies, relational databases are currently the most important ones, although recently the significance of object-oriented and object-relational databases keeps increasing. However, due to the mere fact that enormous amounts of data already exist in relational databases, they will not lose their overwhelming importance in the near future. Also, from their very structure, many kinds of data can more easily be captured in relational databases than in object-oriented ones. They allow efficient management and access to

Relational databases

tables of data which, in practice, frequently occur in the form of tables in the first place. Object-oriented databases will be discussed in more detail in the next chapter.

JDBC

In this chapter, we will present the connection of Java to relational databases. For this purpose a standard exists which has become quite popular, the Java Database Connectivity (JDBC). With JDBC it is possible to access nearly every relational database; and when it is connected to the Internet, this can even be done from (practically) anywhere. It is assumed that the reader has a certain basic knowledge of the functioning of relational databases and the SQL query language.

Development of JDBC

JDBC has been developed out of a series of different standards for relational database access. The most important one is ODBC (Open Database Connectivity). An important goal in the development of JDBC was to facilitate the usability of such a database interface and make it extremely simple for standard cases of application, while allowing at the same time the use of the full bandwidth of possibilities provided by today's relational databases. Advanced mechanisms such as precompiled queries and working with meta-data will only be discussed marginally in this book. JDBC is an integrated part of Java and belongs to the core of the language. Like Java, it has had its development: in the JDK 1.1, JDBC is contained in its version 1.0, while the new version of Java (Java 2, also known as JDK 1.2) already includes JDBC version 2.0, which introduces extensions and improvements, but the core has remained unchanged.

First, the general structure of JDBC will be introduced and the most important interfaces will be presented in more detail. Subsequently, JDBC will be demonstrated with the aid of an example.

8.1 The structure of JDBC

A Java application can establish simultaneous connections to several databases. To make this possible, two layers have been incorporated into JDBC, which help with he management of these connections and make access as simple as possible. For each type of database, a database driver must exist which takes on the direct communication with the database. These drivers are managed by the driver manager, where the drivers are registered once and then handled automatically. The general structure of JDBC is shown in Figure 8.1.

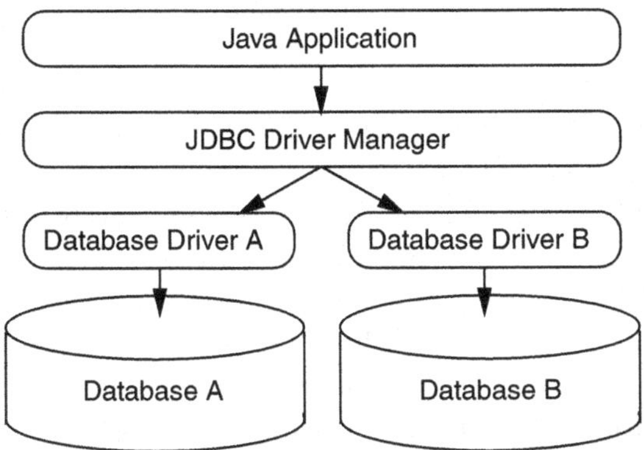

Figure 8.1
The structure of JDBC.

The driver manager

The driver manager is implemented via the DriverManager class and plays a central role inside the JDBC-API. This class is the interface to the different database drivers and establishes the connections with the databases, functioning as a link between the application and the databases. It is not instantiated, but used exclusively via class methods.

With DriverManager.registerDriver(), the drivers automatically register with this class, once they have been activated, and unregister with unregisterDriver(). Once a driver for one kind of database is known, this class does not need to be activated again, because the driver manager now recognizes itself which driver it must activate. Only when a driver is not yet known to the driver manager or has been unregistered, must it be registered again. DriverManager.getDrivers() can be used to find out which drivers are registered. The following paragraphs discuss the drivers in some more detail.

The database drivers

There are four variations of database drivers which chiefly differ by the kind of communication at protocol level. A driver can resort to the existing access protocols of ODBC, use proprietary database protocols, or run protocols standardized for JDBC. The drivers are therefore subdivided into the following four classes:

1. **JDBC/ODBC bridge**. This relatively slim conversion component allows ODBC drivers to be accessed by JDBC. This makes it possible to access every database that provides an ODBC interface even when it has no specific JDBC interface. Since JDBC has been developed on the basis of ODBC, only little frictional loss occurs, but it is slower than a direct link via one of the following alternatives. This driver can only be used by applications or by trusted applets, not by normal applets. It is provided free of charge by Sun and Intersolv.

2. **Platform-specific JDBC drivers**. These drivers convert JDBC calls directly into the proprietary calls of a database. As these are mostly not written in Java, but in C or C++, they cannot be loaded from the server into a browser and can therefore generally not be used for applets.

3. **Universal JDBC drivers**. In this solution, the driver is written in Java and communicates with a server component, also programmed in Java, via a database-independent protocol. The client part can automatically be loaded by an applet, so that nothing needs to be preinstalled on the client.

4. **Direct JDBC drivers**. These are drivers that work directly at the protocol level of the database. This solution is the fastest from the performance point of view, but has the disadvantage that the drivers are nearly exclusively supplied by the database manufacturers.

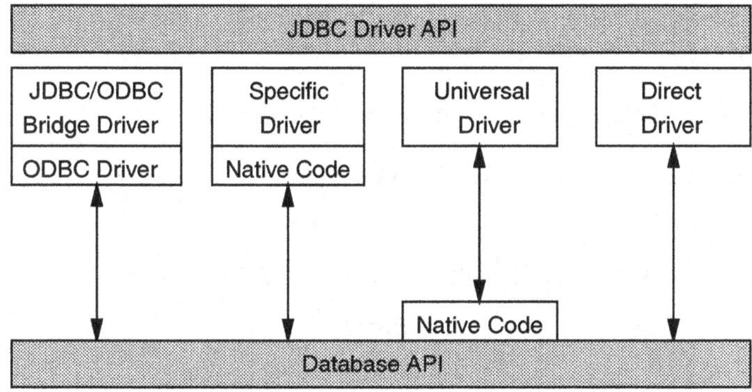

Figure 8.2
The different types of driver.

The two most frequently adopted solutions are the JDBC/ODBC bridge and the universal JDBC drivers. The bridge solution is the financially most economical one as this driver is available free of charge. However, it is also relatively slow and inflexible, while the universal drivers are highly flexible and, under performance aspects, comparable with the direct drivers.

Fortunately the decision as to which driver is going to be used is irrelevant for the programming of database applications. It has repercussions on costs and performance, but not on the interface to be used. However, as mentioned above, not all drivers are suitable for use in applets.

All drivers implement the java.sql.Driver interface, which a programmer has practically nothing to do with. A driver registers automatically with the DriverManager. It can then simply be called via a String that represents its class name or a URL. The JDBC-ODBC bridge driver used in the next example is included in the JDKs from version 1.1 onward.

```
// REGISTER DRIVER
try {
  Driver d = (Driver)Class.forName("sun.jdbc.odbc.JdbcOdbcDriver").newInstance();
} catch (Exception e) {
   System.out.println(e)
}
```

Usually, it is even possible to do without a reference to this driver and simply use the abbreviated form:

Class.forName(sun.jdbc.odbc.JdbcOdbcDriver)

Everything else is controlled via the driver manager.

8.2 Establishing a connection with a database

For a normal sequence of queries, the course of a database application making use of JDBC looks as follows: the central class of JDBC is the DriverManager. This establishes one or more connections to one database each (the Connection). Via the Connection, individual queries (Statement) are created and passed to the database, which returns a set of result lines, the ResultSet. The result lines are read one by one by the application and then processed. Inside one Connection, several Statements can be executed in the context of one transaction, and be confirmed with a commit() or rejected with a rollback(). As the last step, the Connection is closed. The relation between these classes is shown in Figure 8.3.

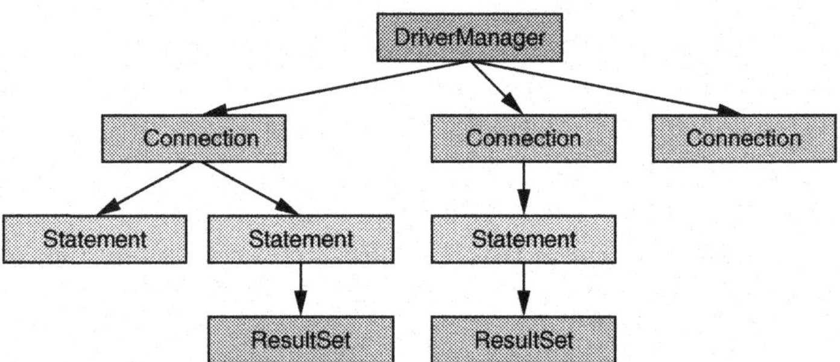

Figure 8.3 *The driver manager handles several connections.*

One of the most important functions of the driver manager is to establish and manage connections with one or more database(s). Each of these connections is handled by one object of the Connection class. The driver manager is passed a URL of a database, a user name, and a password, and will – if possible – return the required connection.

URLs for databases

As with other URLs, the URL for databases has the form: jdbc:<subprotocol>:<resourcename>, where the subprotocol specifies the driver to be used for the transmission. These subprotocol denominations are established by JavaSoft and can be reserved there by database or driver manufacturers. The JDBC/ODBC bridge, for example, has been assigned the subprotocol denomination odbc, so that an ODBC database can be accessed via jdbc:odbc://.... The resource name is the name of a database made available on a local computer or a computer on the Internet or Intranet. The database which will be used in the next examples can be accessed under the URL jdbc:odbc://sun.informatik.uni-hamburg.de/BulletinBoardDb or locally as jdbc:odbc://BulletinBoardDb.

```
// GET CONNECTION
Connection con;
try{
   con = DriverManager.getConnection(
    "jdbc:odbc://sun.informatik.uni-hamburg.de/BulletinBoardDb",userName,password);
}catch(Exception e){
   System.out.println(e);
}
```

8.3 Queries and answers

After a connection has been established, it can be used for putting queries to the database. In the development of JDBC, much care has been taken to make the solution of simple queries as easy as possible, while for more complex queries, users can put up with a more complex interface. Therefore, the queries are subdivided into three categories. For common SQL SELECT queries, the programmer can make use of a very easy-to-handle form, the Statement. For more complicated queries, the classes PreparedStatement and CallableStatement are available. Access to meta-data of a database, such as the structure of the tables, is made possible through a DatabaseMetaData class.

In order to put a normal SQL query, an object of the Statement class is created and passed to the database by means of the executeQuery()call which, as a parameter, contains an SQL query string. The database answers with an object of the ResultSet class, which contains a set of result lines which can be browsed through and read one by one.

```
Statement stmt = con.create();
String query="SELECT * FROM BlackBoard";
ResultSet results=stmt.executeQuery(query);
```

For database operations such as UPDATE, INSERT, and DELETE, Statement provides the executeUpdate() method, which returns a Boolean value.

```
String insert="INSERT INTO BlackBoard VALUES ('A new important message', 'Marko')";
Boolean bool=stmt.executeUpdate(insert);
```

The PreparedStatement class is an extension of Statement which is intended for queries that are often repeated in a similar form, with a view to optimization of performance. PreparedStatement makes it possible to pass a query containing placeholders to the database, which then precompiles the query. The placeholders are set with a set instruction, their actual values are passed at a later stage by means of an executeQuery() call.

```
PreparedStatement prepstmt = con.prepareStatement(
  SELECT * FROM BlackBoard WHERE user = ?);
prepstmt.setString(1,Marko);
ResultSet result1=prepstmt.executeQuery();
prepstmt.setString(1,Harald);
ResultSet result2=prepstmt.executeQuery();
```

CallableStatements are used in connection with *stored procedures* and provide an out parameter in addition to the in parameters.

Finally, the result which, after a query, is present as an object of the ResultSet class, must be processed. The next() method lets you browse through the lines of the result. The individual columns can be read by means of a **get** instruction which must know the type of the data field.

```
while (result1.next()) {
	String msg=result1.getString(Message);
	String user=result1.getString(User);
	System.out.println(Message from +user+ : +msg);
}
```

8.4 Example: a BulletinBoard

As an example we will now present an electronic bulletin board where messages are to be read from a database and displayed. For the sake of simplicity, a message (*Posting*) consists only of a headline and a text body and belongs to a group of subjects (*Category*). This simple structure can easily be extended to include an author or sender, the creation date and, where necessary, the date of expiry or something similar. For our purposes, however, a simple message will suffice.

For this example, two tables are created in a database, one for the categories and one for the actual messages. In principle, this could also be implemented in a single table, but we also wish to show the reader how to work with several tables. The first table contains the categories and consists of the two fields ID and name.

ID	name
1	Giveaway
2	Search
3	Offer

The second table contains the messages and is subdivided into the fields ID, subject, and body; in an additional category field the category is indicated by its ID from the first table.

ID	subject	body	category
1	Vacuum cleaner	giveaway Hoover ...	1
2	Ford Thunderbird	used T-Bird, year ...	3
3	Cat escaped	striped cat, blue ...	2

The graphical interface of the application is split into two windows; the main window is generated by the BulletinBoardFrame class and displays the information from the database. An additional window, created by the NewPostingDialog class, is needed for the generation of new messages. Figures 8.4 and 8.5 show these two classes which are listed and explained in Appendix B.

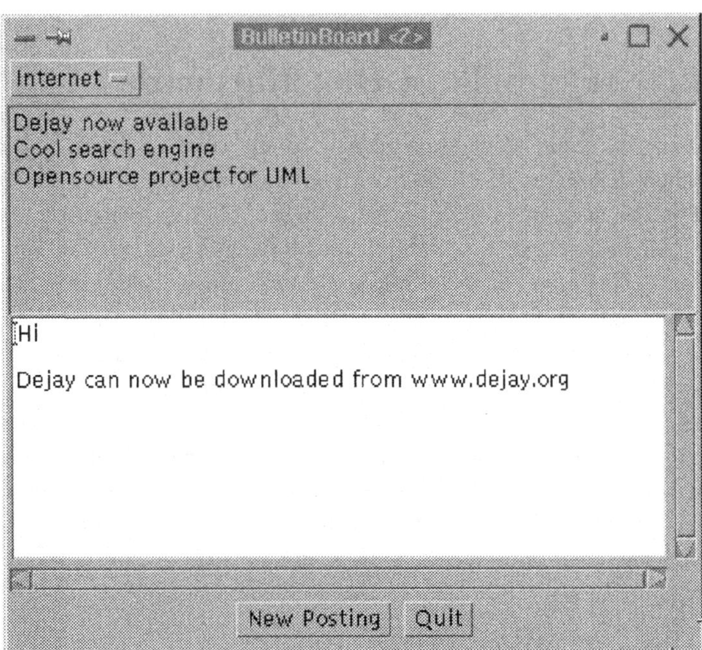

Figure 8.4 *The graphical interface of the BulletinBoard.*

Figure 8.5 *Input window for new messages.*

```
import java.sql.*;

public class BulletinBoard {

  private BulletinBoardFrame gui = null;
  private Connection conn = null;

  public BulletinBoard() {

    gui = new BulletinBoardFrame("BulletinBoard", this);

    // register jdbc driver
    try {
      Class.forName("org.gjt.mm.mysql.Driver");
    } catch (ClassNotFoundException cnfe) {
      System.out.println("Can't load driver. Exiting.");
      System.exit(1);
    }

    // open connection to rdbms
    try {
      conn = DriverManager.getConnection(
          "jdbc:mysql://localhost:3306/jivs?user=jivs;password=jivs");
    } catch (Exception e) {
      System.out.println("Connection to RDBMS failed!");
    }

    try {
      Statement stmt = conn.createStatement();
       ResultSet rs = stmt.executeQuery(
          "SELECT ID, name FROM categories ORDER BY name ASC");
      while (rs.next()) {
        int id = rs.getInt(1);
        String name = rs.getString(2);
        gui.addCategory(id, name);
      }
    } catch (SQLException e) {
      System.out.println("Reading categories failed: "+e);
    }
  }
```

```
public boolean handleQuit() {
  try {
    conn.close();
  } catch (SQLException e) {
    System.out.println("Closing connection failed");
  }
  return true;
}

public synchronized void insertNewPosting(String _subject, String _body,
    int _category) {
  try {
    Statement stmt = conn.createStatement();
     stmt.executeUpdate(
       "INSERT INTO postings VALUES
       (0,'"+_subject+"','"+_body+"',"+_category+")");
    reloadSubjects(_category);
  } catch (SQLException sqle) {
    System.out.println("Insert failed: "+sqle);
  }
}

public synchronized void reloadSubjects(int _category) {
  gui.clearSubjects();
  try {
    Statement stmt = conn.createStatement();
     ResultSet rs = stmt.executeQuery(
       "SELECT ID, subject FROM postings WHERE
       category = "+_category );
    while (rs.next()) {
      int id = rs.getInt(1);
      String subject = rs.getString(2);
      gui.addSubject(id, subject);
    }
  } catch (SQLException sqle) {
    System.out.println("Select failed");
  }
}
```

```
  public String getBody(int _id) {
    try {
      Statement stmt = conn.createStatement();
      ResultSet rs = stmt.executeQuery(
        "SELECT body FROM postings WHERE ID = "+_id);
      String body = null;
      if (rs.next()) {
        body = rs.getString(1);
      }
      if (body != null)
        return body;
      else
        return "";
    } catch (SQLException sqle) {
      System.out.println("Select failed");
    }
    return "";
  }

  public static void main (String[] args) {
    BulletinBoard bBoard = new BulletinBoard();
  }
}
```

8.5 References

As for Java in general, there exists a whole series of good books on JDBC. One of the most frequently quoted books is [Reese 1997]. A very good and sufficiently detailed book is [Hamilton *et al.* 1997], whose authors have been highly influential in the development of JDBC.

For a general introduction to relational databases, we recommend [Date 1995] or [Meier 1998].

9 Object-oriented databases

The relational databases discussed in the previous chapter are widely diffused in practical applications, their implementations are very reliable, highly optimized and perform very well. However, the fact that relational databases make use of data structures that do not quite fit into the object-oriented paradigm, creates a gap between programming language and database model which must be bridged by the programmer with relatively high effort. This fact is also known as *impedance mismatch*.

Disadvantages of relational databases

Relational databases have been developed after the theoretically founded relation model of Codd [Codd 1970], and the bridge towards programming languages has been made only at a later stage. The opposite way is followed by object-oriented databases: after the object-oriented paradigm had revealed itself as highly successful for programming, databases were developed that are compatible with the data structures employed, namely with objects. This database technology is much younger than the relational one, and scalability, stability, and performance have not yet reached a comparable level. However, the use of object databases makes programming substantially easier and permits a considerable increase of productivity. Therefore, object databases are currently given rather favorable odds.

Pros and cons of object-oriented databases

As opposed to relational databases, which possess a standardized query language, SQL, and standardized interfaces, such as ODBC and JDBC, the ways in which object databases are handled and accessed are still very dissimilar. Standardization attempts are being made, in particular by the ODMG (Object Database Management Group), a sub-organization of the

OMG, which is responsible for the standardization of object-oriented databases. However, these attempts have not yet been concluded and are only of limited significance. Therefore, one must today still look at individual products. The most important databases in this field come from companies such as Poet, Versant, Objectory, and ObjectDesign.

ObjectStore

In the following section, we will use the ObjectStore database by ObjectDesign. This has several reasons: on the one hand, ObjectDesign is the market leader in this field, so that the probability of finding this product in practice is extremely high. Also, ObjectStore's support for Java is very good and relatively easy to use. Third, ObjectStore exists in three different versions, the first of which, ObjectStore PSE, is available completely free of charge, while the second one is commercially available at moderate prices in the three-digit range. This version, ObjectStore PSE Pro, is compatible with the full product, so that programming remains the same. This version is designed for single-user systems, but otherwise provides the full range of features. The full product, ObjectStore, provides additional possibilities for multi-user operation and large amounts of data.

9.1 ObjectStore

PSE

When one thinks of databases, one usually imagines big server computers on which huge programs are running. That this must not necessarily be the case is proved by ObjectDesign with their ObjectStore Personal Storage Environment (PSE). PSE is an object database with extremely low storage requirements, which is completely written in Java. It is well suited for storage and management of a larger number or persistent objects and, due to the fact that its memory requirements are so low, can even be used in applets. Nevertheless it provides very much of the functionality of fully-fledged databases, such as transactions and a query feature. For very large databases in which performance plays a major role, however, one should revert to the big brother.

PSE exists in two different variations. Initially, PSE was free of charge and was integrated, for example, into Netscape Navigator. Unfortunately, this version is no longer supported by ObjectDesign, but should still be available on the Web for quite a while. It has been designed for smaller amounts of data and single users, and does not allow parallel access to the database, but apart from these limitations, it offers nearly the complete functionality of an object-oriented database. Here the database is written to a file which is completely read into RAM when the database is opened. Therefore, PSE databases are subject to restrictions with regard to size and performance.

This version has been further developed by ObjectDesign to become ObjectStore PSE Pro which is, however, no longer free of charge. The cost, however, is more than reasonable. It can also be downloaded from ObjectDesign (currently in version 3) [ObjectDesign 1998] and be freely used for evaluation purposes for a period of 30 days. This version promises a good performance with data amounts of up to several hundred megabytes, and allows efficient indexing and garbage collection in the persistent storage. In this version, the entire database is not read, but only its currently relevant parts. This makes PSE Pro well suited even for large amounts of data. The following discussion is based on PSE Pro.

9.2 Accessing persistent objects

To access objects in a PSE Pro database, three preparatory steps are needed:

1. open a session,
2. open or create the database,
3. start the transaction.

Opening a session

All activities on a database are performed inside so-called *sessions* (Session). A session must first be created, then several threads of an application can participate in this session (join()). PSE supports exactly one session, while PSE Pro also supports several sessions opened in parallel.

```
Session session = Session.create(null,null);
session.join();
```

Opening a database

Before a database can be accessed, it must be opened. To do this, PSE/PSE Pro uses the Database.open() method. Databases have a name through which they are identified. Closed databases are kept on non-volatile storage media in the file system. In simple cases, the database file is located in the same directory as the Java application. Thus it can be simply identified via the file name. When the database is opened, you can specify whether it is to be accessed read-only or read and write. This is indicated in the second parameter via the READ_ONLY or UPDATE constants defined in the ObjectStore class.

```
Database db = Database.open("CounterDb.odb", ObjectStore.UPDATE);
```

Obviously, a database must exist in order to be accessed. If a database does not yet exist, it is created by means of the Database.create() method. Databases can be protected through the definition of access rights, in a similar way as, under Unix, files have read and write privileges for different user groups. For this purpose, constants such as ALL_READ, ALL_WRITE, and OWNER_WRITE are available. However, Java does not allow overriding of file system modes.

```
Database db = Database.create (
"CounterDb.odb", ObjectStore.ALL_READ|ObjectStore.ALL_WRITE);
```

The framework for all actions performed on the data of a database is the transaction. Inside a transaction, data can be accessed in reading or writing. When the transaction is terminated, all (modified) data items are written persistently in the database. But only then: prior to the end of a transaction, the changes are not visible to others. A transaction is started with begin() and terminated with commit(). Both methods have a parameter which controls the access to the data. During opening, an access mode must be specified. Transactions can be

Starting a transaction

defined as read-only. Then, several such transaction can exist at the same time. For write access, however, only one single transaction may be open. This is indicated by means of the constants UPDATE and READ_ONLY.

```
Transaction trx = Transaction.begin(ObjectStore.UPDATE);
```

Now, persistent objects can be accessed. Objects are persistent if and only if they are either a *root object* of the database or can be reached from a root object. Several root objects can be defined for one database. Usually, these are objects through which many other objects are referenced, such as a hash table or a vector. Unfortunately, in the JDK up to version 1.1, exactly these structures cannot be made persistent. For these cases, replacement structures exist which fulfill the same purpose and can be persistent. Here, ObjectStore provides special classes, such as OSHashtable and OSVector. However, with JDK 1.2 and the introduction of collections, this deficiency has been remedied.

Root objects

A root object is created by means of createRoot(), which binds a name to an object. Root objects are the entry points in the persistent object graph and starting points of the navigation – the only way persistent objects can be reached.

```
OSHashtable counterHash = new OSHashtable();
db.createRoot("MyCounterHash", counterHash);
Counter accesses = new Counter();
accesses.set(42);
counterHash.put("AccessCounter", accesses);
trx.commit();
```

The name can later be used to access a root object, and subsequently all persistent objects, by applying the getRoot() method.

```
Transaction trx2 = Transaction.begin(ObjectStore.UPDATE);
counterHash = (OSHashtable) db.getRoot("CounterHash");
accesses = (Counter) counterHash.get("AccessCounter");
```

As already mentioned, transactions can be terminated by means of commit(), thus making the modifications persistent. All changes are stored simultaneously and undivided. All objects that can be reached from the root objects are made persistent. Thus the storage of persistent objects is carried out in a simple and transparent way for the programmer. It is also possible to reject the changes of a transaction and restore the state prior to the transaction. All changes to the data are either taken over completely into the database or not at all. To reject the changes, the abort() method is called.

```
accesses.increase();
if (accepted) {
  // the counter is incremented
  trx2.commit()
} else {
  // the counter is NOT incremented
  trx2.abort()
}
```

Access to persistent objects is (by default) only possible inside transactions. After a commit() has been executed, all persistent objects are made unreachable from the Java program.

Stale objects

They are then called *stale*, and their values are deleted – obviously only in the program, and not in the persistent storage. When a stale object is accessed, the database system generates an exception. When a new access is to be made to one of these objects, a new transaction must be started and the required object must be reached from the root object. This is sensible, on the one hand, since in this way, changes made outside transactions cannot be written to the database, and the system cannot change into an inconsistent state. On the other hand, however, it is very useful to maintain certain states and be able to use them, for example, in new transactions. When the programmer so wishes, this can be specified through an additional parameter in the commit() method (as well as in the abort() method). This parameter too is an int for which again constants are available to express the required state. The constant RETAIN_STALE is equivalent to the default case without a parameter. With RETAIN_HOLLOW, references to persistent objects remain valid also outside the transaction, although any access is still forbidden and generates an exception. In a new transaction, however, the objects can again be freely accessed. To be able to perform at least a reading access to such objects, RETAIN_READONLY is set. RETAIN_UPDATE even allows modifications, but as soon as the next transaction begins, these modifications are rejected.

One disadvantage of these procedures is that the corresponding objects cannot be collected by the garbage collector and thus encumber the main memory even when they are no longer needed. Therefore, one should from time to time terminate a transaction with RETAIN_STALE.

Terminating a session

Finally, the database must be closed and the session must be terminated. If this is not done, the database remains locked and cannot be opened again until the lock is deleted. In PSE, this lock is realized by creating and deleting an (otherwise empty) directory which bears the name of the database with the extension .odx.

```
db.close();
session.terminate();
```

Now that all of the individual steps have been explained, we will present a short but complete example. Here, objects of the already known Counter class are to be kept persistent.

```
import COM.odi.*;
import COM.odi.util.*;

public class CounterManager {

  public static void main(String[] args) {

    Session session = Session.create(null,null);
    session.join();
    Database db;
    OSHashtable counterHash = new OSHashtable();
    Counter accesses = new Counter();
    try {
      db = Database.open("CounterDb.odb", ObjectStore.UPDATE);
      Transaction trx = Transaction.begin(ObjectStore.UPDATE);
```

```
      db.createRoot("CounterHash",counterHash);
      accesses.set (42);
      System.out.println("Counter set to "+accesses.read());
      counterHash.put("AccessCounter",accesses);
      trx.commit();
    } catch (DatabaseNotFoundException e) {
      db = Database.create("CounterDb.odb",
         ObjectStore.ALL_READ|ObjectStore.ALL_WRITE);
    }

    Transaction trx2= Transaction.begin(ObjectStore.UPDATE);
    counterHash = (OSHashtable) db.getRoot("CounterHash");
    accesses  = (Counter) counterHash.get("AccessCounter");
    accesses.increase();
    System.out.println("Counter increased to "+accesses.read());
    trx2.commit(ObjectStore.RETAIN_READONLY);

    db.close();
    session.terminate();
  }
}
```

9.3 The postprocessor

With the mechanisms described above, ObjectStore offers a very easy-to-handle usage of persistence. To make this possible, however, classes must be postprocessed and prepared for persistence. This task is carried out by a postprocessor which reads the translated Java code and outputs it in modified form.

This postprocessor, named osjcfp (ObjectStore Java Class File Postprocessor), must be called after compilation with javac.

Mandatory parameters

It is controlled through a number of parameters, some of which are mandatory, while others are optional. In the easiest case, where the existing .class file is simply to be overwritten, the output must be redirected into the current directory (-dest .) and the postprocessor must be allowed to actually overwrite the existing file (-inplace). As the processor possesses two different modes, it also needs to be told whether the specified class is to be *persistence capable* (-pc) or only *persistence aware* (-pa). Here are the necessary steps, together with the output of the program:

```
sun> javac Counter.java CounterManager.java
sun> osjcfp -dest . -inplace -pc Counter.class
sun> java CounterManager
sun| Counter set to 42
sun| Counter increased to 43
```

To obtain information on an existing database, an additional tool is provided (together with several others): the osjshowdb command displays the class names and the number of objects in the database together with their size. For the database created in the above example, the following information is shown:

```
sun> osjshowdb CounterDb.odb
sun| Name: CounterDb.odb

sun| There is one root:
sun|  Name: CounterHash   Type: COM.odi.util.OSHashtable

sun| Segment: 0
sun| Size: 4111 (5 Kbytes)

sun|     Count  Tot Size  Type

sun|         2        64  COM.odi.util.OSHashtable
sun|         2        64  COM.odi.util.OSHashtableEntry
sun|         2        72  COM.odi.util.OSHashtableEntry[]
sun|         1        16  Counter
sun|         2        88  java.lang.Object[]
sun|         3       384  java.lang.String
sun|         1        16  java.lang.String[]
```

9.4 The BulletinBoard with ObjectStore

The following example shows how to make data persistent in an object-oriented database in a slightly more realistic application.

We will use the same example as with JDBC, the BulletinBoard. Messages are sorted by categories and include a subject, the message body itself, plus a category number which stores the category to which the message belongs. For internal identification, the message is assigned an ID number. The complete object together with its access methods presents itself as follows.

```
public class Posting {
  private int id;
  private String subject;
  private String body;
  private int category;
  public Posting() {
    id=0;
    subject = "";
    body = "";
    category = 0;
  }

  int getID() { return (id); }
  String getSubject() { return (subject); }
  String getBody() { return (body); }
  int getCategory() { return (category); }

  void setValues(int _id, String _subject, String _body, int _category) {
    id = _id;
    subject = _subject;
    body = _body;
    category = _category;
  }
}
```

Similarly to the JDBC example, there is also a simple class, Category, in which only the name of the category and the internal ID are defined together with the access methods.

Output and interaction with the user are performed via the same user interfaces defined in the BulletinBoardFrame class and listed in Appendix B. This generates the window shown in Figure 9.1.

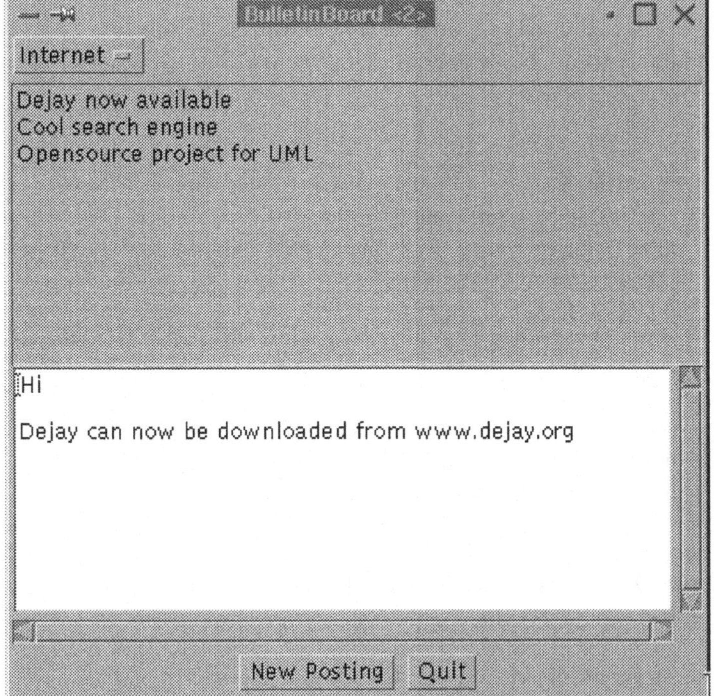

Figure 9.1 *The graphical interface of the BulletinBoard.*

When the user wishes to create a new message, pressing the "New Posting" button opens a new window in which the new message can then be entered.

The BulletinBoard class controls the storage of data and the communication with the BulletinBoardFrame, which in turn is responsible for the interaction with the user and the graphical presentation.

As root objects which house the postings and the categories, we will use two hash tables which have been adapted by ObjectDesign to suit the requirements of persistence (OSHashtable). Hash tables assign an entry a key (the hash code) through which it can again be reached.

```
// two root objects...
OSHashtable entryHash = new OSHashtable();
OSHashtable categoryHash = new OSHashtable();
```

Either, a database is generated in the constructor of the BulletinBoard class and the appropriate categories (search, offer) are created, or an existing database is opened and the data contained in it is read. This is carried out in the following try/catch clause:

```
try {
  db = Database.open("BulletinDb.odb", ObjectStore.UPDATE);
} catch (DatabaseNotFoundException e) {
  db = Database.create("BulletinDb.odb", ObjectStore.ALL_READ |
    ObjectStore.ALL_WRITE);}
```

Then a new transaction is generated in which the database can be accessed.

```
  Transaction trx = Transaction.begin(ObjectStore.UPDATE);
  db.createRoot("entryHash",entryHash);
  db.createRoot("categoryHash",categoryHash);
```

To set up the categories in the database, the put() method of the OSHashtable object is used. As soon as the transaction is terminated, this data is persistent in the database.

```
  categoryHash.put("1", new Category(1, "Search"));
  categoryHash.put("2", new Category(2, "Offer"));
  trx.commit(ObjectStore.RETAIN_HOLLOW);
}
```

The Objectstore.RETAIN_HOLLOW switch ensures that references to persistent objects in the database are maintained and can be used in subsequent transactions. The counterpart would be the default setting Objectstore.RETAIN_STALE which deletes the database cache, causing references to objects in the database to be lost.

The following listing shows a typical query to the database. All categories are read and passed to the BulletinBoardFrame for output. As the stored object is a hash table, querying the data is reduced to looking up this hash table. First, a new transaction is opened, then the getRoot() method is used to fetch a reference to the categoryHash object stored in the database. Via an iterator, all categories are read in a while loop and passed to the BulletinBoardFrame. After the current transaction has been terminated, the session can be exited to make it available to other threads.

```
Transaction trx = Transaction.begin(ObjectStore.READONLY);
categoryHash = (OSHashtable)db.getRoot("categoryHash");
Iterator categoryIter = categoryHash.values().iterator();
Category tempCategory = new Category(0, "no_matter");
while (categoryIter.hasNext()) {
  ecounter++;
  tempCategory = ((Category)categoryIter.next());
  int catID = tempCategory.getID();
  String name = tempCategory.getName();
  gui.addCategory(catID, name);
}
trx.commit(ObjectStore.RETAIN_HOLLOW);
session.leave();
```

The three methods (see source text) insertNewPosting(), reload-Subjects(), and getBody() control the further accesses to the database. Finally, it is important that, upon termination of the application, the functions close() of the database and terminate() of the session are called to terminate the transaction in an orderly way and to close the database.

```
// close database and terminate session
  public boolean handleQuit() {
    db.close();
    session.terminate();
    return true;
  }
```

The following listing shows the complete source code of the BulletinBoard class.

```
import COM.odi.*;
import COM.odi.util.*;

public class BulletinBoard {

  private BulletinBoardFrame gui = null;

  // define a session...
  Session session = Session.create(null,null);

  // ... and a database
  Database db;

  int ecounter = 0;

  // two root objects...
  OSHashtable entryHash = new OSHashtable();
  OSHashtable categoryHash = new OSHashtable();

  // constructor opens/creates the database and fills the GUI
  public BulletinBoard() {
    session.join();
    gui = new BulletinBoardFrame("BulletinBoard", this);
    Posting posting = new Posting();

    // try to open the database, otherwise create one and fill it with categories
    try {
      db = Database.open("BulletinDb.odb",ObjectStore.UPDATE);
    } catch (DatabaseNotFoundException e) {
      db = Database.create("BulletinDb.odb", ObjectStore.ALL_READ |
        ObjectStore.ALL_WRITE);
      Transaction trx = Transaction.begin(ObjectStore.UPDATE);
      db.createRoot("entryHash",entryHash);
      db.createRoot("categoryHash",categoryHash);
      // fill category
      categoryHash.put("1", new Category(1, "Search"));
      categoryHash.put("2", new Category(2, "Offer"));
      trx.commit(ObjectStore.RETAIN_HOLLOW);
    }
```

```
    // get all categories and pass them to the GUI
    Transaction trx = Transaction.begin(ObjectStore.READONLY);
    categoryHash = (OSHashtable)db.getRoot("categoryHash");
    Iterator categoryIter = categoryHash.values().iterator();
    Category tempCategory = new Category(0, "no_matter");

    // iterate over all categories...
    while (categoryIter.hasNext()) {
      tempCategory = ((Category)categoryIter.next());
      int catID = tempCategory.getID();
      String name = tempCategory.getName();
      gui.addCategory(catID, name);
    }
    trx.commit(ObjectStore.RETAIN_HOLLOW);
    session.leave();
    reloadSubjects(1);
  }

  // create new entry
  public synchronized void insertNewPosting(String _subject, String _body,
      int _category) {
    session.join();
    Transaction trx = Transaction.begin(ObjectStore.UPDATE);
    Posting tmpPosting = new Posting();
    ecounter++;
    tmpPosting.setValues(ecounter, _subject, _body, _category);
    Integer tmpecounter = new Integer(ecounter);
    entryHash.put(tmpecounter.toString(), tmpPosting);
    trx.commit(ObjectStore.RETAIN_HOLLOW);
    session.leave();
    reloadSubjects(_category);
  }

  // fetch the subjects from the database
  public synchronized void reloadSubjects(int _category) {
    session.join();
    gui.clearSubjects();
    Transaction trx = Transaction.begin(ObjectStore.READONLY);
    entryHash = (OSHashtable)db.getRoot("entryHash");
    Iterator postingIter = entryHash.values().iterator();
```

```
  Posting tempPosting = new Posting();
  ecounter=0;
  while (postingIter.hasNext()) {
    ecounter++;
    tempPosting = ((Posting)postingIter.next());
    int catID = tempPosting.getCategory();
    if (catID == _category) {
      String subject = tempPosting.getSubject();
      int id = tempPosting.getID();
      gui.addSubject(id, subject);
    }
  }
  trx.commit(ObjectStore.RETAIN_HOLLOW);
  session.leave();
}

// get the body for a posting
public String getBody(int _id) {
  session.join();
  Transaction trx = Transaction.begin(ObjectStore.READONLY);
  Iterator postingIter = entryHash.values().iterator();
  Posting tempPosting = new Posting();
  String body = null;
  while (postingIter.hasNext()) {
    tempPosting = ((Posting)postingIter.next());
    int id = tempPosting.getID();
    if (id == _id) {
      body = tempPosting.getBody();
    }
  }
  trx.commit(ObjectStore.RETAIN_HOLLOW);
  session.leave();
  if (body != null) {
    return body;
  }
  else {
    return "";
  }
}
```

```
  // close database  and terminate session
  public boolean handleQuit() {
    db.close();
    session.terminate();
    return true;
  }

  // main method
  public static void main (String[] args) {
    BulletinBoard bBoard = new BulletinBoard();
  }
}
```

9.5 Reactivation of objects

In distributed systems, individual components may fail and thus lose information about their state. Persistence can make sure that the data or the objects themselves are not lost; however, the consistency of remote references to these objects cannot be guaranteed. To solve this problem, further-reaching concepts are needed which can reactivate objects from a database as soon as they are accessed via remote references. This process is called activation. In Voyager, ObjectSpace provides a so-called *Activation Framework*, which does exactly this and which is particularly suited for use in distributed systems. The classes of the objects to be made persistent do not need to be modified or prepared in any way. Also, there are no additional precompilers or postcompilers. The mechanism presumes, however, the use of Voyager and, in particular, the use of proxies. This capability of Voyager can well be connected with an object-oriented database, as we will demonstrate with the aid of ObjectStore.

Activation Framework

When an object no longer exists in main memory, it can also no longer be referenced or called, not even via remote references. The Voyager Activation Framework ensures that this can nevertheless function. A persistent object can be reactivated, as soon or as long as a Voyager runtime environment is running under the appropriate port number on the original computer. Proxies pointing to such a persistent object can obviously still exist in other programs. When an object is called via such a proxy (which must contain some special activation information) and tries to contact the real object, it will notice that the object no longer exists. In this case, it sends the activation information to the Voyager runtime environment which then reactivates the object. Subsequently, the call can be executed as normal. For the developer, this mechanism, which is sketched in Figure 9.2, is transparent.

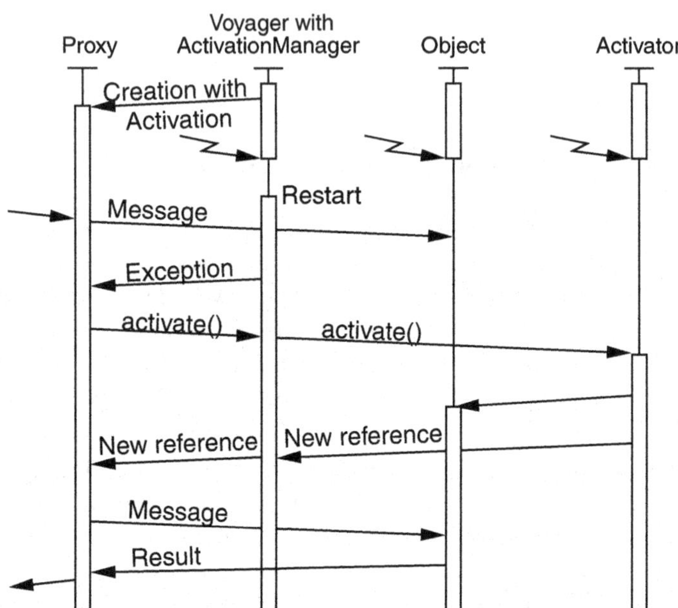

Figure 9.2 *Activation of a persistent object.*

Each Voyager runtime environment includes an ActivationManager which manages a series of Activator objects. Each of these objects can in turn be connected with a database which either simply writes the serialized object into a file, or stores it in tables in a relational database, or makes it persistent in an object-oriented database. For each type of database, a class must exist which performs the mapping onto the database structure. This can either be written for arbitrary objects or developed for special applications. Thus, for example, an object can be mapped onto an existing table structure of a relational database. This mapping class must implement Voyager's IActivator interface and is then called Activator.

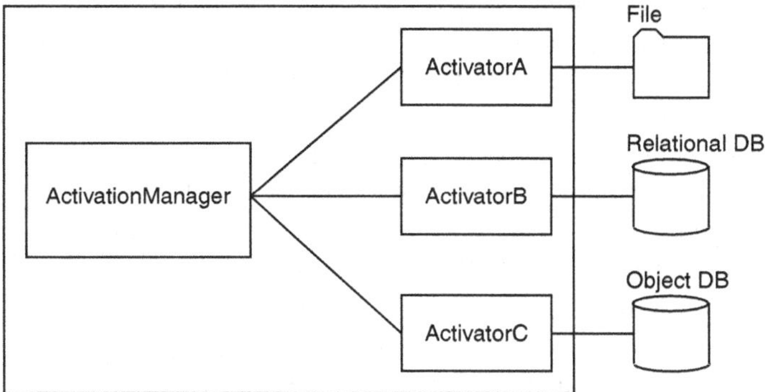

Figure 9.3
The Voyager ActivationManager.

A new activator is registered with the manager via the call Activation.register(). This interface prescribes the methods getMemento() and activate(). The first method is passed a proxy for an object. It returns a string which is used to retrieve the object in the database. This string is called *Memento*, which means something like bookmark. The second method is passed this memento, with which the object is woken up from its persistence sleep and activated. Subsequently, it can again be accessed via the proxy.

The Memento

These methods must, however, not be called by the developer, but by the ActivationManager. The developer must decide in the program, which objects are to be made persistent and which Activator should be used. Depending on the implementation, the Activator must be passed the name or the URL of the database and is then registered by calling Activation.register(). Subsequently, the Activator is told which objects are to be made persistent, by passing it a reference to an object or its proxy by means of the Activation.enable() method. Then all newly created proxies of this object receive the information required for the activation of the object. This consists of the URL of the program, the Memento of the object, and the class name of the Activator that has generated the Memento.

Upon the call of this method, the Activator writes the object into the database, before the object is destroyed by the garbage collector, or the program is exited, or the Voyager runtime environment is terminated by means of Voyager.shutdown(). With this, the object has become persistent and can be reactivated.

Let us demonstrate this mechanism with the aid of a simple example. We will again use the example of the bat and the ball, in which the Bat is supposed to remotely access an instance of the Ball type. The server on which the Ball object is located will, in the meantime, be shut down and restarted. The bat should access the ball once before and once after the server shutdown, reactivating the Ball at the second access. The following class, BallMachine, prepares the Ball for activation. As a database, ObjectStore PSE Pro is employed, for which a generic Activator class exists, the OSVoyagerActivator. Please note that at this point alternative Activators for different databases can be used as well; this merely requires a different instantiation of the Activator.

```
import com.objectspace.voyager.*;
import com.objectspace.voyager.activation.*;

public class BallMachine {

  public static void main(String[] args) {
    try {
      Voyager.startup("8000"); // start as server
      Ball ball = new Ball();
      Proxy.export(ball);
      Namespace.bind("ABall",ball);
      OSVoyagerActivator activator =
        new OSVoyagerActivator("testdb.odb");
      Activation.register(activator);
      Activation.enable(ball);
    } catch( Exception exception ) {
      System.err.println( exception );
    }
  }
}
```

The Ball class must only support serialization and is listed in the following code fragment. To simulate the termination of the server, Voyager is shut down by calling shutdown() at each call of the hit() method. Due to a flaw in the implementation of the OSVoyagerActivator, the ObjectStore session must also be terminated at this point with a call to terminate().

```
import com.objectspace.voyager.*;

public class Ball implements java.io.Serializable {

  public void hit() {
    System.out.println("Ball has been hit");
    COM.odi.Session.getGlobal().terminate();
    Voyager.shutdown();
  }
}
```

The Bat class receives a proxy for the Ball object through the name service where it has been registered by BallMachine and calls it twice. Between these two calls, the program stops and waits for user input, which gives enough time to restart the server which is, as we know, terminated with each call of hit().

```
import com.objectspace.voyager.*;

public class Bat {

  public void play(IBall ball) {
    System.out.println("Hitting the new Ball");
    ball.hit();
  }

  public static void main(String[] args) {
    try {
      Voyager.startup(); // start as client
      Bat bat = new Bat();
      IBall ball = (IBall) Namespace.lookup(
        "//vsyspc5.informatik.uni-hamburg.de:8000/ABall");
      bat.play(ball);
      System.out.println("Press key when Server restarts");
```

```
      System.in.read();
      bat.play(ball);
    } catch(Exception exception) {System.err.println(exception);}
    Voyager.shutdown();
  }
}
```

The server is restarted through the BallMachine2 class, which contains no information whatsoever about a Ball. Thus, when a new call of Ball occurs, this is reactivated exclusively through the Activation Framework and the activation information contained in the proxy.

```
import com.objectspace.voyager.*;
import com.objectspace.voyager.activation.*;

public class BallMachine2  {

  public static void main(String[] args) {
    try {
      Voyager.startup("8000"); // start as server
      OSVoyagerActivator activator =
        new OSVoyagerActivator("testdb.odb");
       Activation.register(activator);
    } catch( Exception exception ) { System.err.println(exception);}
  }
}
```

9.6 References

The field of object-oriented databases is still young and, as opposed to relational databases, the development of the market has not yet reached its peak. Therefore it is more difficult to find good, up-to-date literature. A book which lays a good foundation, explains the concepts, and discusses the differences against relational databases is [Heuer 1997]. Equally recommendable books are [Meier and Wüst 1997] and [Saake *et al.* 1997].

Information on ObjectStore can be found on the Web pages of the company [ObjectDesign 1998]. Also for other products, such as Poet, Versant, Objectory, and Gemstone, information can best be found on the Internet.

The description of Voyager and the Activation Framework is contained in the Voyager documentation [ObjectSpace 1998b]. Also JDK 1.2 by now includes an activation mechanism for RMI.

10 A persistent programming language

Now that we have described the mechanisms for persistent storage of data from within Java, the question arises as to whether it might not be possible to integrate the property of persistence into a language like Java as an elementary component of the language environment. The vision is to hide the complexity of previous approaches to persistence completely from the programmer and make the data of an application or even an application as a whole persistent in the easiest possible way. This chapter presents a project in which exactly this attempt is made.

10.1 PJama

PJama is an experimental, persistent programming environment for the Java programming language. PJama is being developed by the members of the "Persistence and Distribution" research group of the Department of Computing Science at Glasgow University in cooperation with the Sun Microsystems Laboratories in the framework of the "Forest" project. Originally, this programming environment was to be called "PJava" as an abbreviation for "Persistent Java", but this collided with the "Personal Java", equally developed by Sun. Therefore, PJama was chosen as an *ersatz* (which I find a lot funnier). By the way, the mascot of PJama is a duke in pyjamas.

Orthogonal persistence

PJama implements the principles of orthogonal persistence. This means that any data type occurring in the language can be made persistent without a transformation into another data format and loaded back into main memory. In the case of Java, these are the base types and the compound types such as arrays or objects. However, this also includes threads and the graphical interface of an application together with their states. In addition, the code that belongs to an object is stored as well.

PJama consists of the implementation of its own virtual machine, several modified Java base classes, its own specific APIs, and modified Swing classes. Basically it is an alternative JDK which can be employed instead of the normal JDK and which automatically integrates persistence into an application. Only a minimum effort is required by the application programmer.

The current prototype is version 0.5.7.10 and is based on the JDK 1.1.7. It is, however, not freely available, but can under certain circumstances be obtained from the developers on request.

Persistence through reachability

To be able to work with persistent data structures, these must be kept on a non-volatile storage medium. The file in which PJama stores objects is the so-called *persistent store*. Individual objects are registered by their names as *persistent roots*, a process in which – according to the "persistence through reachability" principle – all classes related to these objects (superclasses, interfaces, other used classes, etc.) are also made persistent (transitive persistence). The procedure of employing PJama can thus be summarized as follows:

1. Creation of a persistent store
2. Registration of persistent roots ("filling" the store)
3. Program runs with access to the objects and classes stored as persistent roots.

The persistent store is provided by PJama through the PJStore API. For reasons of consistency, a store can only be used by one running application; vice versa, in the current version, an application can also access only one store (this limitation will, however, be eliminated in future versions). Moreover, PJama supports the evolution of single classes, class hierarchies, and persistent data, that is, classes of a persistent store can be replaced with more recent versions, new classes can be inserted, and old classes be deleted.

The following tools are available for working with the store:

- opj – the PJama interpreter
- opjcs – creates a new store (without persistent roots)
- opjgc – an off-line garbage collector for persistent stores
- opjsubst – replaces classes of an existing store (off-line)
- opjc – a special compiler which supports opjsubst.

opj = orthogonally persistent Java

All of these tools (except opjcs) work on an existing store which is passed to them as an argument through the -store option, for example. As any other Java program, PJama applications are compiled with the javac compiler. The opjc compiler is a part of the PJama evolution system opjsubst and is only employed in user-defined conversion of already persistent data.

Step by step, the following sections will describe the usage of PJama.

10.2 The persistent store

PJama stores both the code and the state of objects together in a persistent store. The store is not opened in the classical way by programs, but passed as an argument to the PJama interpreter, together with the name of an executable class. This searches the store for that particular class and calls its main method. If this class does not exist in the store, the usual class path is searched. The rules of "persistence through reachability" guarantee that all classes needed by a class that has once been made persistent are also persistent. In this sense, a persistent store can also be seen as a virtual machine which has been "frozen" (*stabilized*) at a specific point in time.

Tool-supported creation of the store

The easiest way to create a persistent store is to use the opjcs tool, with the path name of the store specified as argument (by convention with the .pjs extension):

```
sun> opjcs /home/user/stores/TestStore.pjs
```

If the specified path is relative, opjcs starts with the current working directory or the directory defined by the STOREPATH environment variable:

```
sun> setenv STOREPATH /home/user/stores
sun> opjcs TestStore.pjs
```

A newly created store contains an instance of the implementation of the PJStore interface, an empty table of the objects registered as persistent roots, all classes required for the functioning of the virtual machine, plus the classes that can be reached from there. By default it is also initialized with determined properties ("AutoWindows") which make it possible to render existing AWT programs pseudo-persistent without changes to their code, or even to write completely "persistence-independent" programs. Finally, for each store a file with the additional extension .log is created, which is used during the *stabilization* of the store (see Section 10.3) to allow the current state to be restored in the case of a system crash.

In opjcs, options are indicated *after* the path name of the store:

- **overwrite.** An existing store of the same name is deleted before the new store is created.
- **verbose.** Causes the screen output of various items of information on the created store and the actions performed by opjcs.
- **autoWindowsOff.** A store created with this option does not provide the above-mentioned possibility of making AWT programs persistent at a later stage.

If opjcs is called without arguments, the program starts in an interactive mode in which the user can enter the path name of the store and the required options via a graphical interface (AWT).

Creating the store from a program

As a second alternative, a persistent store can be created from within a program. A typical reason for this procedure is the need to store a number of persistent, application-specific objects together with the creation of the store. Objects and classes that are made persistent at the first stabilization (see Section 10.3) of a new store are stored in a special bootstrap region which is loaded immediately at the start-up of a persistent application, which may lead to improved performance.

A program that creates a new store must first import the PJStore interface and its implementation:

```
import org.opj.store.PJStore;
import org.opj.store.PJStoreImpl;
```

To create a store, a new instance of PJStoreImpl is created by passing the constructor a String with the name of the store:

```
PJStore ps = new PJStoreImpl("/home/user/stores/TestStore.pjs");
```

If this String describes a relative path name, either the current working directory is used, or the directory defined by the STOREPATH environment variable. The contructor PJStoreImpl() can be used without arguments if the name of the store was previously defined by setting the PJSTORE variable. A combination of the two vaiables is allowed.

Once a persistent store has been created, an arbitrary object is made persistent by registering the object itself as a persistent root or by referencing it through a root object. Persistent roots can be registered by means of the newPRoot method which is passed a String with the name under which the object is to be registered and a reference to the object itself as arguments:

```
Object anObject = new Object();
ps.newPRoot("My Object", anObject);
```

The program (let us call it CreateTest.java) is translated by means of the javac compiler and subsequently executed by the opj PJama interpreter:

```
sun> javac CreateTest.java
sun> opj CreateTest
```

After successful termination of the program, the files TestStore.pjs and TestStore.pjs.log will have been created in the appropriate directory.

Besides all of the options also accepted by the Java interpreter, the PJama offers, amongst others, the additional option -store, which specifies the path name of the store. This option is equivalent to a temporary setting of the PJSTORE environment variable. Thus, if in the program the PJStoreImpl() constructor has been used without arguments, the call could also be:

```
sun> opj -store /home/user/stores/TestStore.pjs CreateTest
```

Here, the current value of PJSTORE plays no role and remains unchanged.

Use of an existing store

To access an existing store, the static method getStore() of the PJStoreImpl class is called:

```
PJStore ps = PJStoreImpl.getStore();
```

The objects of the store can then be modified through the persistent roots. The getPRoot() method is passed a String with the name of the root object and returns a reference of the Object type:

```
Object anObject = ps.getPRoot("My Object");
```

Obviously (as described above), additional objects can be registered as persistent roots. For this purpose, the newPRoot() method is used:

```
Object anotherObject = new Object();
ps.newPRoot("2nd Object", anotherObject);
```

Deleting and moving persistent objects

A root object can obviously also be removed.This is done by calling the ps.discardPRoot("2nd Object") method. This only deletes the corresponding name entry from the table of persistent roots, while the object itself remains in the store. It is the task of the garbage collector (see Section 10.4) to remove the object when it is no longer reachable.

If a different object is to be registered as a root object under an already existing name, it is not necessary to delete the name of the original object first and only then set a new persistent root – the setPRoot() method combines these two steps:

```
Object oneMoreObject = new Object();
ps.setPRoot("My Object", oneMoreObject);
```

In its present version, PJama has the limitation that an application can at runtime work on only *one* store: PJStoreImpl.getStore() does not provide the possibility of explicitly specifying the store to be used. This is passed to the interpreter as an option at the start of the program (UseTest.java):

```
sun> opj -store /home/user/stores/TestStore.pjs UseTest
```

10.3 Stabilization

When changes are made to persistent objects, the store must be updated accordingly. This procedure is known as stabilization of the store: all objects that have been directly or indirectly made persistent are checked and all modified states are written into the store. Stabilization of a store is an atomic process, so that even in case of a system crash the store is left in a consistent state (although, at the new call of the interpreter, some error recovery routines might be executed in the background).

The PJama interpreter stabilizes the used store *automatically* upon normal termination of the program. Programmers do not need to care explicitly about stabilization. In case of a program crash, the store is still in exactly the same state as at the beginning of program execution.

When a store, in addition, is to be stabilized at runtime of an application, its stabilizeAll() method can be called at any point in time. As with the implicit stabilization at the end of the program, the explicit stabilization too is atomic: in case of a crash during stabilization, the store is left in the state it assumed at the point of the last stabilization.

```
PJStore ps = PJStoreImpl.getStore();
...
ps.stabilizeAll();
...
```

Stabilization and threads

In applications with several threads, stabilization may become problematic when the threads do not cooperate with each other. During a stabilization, all threads are halted – the stabilization is atomic, isolated, and durable. However, as long as it refers to *all* persistent objects, there is no guarantee for the semantic consistency of the halted threads (except for the thread that has triggered the stabilization). For future versions of PJama, support of persistent threads is planned which can continue with their execution during a stabilization until they have possibly reached a consistent state.

10.4 Garbage collection

Memory management for *non*-persistent objects is the same in PJama and Java: when non-persistent objects are no longer reachable, that is they are no longer referenced, their memory space is released at runtime by the garbage collector.

Even persistent objects that are stored in a store can become unreachable, for example through the explicit management of the store's root objects: the discardPRoot method deletes the entry of an object from the table of persistent roots. If the object itself is no longer referenced by any other persistent object, it has become unreachable (and with it, all objects that were reachable only via this object). The setPRoot method, which registers a new object as a persistent root under an already existing name, has the same effects. Even the mere usage of a store creates a certain overhead, which every time increases the size of the store.

The self-contained opjgc program is available for garbage collection in a persistent store. Again, the store is specified via the -store option or the environment variables PJSTORE and STOREPATH:

```
sun> opjgc -store /home/user/stores/TestStore.pjs
```

Garbage collection with opjgc can only be performed on a store which is not in use in any other way. Concurrent garbage collection is not supported in the current version of PJama.

10.5 A simple example: a persistent counter

To exemplify the use of PJama, as it has been explained in the previous sections, once again in a specific context, we will use this example to show how a single class, which implements a simple counter, can be made persistent. The class contains a variable of the int base type, plus two methods that allow the value of the variable to be incremented or read:

```
class Counter {
  private int count;

  public Counter() {
    count = 0;
  }

  public void increase() {
    count++;
    System.out.println("increasing counter...");
  }

  public int getCount() {
    return count;
  }
}
```

To make the counter persistent, first a new store is created. We assume that the environment variable STOREPATH is not defined – thus the new store named CounterStore.pjs is created in the current working directory:

```
sun> opjcs -store CounterStore.pjs
```

The following program then instantiates a counter and registers it as a persistent root:

```
import org.opj.store.PJStore;
import org.opj.store.PJStoreImpl;
import org.opj.store.PJSException;

class SetupCounter {
  public static void main(String[] args) {
    try {
      PJStore ps = PJStoreImpl.getStore();
      Counter aCounter = new Counter();
      ps.newPRoot("Counter", aCounter);
      System.out.println("Persistent Counter registered!");
    } catch (PJSException e) {
      System.out.println("PJSException occured:");
      e.printStackTrace();
    }
  }
}
```

After the classes have been compiled, the PJama interpreter can now be used to execute the SetupCounter program on the newly created store:

```
sun> javac Counter.java SetupCounter.java
sun> opj -store Counter.pjs SetupCounter
```

To conclude, the now persistent counter is actually used in the context of a further propram, which accesses the counter, increments its value, and finally displays it:

```
import org.opj.store.PJStore;
import org.opj.store.PJStoreImpl;
import org.opj.store.PJSException;

class RunCounter {
  public static void main(String[] args) {
    try {
      PJStore ps = PJStoreImpl.getStore();
```

```
        Counter theCounter = (Counter)ps.getPRoot("Counter");
        theCounter.increase();
        System.out.print("This was run no. ");
        System.out.println(theCounter.getCount());
      } catch (PJSException e) {
        e.printStackTrace();
      }
    }
}
```

The (repeated) call of RunCounter is:

```
sun> opj -store Counter.pjs RunCounter
```

Upon successful termination of the program, the store is automatically stabilized, and thus the new counter value is stored.

10.6 References

As PJama is still a research project, we cannot yet refer the reader to books in which it is discussed more in detail. However, you will find scientific reports and publications, plus up-to-date information, on the Web.

For a more extensive approach to the subject of orthogonal persistence for Java, we recommend [Atkinson *et al.* 1996] and [Atkinson and Jordan 1998]. The problems that arise when this approach to persistence is combined with distribution are discussed in [Spence 1997]. On the Web, PJama can be found under http://www.dcs.gla.ac.uk/pjama/, where a more extensive tutorial is available as well.

11 Tuplespaces in Java

Up to now, we have presented mechanisms for concurrency, for distributed communication, and for persistence, and implemented them by means of techniques completely independent from each other. There is, however, a communication mechanism which carries elements of all three areas: Tuplespaces. In Tuplespaces, pairs of values (tuple, triple, quadruple, ...) can be stored in a memory space and taken out again. This Tuplespace can be accessed from within a distributed system, so that an arbitrary computer can deposit a tuple and another one can go and fetch it. This gives rise to a communication mechanism which is extremely useful for distributed and parallel systems: the communication is asynchronous, anonymous, distributed, and persistent.

The idea that underlies these Tuplespaces is not new, but has been developed in the 80s by Nicholas Carriero and David Gelernter at Yale University. The project, as well as the language that originated from it, was called *Linda*. The idea found great resonance in the small community of programmers of parallel computing systems, but was practically ignored outside this community.

Linda

The principle of Linda is very simple: arbitrary tuples of values can be deposited in a globally visible Tuplespace by means of an out command, read by means of a read command, and taken out of that space again by means of an in command. Addressing of the tuples is associative, that is, they are not written to a specific address location, but can be addressed through their contents: to find a tuple, a pattern is specified which contains part of the information of the desired tuple. The system then returns a tuple that matches this pattern.

Associative addressing

For example, one computer might generate a request, say, of the form out(calculate, 42, 933), and another computer might look for a request, in(calculate, *, *); the latter is returned a matching request which it can then process. The communication that arises is asynchronous because the communication partners do not have to communicate with each other at a specific time. It is anonymous because none of the communication partners needs to know who the other partner is. It is distributed because spatially separated computers can cooperate as long as both of them can reach the Tuplespace. And it is persistent because the data objects in the Tuplespace can live longer than the programs that generated them.

Communication through Linda

With such a communication mechanism, extremely different communication models can be realized. As already mentioned, it is very easy to implement "producer-consumer" relationships in which the Tuplespace serves as request buffer. The number of producers, as well as the number of consumers, can be arbitrarily extended without any of the parties involved having to be notified of this fact. In this form, Tuplespaces are often employed in parallel processing. However, Tuplespaces can also function as a lightweight database in which a device or program writes its data before it is switched off and from where it loads its data again when it is switched back on. This would, for example, make the implementation of a mail server a very easy task. Mail messages are simply labeled with the address and put into the Tuplespace, where the addressee can inquire whether any messages bearing its address have arrived. This mechanism can also be used to make events known, so that the Tuplespace can also function as an event service.

Linda is a communication mechanism. You still need a programming language into which Linda is integrated to create and process the tuples. Links for Linda have been developed for a series of languages, such as PASCAL, C, and Fortran. But as simple and elegant as Linda is, it has a big disadvantage: Linda *per se* is not object-oriented. It only permits simple data types and compound data types made out of these simple types, but no objects.

Sun have taken on the idea of Linda and extended it with object-oriented concepts, integrated it into Java, and developed a mechanism they call JavaSpaces. A beta version of the specification was published in Summer '98 and has aroused vivid interest in the community. Meanwhile, JavaSpaces has become an integral part of Jini. A sample implementation can be downloaded from the Sun Web server; however, it is still rather unstable and requires installation and running of Jini, plus JDK 1.2. Sun emphasize that this is only a sample implementation intended to demonstrate the feasibility, but that it is far from having reached product level. ObjectSpace, by the way, have announced an implementation integrated into Voyager before the end of '99.

JavaSpaces, an object-oriented Linda

Besides Sun, IBM too have shown an interest in this technology and developed their own version of this technique which they call TSpaces. Unfortunately, the interfaces of the two approaches do not match, so that they are not compatible with each other.

TSpaces

These two approaches will be presented in the following sections. First of all, the principal functioning and the interface are demonstrated with the aid of JavaSpaces, which will probably be more successful due to Sun's leading position in the market. Subsequently, TSpaces and its differences against JavaSpaces will be discussed and shown in a sample program.

11.1 JavaSpaces

JavaSpaces has been developed as an independent project in Sun's research labs, but has subsequently become an integral part of Jini, which will be discussed in the next chapter. For this reason, the interfaces of JavaSpaces are to be found in the `net.jini.space` package.

In JavaSpaces, tuples are called *Entries*. An object must implement the `net.jini.space.Entry` interface in order to be written into a space, but otherwise it can be a utterly common Java object. The attributes of such an object are called *Fields*. As an example, let us take a message with three fields for our well-known BulletinBoard:

```
public class Message implements net.jini.space.Entry {
  public String subject;
  public String body;
  public int category;

  public Message(String _subject, String _body, int _category) {
    subject = _subject;
    body = _body;
    category = _category;
  }
}
```

Such an object can be created in the usual way and then deposited in a Tuplespace. In JavaSpaces, Tuplespaces are simply called *Spaces* and are centrally managed by a server. A client accesses this server via a network and can remotely use its interface. To ensure that programmers have as little as possible to do with distribution, a local object is generated which represents the server and makes the interface locally available to the client. From the point of view of functionality, the methods provided by this interface more or less correspond to those of Linda, but have been renamed to improve readability and intuitive comprehension. Writing into a space is now called write(), reading is called read(), and taking out objects is called take().

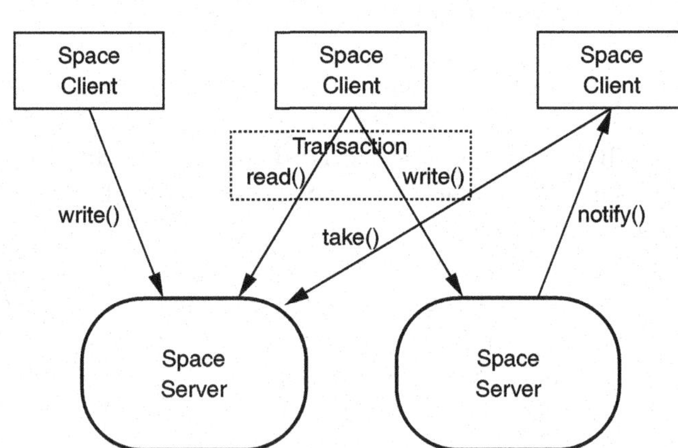

Figure 11.1 *Operations on a JavaSpace.*

When writing an entry, its validity period is specified as well, so that obsolete objects can be removed from the space and the space is not cluttered with abandoned garbage. However, the validity period of an entry can be extended through a mechanism based on leasing, which will be discussed in more detail in the chapter on Jini. The result of a write operation is a Lease object, which can be used to extend the validity.

```
JavaSpace space = getSpace();
Message message = new Message("Ford TBird","used Thunderbird, 1966 ...", 2);

long oneday=24*60*60*1000; // 24 hours in milliseconds
Lease lease = space.write(message, null, oneday);
```

read() and take() each return an entry from the space, where read() only copies the entry and leaves it in the space, while take() also deletes the entry from the space. Both commands are of the locking kind, that is, when no matching entry is present, they wait until such an entry arrives. Therefore, the waiting time of both operations must be limited by specifying a timeout in milliseconds. To be able to search for an entry, the two functions are passed an entry pattern. This pattern, also known as *template*, is of the same type as the entry to be found, but can contain placeholders which are not specified, that is, which are set to null. These placeholders are called *wildcards*.

```
Message msgTemplate = new Message("Offer", null, null);
Message result = space.read(msgTemplate, null, 100);
```

The space server compares the existing entries field by field with the template and returns an entry in which all fields are identical that are not occupied by a wildcard. Therefore, in this case, a message of the "Offer" category would be returned. Exactly one entry is returned. To access all entries of the "Offer" category, a relatively big effort must be made, since a repeated read() does not return the next matching entry, but again any matching entry, including the one just returned. This is an essential difference to the IBM approach, as we will see later.

Storage of entries The server stores entries in a serialized form, however, not the entire object, but the individual fields of the object are serialized. Thus the server can access these fields without having to deserialize the whole object first. The comparison with templates takes place in exactly this way: the serialized fields are compared with the serialized fields of the template. The comparison is carried out bitwise. If no matching entry is found, the call blocks until a new entry arrives that matches the request or until the timeout expires. Both calls also have non-blocking variations, called readIfExists() and takeIfExists().

Notification Another interesting method is the notify() method, which a client can use to manifest its interest in a newly arriving entry that matches a template. When such an entry arrives, an event handler is called which can catch the event and take the appropriate measures.

All methods of JavaSpaces can be handled as transactions by specifying a transaction object as a parameter of the call. If no transaction is to be used, as in our case, null can be indicated instead.

The following listing shows the (JavaSpace) interface. Please note that this is the complete public interface which includes everything that is needed to operate on a space.

```
import java.rmi.*;
import net.jini.event.*;
import net.jini.transaction.*;
import net.jini.lease.*;

public interface JavaSpace {

  Lease write(Entry e, Transaction txn, long lease)
    throws RemoteException, TransactionException;

  public final long NO_WAIT = -1 // don't wait at all

  Entry read(Entry tmpl, Transaction txn, long timeout)
    throws TransactionException, UnusableEntryException,
      RemoteException, InterruptedException;
```

```
  Entry readIfExists(Entry tmpl, Transaction txn, long timeout)
    throws TransactionException, UnusableEntryException,
      RemoteException, InterruptedException;

  Entry take(Entry tmpl, Transaction txn, long timeout)
    throws TransactionException, UnusableEntryException,
      RemoteException, InterruptedException;

  Entry takeIfExists(Entry tmpl, Transaction txn, long timeout)
    throws TransactionException, UnusableEntryException,
      RemoteException, InterruptedException;

  EventRegistration notify(Entry tmpl, Transaction txn,
      RemoteEventListener listener, long lease, MarshalledObject handback)
    throws RemoteException, TransactionException;
}
```

11.2 TSpaces

The second approach to Tuplespaces with Java comes from the IBM research labs. This approach is more pragmatic, more compact, easier to learn, and oriented much more towards the aspect of persistence than JavaSpaces. Unfortunately, the two approaches are not compatible with each other, but have clearly the same origin and can be well compared with each other.

To create a Tuplespace in TSpaces, and also to connect to an existing Tuplespace, the constructor of the TupleSpace class is called with the name of the Tuplespace and the name of the server (URL).

```
TupleSpace space = new TupleSpace( spaceName, server );
```

For this purpose, a Tuplespace server must be running on the computer denoted as server, which is a lot easier in TSpaces than in JavaSpaces and can be simply handled with a call to a shell script.

Subsequently, tuples can be created and deposited in the Tuplespace. A tuple contains an ordered sequence of *Fields*, where a field consists of a type (a Java class name or simply a string), a value which contains an appropriate object, and, optionally, a field name which will be used in later searches for this field.

```
Field subject = new Field (String.class, _subject);
Field body = new Field(String.class, _body);
Field category = new Field("ID", new Integer(_category));
Tuple message = new Tuple(subject, body, category);
```

The most important functions for non-blocking access to a Tuplespace have the same names as in JavaSpaces: write(), read(), and take(). The blocking variations are called waitToTake() and waitToRead(). They are, however, easier to use than in JavaSpaces and always require just one parameter, namely the tuple that is to be written or serves as a pattern for the search.

```
space.write(message);
```

A pattern or *template* is created by assigning one or more fields of a tuple only a type, but not a value. In the following example, a message is specified as a template, of which only the category and the headline, but not the message body, are known. A message is to be found that matches this template.

```
Tuple template = new Tuple(subject, new Field(String.class), category);
Tuple aMessage = (Tuple)space.read(template);
```

The individual fields of a tuple can then be accessed with getField(), and their values can be read by means of the value() method.

```
body = (String) aMessage.getField(1).value();
```

There is, however, an additional function which does not exist in JavaSpaces, but which is very useful and interesting. This function does not only allow individual tuples to be read one after the other, but all tuples matching a request together at the same time. This method is called scan() and returns a tuple of tuples.

```
Tuple allMessage = (Tuple)space.scan(template);
```

All of these features will now be summarized in a complete example. Once again, as with the examples used in the discussion of persistence, we will show a BulletinBoard whose graphical interface can, as usual, be found in Appendix B. In the constructor, a connection is established with a Tuplespace which we assume already exists and also that it contains categories of messages. New messages are created by means of the insertNewPosting() method and written as tuples into the Tuplespace. The getCategories() method reads the categories and notifies them to the interface. The set of messages is read by means of the reloadSubjects() method. The messages remain in the Tuplespace and can be read by an arbitrary number of other clients.

```
import java.util.*;
import com.ibm.tspaces.*;

public class BulletinBoard {

  BulletinBoardFrame gui;
  TupleSpace space;
  Vector messages = new Vector();

  public BulletinBoard(String spaceName, String server) {
    gui = new BulletinBoardFrame("BulletinBoard mit TSpaces",this);
    try {
      space = new TupleSpace( spaceName, server );
    } catch(TupleSpaceException e) {
      System.out.println(e);
    }
    getCategories();
    reloadSubjects(1);
  }

  public void insertNewPosting(String _subject, String _body, int _category) {
    try {
      Field subject = new Field (String.class, _subject);
      Field body = new Field(String.class, _body);
```

```
      Field category = new Field("ID", new Integer(_category));
      Tuple message = new Tuple(subject, body, category);
      space.write(message);
    } catch(TupleSpaceException e) {
      System.out.println(e);
    }
  }

  public void getCategories() {
    try {
     Tuple template = new Tuple(new Field(String.class),new Field(Integer.class));
      Tuple allCategories = (Tuple)space.scan(template);
     for (Enumeration enum = allCategories.fields(); enum.hasMoreElements();) {
        Field f = (Field) enum.nextElement();
        Tuple category = (Tuple) f.value();
        String name = (String) category.getField(0).value();
        Integer id = (Integer) category.getField(1).value();
        gui.addCategory(id.intValue(), name);
      }
    } catch(TupleSpaceException e) {
      System.out.println(e);
    }
  }

  public String getBody(int subjectId) {
    String body = "";
    try {
      Tuple message = (Tuple) messages.elementAt(subjectId);
      body = (String) message.getField(1).value();
      return body;
    } catch(TupleSpaceException e) {
      System.out.println(e);
    }
    return body;
  }

  public void reloadSubjects(int _category) {
    try {
      gui.clearSubjects();
      messages.removeAllElements();
```

```
      Field subject = new Field (String.class);
      Field body = new Field(String.class);
      Field category = new Field("ID", new Integer(_category));
      Tuple template = new Tuple(subject, body, category);
      Tuple allSubjects = (Tuple)space.scan(template);
      int i = 0;
      for (Enumeration enum = allSubjects.fields(); enum.hasMoreElements();) {
        Field f = (Field) enum.nextElement();
        Tuple message = (Tuple) f.value();
        String subj = (String) message.getField(0).value();
        gui.addSubject(i++, subj);
        messages.addElement(message);
      }
    } catch(TupleSpaceException e) {
      System.out.println(e);
    }
  }

  public boolean handleQuit() { return true; }

  public static void main(String[] args) {
    if (args.length == 2) {
      BulletinBoard bboard = new BulletinBoard(args[0], args[1]);
    } else {
      new BulletinBoard("BulletinBoard", "localhost");
    }
  }
}
```

11.3 References

Both implementations of Tuplespaces for Java are freely available on the Internet. JavaSpaces is a part of Jini and can be downloaded from the URL http://developer.sun.com/developer/products/jini/index.html. You must, however, register as a Java developer, which gets you an e-mail message about once a month. Also when you download TSpaces from the URL http://www.almaden.ibm.com/cs/TSpaces/ you are requested to leave your name and address. Specifications and descriptions too can be obtained under these addresses, with Sun's material being limited to the bare specification, while IBM provides several documents for different requirements and is better suited for a first approach.

Information about Linda can best be obtained directly from the publications of Carriero and Gelernter, for example [Gelernter 1985], [Carriero and Gelernter 1989], and [Carriero and Gelernter 1990].

12 Jini

Java can be used on a very wide range of devices, from chip cards to mainframe computers, and anything lying between these extremes. Java has solved the problem of heterogeneity of these platforms. The communication between the applications that run on these devices is handled by various techniques more or less suited to the different situations and requirements. The palette reaches from sockets via RMI to CORBA and agents, and has been discussed in several chapters of this book. But how do different applications, services, or devices recognize the existence of other ones? Here too, we find various approaches, such as the RMI registry or the CORBA name service. The farthest-reaching approach to this problem is represented by Jini.

Jini allows services to find each other without any knowledge about their names or locations. A program can provide a service without knowing who is managing the service offers and where this takes place. A service user can look for a service and only needs to know which Java interface the service should implement.

Services

All services can be offered, searched for, and connected in Jini. This applies both to hardware devices, such as hard disks, digital cameras, printers, or CD players, and to software services, such as spell check, address books, format converters, or persistence mechanisms. Such services can be dynamically added to and removed from a system without having to be managed by users or administrators as in the old days.

Lookup service

The central service in Jini is the lookup service, where all other services register and by which they are mediated. Services are registered by the lookup server according to the interfaces they implement, after which they are available. When a service user looks for a service, it also specifies an interface for which it searches an implementation. The lookup service will then determine all implementations matching this request and return them. A service can be further specified by means of additional attributes which, for example, describe the quality or similar features and are indicated in both human- and machine-readable form, so that a service user can select one of the returned services on the basis of this attributes. These attributes can also be used to limit the set of results returned in the first place.

Discovery and Join

Even the lookup service itself need not be known to a service, but can be detected automatically in a network. The procedure used for this purpose is called *Discovery and Join.*

Leasing

In Jini, services are not registered permanently, but only for a specific time during which access to this service is guaranteed. This mechanism is called, *leasing* and the object over which it is managed, is known as *lease.* When a lease is about to expire, it can be extended (if this is legal for the corresponding service). If it is not extended, either because the service is no longer to be offered, no longer exists, or can no longer be reached, the lease expires, and the lease is removed from the lookup server. This guarantees maximum availability on the one hand, and a careful management of memory resources on the other. Services do, in fact, not deregister from the lookup server at all – this process is realized through the leasing.

When a service is removed, events are sent via a distributed event service to all parties interested in this service, so they can prepare for the lack of this service. Such events can also be sent upon registration of new services. This distributed event service is a further cornerstone of the Jini infrastructure. It is based on the event mechanism of JavaBeans and has been further developed to meet the needs of distributed services.

Jini also supports transactions, insofar as a transaction interface and the corresponding protocol are specified. However, the implementation is left to the individual services. A transaction manager could in turn be implemented as a Jini service and offered via Jini.

12.1 Requirements

In Jini, services are not only programs, but also devices. In order to be integrated into the Jini infrastructure, every Jini-capable device must have its own processor with enough memory to run a JVM. A device which does not meet this requirement has the possibility of being substituted by another device that has the necessary power.

JVM and memory

Furthermore, such a device must have an infrastructure at its disposal that can be used for communication. This can be a local network as can be found in many offices, but also an internal bus such as USB or a radio LAN, an infrared transmission interface or a data network via the building's power supply lines. A whole series of such techniques is available today or preparing its entry on the market.

Network connection

Java

Java is a key technology for Jini. Java's property of being able to let code migrate from one device to another represents an important cornerstone for Jini. Therefore Java is assumed as the essential implementation language for Jini devices; however, other languages as well are to be supported through appropriate adapters or bridges.

One problem resides in the configuration of the underlying network technology. Today, a large number of networks make use of the Internet protocol, TCP/IP. In its current version (IPv4), it is not capable of automatically assigning IP addresses to new devices. Even Jini cannot remedy this. Thus, the minimum part of the configuration process, the setting of the network address, will unfortunately be maintained in many cases. Here too, however, we find further developments, such as, for example, Mobile-IP and IPv6.

Jini is based on several techniques that are only contained in Java version 1.2 (alias 2.0). Since up to now the JDK 1.2 is only available for very few platforms and with different degrees of stability, Jini is usable only to a limited extent.

JDK 1.2

On the whole, the usability of Jini is still insufficient because there are no mature products as yet that implement Sun's specification. Sun makes an implementation available for downloading which is, however, called a sample reference implementation and therefore shows the corresponding limitations. However, fully-fledged implementations will shortly be available on the market.

12.2 Services

All services in Jini are represented by objects, no matter whether they are devices or programs. Jini essentially carries out the mediation of service offer and service request. Jini itself uses RMI for remote communication, and service user and service provider too can communicate via RMI after the mediation.

The example we are going to use for a Jini service is the same as we already used in the chapter on RMI, Bat and Ball, where the ball represents a service which is called by the bat. In Jini, each service is assigned a unique identification. This is assigned at registration time by the lookup server and returned to a ServiceIDListener by calling the listener's serviceIdNotify()method. In this simple case, the Ball class implements the ServiceIDListener interface and the related serviceIdNotify() method in addition to the implementation shown in the chapter on RMI.

```
import java.rmi.*;
import java.rmi.server.*;
import net.jini.core.lookup.*;
import sun.com.jini.lookup.*;
import sun.com.jini.lease.*;

public class Ball extends UnicastRemoteObject implements RemoteBall,
ServiceIDListener {

  public Ball() throws RemoteException {
    super();
  }

  public void serviceIdNotify(ServiceID id) {
    System.out.println("ServiceId is "+id);
  }
```

```
  public hit() {
    System.out.println("Ball has been hit");
  }
}
```

12.3 Discovery and Join

A really decisive idea of Jini is that new devices or new services that are added to a Jini network do not need to have any previous knowledge. Thus they need not know any address or central instance and nevertheless can link in. All the same they must register with a lookup server which, however, they do not need to know.

To cope with this first step, Jini includes a protocol which permits the initial finding of the lookup server. It is known as *Discovery*. Once a lookup server has been found, the new service registers with it and passes it all information it requires. This includes, in particular, the interface the service implements and the service attributes which additionally describe the service. This step is known as *Join*. Together these two steps constitute the registration with the lookup server.

Precisely speaking, the Discovery can be carried out via three different protocols. Typically it is realized through a multicast protocol, the so-called *Multicast Request Protocol* shown in Figure 12.1. The new service sends a UDP datagram packet into the local network, to the IP address and port reserved for multicast, that is 224.0.1.85:4160, and waits for an answer. The lookup server listens at the specified address and reports to the new service. Since multicast packets are by default not forwarded beyond the routers, this process works only for local network segments.

Discovery via Multicast

A service can also address a lookup service directly; however, it needs to know the service's IP address. This is carried out via the *Unicast Discovery Protocol*, which can also be employed beyond the limits of the local network.

Discovery via Unicast

When a new lookup server is set up in a network or the network has been out of service for a period of time, the

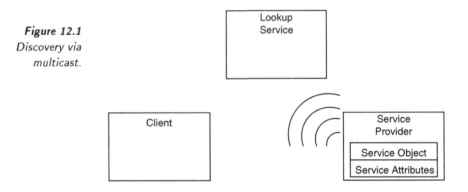

Figure 12.1
Discovery via multicast.

Discovery via Announcement

Multicast Announcement Protocol announces the (re-)availability of a lookup server. For this purpose, the new lookup server too sends a multicast message, this time to multicast address 224.0.1.**84**:4160. Interested services can intercept this message and react accordingly.

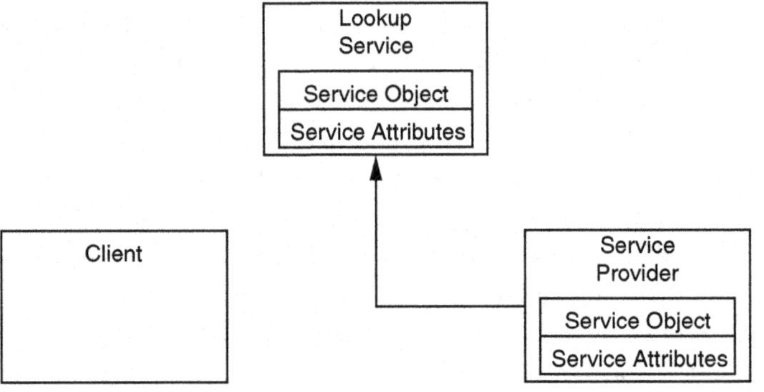

Figure 12.2
Join, information is being transmitted.

Groups of services

Services are organized in groups to which they are logically associated. A service may belong to exactly one or to several groups. A group is exclusively defined through its name and exists only through the fact that the same group name is used for several services. Structuring of group names is left to the user and can be organized, for example, by device or service types, such as "Printer" or "General Tools", or spatially, such as "Block F" or "Conference Room". It is recommended to follow the naming conventions of the DNS, thus, for example, drucker.informatik.uni-hamburg.de. The most general group is public, to which a service belongs automatically if it has not been assigned to any other group.

Lookup servers can be responsible for different groups. Thus, when a service from the "Printer" group is looked for, a lookup server must be found which manages this group. A service must register with every lookup server that manages a group to which the service shall belong.

Discovery and Join are defined in the Sun specification as a protocol, not as a programming interface. It specifies the exact format and contents of data streams. The protocol is relatively easy to implement with the aid of sockets, however, in the Jini package, Sun have included a (sample) class which hides this protocol behind an interface, which makes its use relatively easy for the programmer. This class is called JoinManager and can handle both the Discovery and the Join. For simple cases, it is sufficient to call the JoinManager with the appropriate constructor, and all the rest is carried out automatically. The constructor is passed an instance of the service to be registered and a set of descriptive attributes of this service, plus a ServiceIDListener. The lookup service, in turn, passes the ServiceIDListener the service ID and a LeaseRenewalManager which takes care of the Leases.

Registration of services

```
JoinManager(java.lang.Object obj,
          Entry[] attrSets,
          ServiceIDListener callback,
          LeaseRenewalManager leaseMgr)
```

In the following example, our well-known Ball service is to be registered. As already mentioned, Ball itself implements the ServiceIDListener. The use of LeaseRenewalManager and Entry is explained further below.

```
Ball ball = new Ball();
LeaseRenewalManager renewal = new LeaseRenewalManager();
Entry[] attributes = new Entry [] { new Name("Jini enabled ball")};
JoinManager join = new JoinManager( ball, attributes, ball, renewal );
```

If the service is to be registered with determined groups or specific lookup servers, the following constructor is available which, in addition, can be passed a set of group names and a set of already known lookup servers.

```
JoinManager(java.lang.Object obj,
        Entry[] attrSets,
        java.lang.String[] groups,
        LookupLocator[] locators,
        ServiceIDListener callback,
        LeaseRenewalManager leaseMgr)
```

The simple service of the Ball class shown above will now be registered in a complete example. In this case, we will use a separate class for the purpose, the BallStarter.

```
import java.rmi.*;
import net.jini.core.entry.*;
import net.jini.lookup.entry.*;
import com.sun.jini.lookup.*;
import com.sun.jini.lease.*;

public class BallStarter {
  public static void main(String[] args) {
    try {
      System.setSecurityManager(new RMISecurityManager());
      RemoteBall ball = (RemoteBall) new Ball();
      LeaseRenewalManager renewal = new LeaseRenewalManager();
      Entry[] attributes = new Entry [] { new Name("Jini enabled ball")};
      JoinManager join = new JoinManager( ball, attributes, (Ball) ball, renewal );
      System.out.println("Ball started and registered at Lookup-Server");

    } catch (Exception e) {
      e.printStackTrace();
    }
  }
}
```

After this class has been executed, the service is available. Now, how can others access it?

12.4 Lookup

From the client's point of view, the lookup service is the central instance that can be used, like the Yellow Pages, to find services on offer. The lookup server contains the collection of all existing services and their descriptions, and can answer queries regarding a specific type of service and, if possible, return matching services. A service user asks for a service by specifying a Java interface or a class to which the service needs to conform. In case they exist, the user is returned a set of matching objects each of which represents a remote service. This is schematically shown in Figure 12.3.

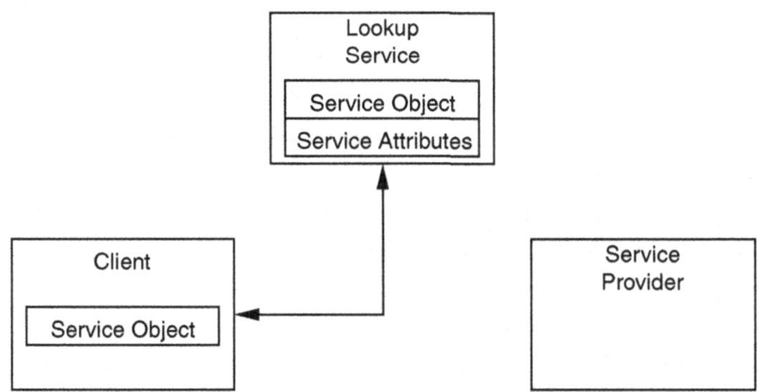

Figure 12.3 Lookup.

Search by template

To look for a service, a ServiceTemplate can be set up and specified to which services are to conform. Such a template can contain three entries that describe the service to be found. In the first parameter, the ServiceID of an already known service that one wishes to use again can be specified. Usually, however, this is not the case, then null is specified. In the second parameter, the type of service can be determined. Since this must possibly implement not only one, but several interfaces, it is defined as an array. Finally, attributes of a service can be specified. This is done in the same way as in JavaSpaces, via the Entry class. JavaSpaces, which has been described in the previous chapter, is an integral part of Jini and is itself available as a Jini service. Internally, JavaSpaces is used for management and retrieval of matching services in the lookup service, so that services and service attributes are described in the JavaSpaces way in the first place. Here too, several attributes can be specified in an array.

```
public ServiceTemplate( ServiceID serviceID,
                        Class[] serviceTypes,
                        Entry[] attributeSetTemplate );
```

To keep the example simple, we will do without attributes and simply search for a class that implements the Ball service.

```
Class[] classes = new Class[] { RemoteBall.class };
ServiceTemplate template = new ServiceTemplate( null, classes, null);
```

Accessing the lookup server

Now we need a lookup service to which we can pass this ServiceTemplate for the actual search. The lookup service is represented by an object of the ServiceRegistrar type. This is a proxy of the true lookup server. It is loaded onto the local computer and handles the remote access to the server. A ServiceRegistrar can be obtained by applying the Discovery protocols described above. For the unicast, a class is available which carries out this task, the LookupLocator. This class is passed the URL of a computer on which the lookup service is running and, after applying the getRegistrar() method, it returns a ServiceRegistrar. This, in turn, can be passed the ServiceTemplate and set to search for suitable services.

```
LookupLocator locator = new LookupLocator("jini://sun");
ServiceRegistrar registrar = locator.getRegistrar();
RemoteBall remoteBall = (RemoteBall) registrar.lookup(template);
```

In this way, a proxy of the requested service will be transmitted, which in this case corresponds to an RMI stub, and which can be used to issue remote calls to the service via RMI (see Figure 12.4). This can now be used to set up a complete example of a service user. In the main() method, the Bat class uses Jini to find a Ball service, and invokes the remote service in the play() method.

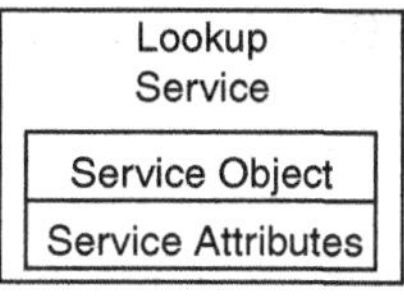

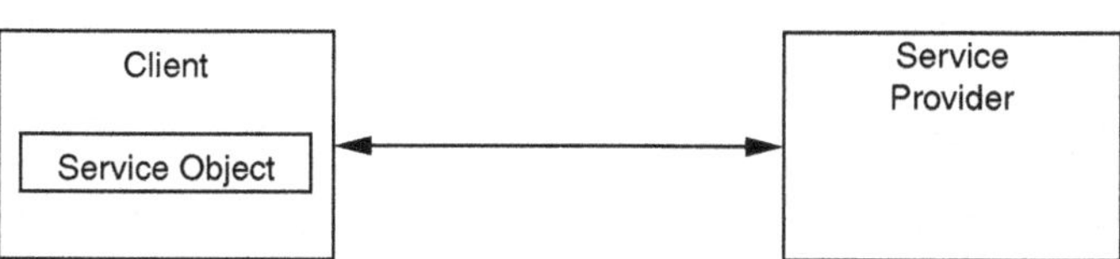

Figure 12.4
Invoking the service via RMI.

```
import java.rmi.*;
import net.jini.core.discovery.*;
import net.jini.core.lookup.*;

public class Bat {

  public Ball ball;

  public void play(RemoteBall ball) {
    try {
      ball.hit();
      System.out.println("I hit the ball");
    } catch (RemoteException e) {
      System.out.println(e);
    }
  }

  public static void main (String[] args) {
    Bat bat = new Bat();
    try {
      System.setSecurityManager(new RMISecurityManager());
      LookupLocator locator = new LookupLocator("jini://sun");
      ServiceRegistrar registrar = locator.getRegistrar();
      Class[] classes = new Class[] { RemoteBall.class };
      ServiceTemplate template = new ServiceTemplate( null, classes, null);
```

```
      RemoteBall remoteBall = (RemoteBall) registrar.lookup(template);
      bat.play(remoteBall);
    } catch (Exception e) {
      e.printStackTrace();
    }
  }
}
```

To be able to start this example, first of all a Jini lookup server needs to be running. This will be discussed in Section 12.6 because, usually, the network administrator sets this up once and for all, and it is of no further interest to the programmer. Subsequently, the Ball must be registered by means of the BallStarter class. For this purpose, the Java runtime environment must be given some additional information regarding storage location and security. To allow other classes to access the Ball, the code must be reachable from an HTTP server, whose URL must be specified here. Finally, the access rights to this service must be listed, a new feature of JDK 1.2. All required privileges are simply validated in the file policy.all.

```
sun>java -Djava.rmi.server.codebase=http://localhost:8080/example/batball/ -
Djava.security.policy=/jini1_0/example/batball/policy.all BallStarter
sun| Ball started and registered at Lookup-Server
sun| ServiceId is f7a17bde-e40b-42cb-94d4-bb6d37a999b8
```

Now the client can be started, again with a specification of the access rights. Then the Bat can call the Ball on a remote, unknown computer.

```
lin> java -Djava.security.policy=/jini1_0/example/batball/policy.all Bat

sun| Ball has been hit

lin| I hit the ball
```

12.5 Leasing

In distributed systems, relations between resources or services and their users are not as tight and reliable as in traditional local systems. Connections may be interrupted, devices switched off or taken off the network or occupied by other users. When the devices involved are mobile, which is increasingly the case, these will be inherent features of the system instead of exceptional situations. To be able to cope with this inconstancy, different linkage and communication patterns are required than the traditional rigid connections.

To cope with this, Jini proposes the mechanism of *Leasing*. A lease confers the user of a service certain rights, but also certain obligations, for a specific period of time. A lease is comparable to the mechanism we know from everyday life, such as the lease of cars or similar things.

Leases have a determined period of time after which they expire. This is the conventional normal case upon which both provider and user of a lease can more or less safely rely. Leases can be extended beyond this normal case, but can also be terminated prematurely. The agreed period of time can reach from very short to very long, even to infinity, and is freely negotiable. Very short periods (less than minutes or seconds) are, however, rather untypical. The mechanism of leasing allows information and resources to be kept up-to-date, and obsolete information can be reliably discarded. The user of a resource does not need to care about termination of the service and deletion of information, but can simply forget a service no longer in use without putting any stress on the remaining system.

During the usage of many objects which represent a Jini-capable service, a Lease object is returned as a result. The most important elements of the interface of such an object are the following (shown here only in excerpts):

```
public interface Lease {
  long getExpiration();
  void renew(long duration) throws LeaseDeniedException,
            UnknownLeaseException, RemoteException;
  void cancel() throws UnknownLeaseException, RemoteException;
```

The getExpiration() method can be used to find out the remaining time for which the lease stays valid. As usual in Java, it is specified in milliseconds and must be interpreted as remaining duration and not as a point in time. With renew() a lease can be extended. Please note that the specified time is set as a new duration and is not added to the remaining time. If the provider of the lease is not willing or not able to extend the lease, a LeaseDeniedException is generated. The user of a lease can terminate a lease prematurely by calling cancel() which, in the end, has the same effect as the expiration of the lease.

An object must not necessarily care itself for a renewal of leases, but can delegate such tasks to helper classes and charge these with the management. An example is the LeaseRenewalManager class already mentioned in the example. This class can manage a whole group of leases, which it renews automatically until the program from which it has been started is terminated.

12.6 Starting Jini

Today Jini is still in a rather early stage of development. As yet, no implementation exists which could claim to be seriously applicable in practice. Neither are there any fully developed services or devices conformant to Jini. However, the problem that Jini tries to solve has become pressing for many manufacturers. A very large number of companies cooperate with Sun or support the enterprise. The only currently existing alternative for this kind of problem is the "Universal Plug and Play", presented by Microsoft shortly after the publication of Jini.

However, some merchantable products can be expected in the near future. ObjectSpace, for example, have announced an implementation of Jini in connection with their Voyager product before the end of 1999.

The Jini Starter Kit

For the purpose of experimenting and getting acquainted with Jini, Sun supplies a reference implementation, which is available for downloading from the Internet and includes even the source code. It certainly still has its quirks and flaws, but is definitely well suited for first experiments. Unfortunately, the implementation requires Java 1.2, which is not yet available for all platforms. However, Java 1.2 is available for Windows (95/98/NT) and Solaris and, last not least, also for Linux.

Jini builds on a series of further services which must have been started individually for Jini to function. First of all, an HTTP server is needed from which clients can load the necessary code, such as proxies. This can be a standard Web server which contains the required classes in its search path, or a simple HTTP server from the Jini package. Since Jini builds on RMI, an RMI daemon and the RMI registry must be started as well. The sample implementation of the lookup server bears the name of "Reggie". The package also includes a prototype of a transaction manager which responds to the name of "Outrigger".

The easiest way to start the whole system is by running an applet which is also included in the package. It can be called with

```
java -cp /usr/remote/java/jini1_0/lib/jini-examples.jar
        com.sun.jini.example.service.StartService
```

The applet must still be configured a bit for the actual environment, but is then capable to start the individual components with a click of the mouse. The most important parameter that needs to be set is the path name leading to the Jini program packages, which are typically located in a directory like /usr/local/jini1_0. The default setting is /files/jini1_0 and must be changed at several points. Then the HTTP server, RMI and, finally, the lookup server can be started, and the experiments can begin.

12.7 References

Sun provides Jini for downloading under http://developer.java.sun.com/developer/products/jini/index.html. Jini is subject to a license specifically created for this purpose, which is finding more and more adherents. This allows Jini to be used for research purposes and also for non-commercial projects, such as in-house applications, free of charge and including use of the source code. Only commercial applications are subject to the payment of a fee.

General information on Jini is available on the Internet and can, for example, be found under http://www.sun.com/jini.

Part II

A distributed Java

13 Distributed programming languages and concurrency

"Making the impossible possible,
the possible easy, the easy elegant..."
– Moshé Feldenkrais

In the first part of this book, several techniques were introduced of how Java can be employed in distributed systems. Widely different mechanisms for concurrency, distribution and persistence were needed and described. Why do we need all these different techniques? Is there no easier solution? Instead of finding lots of extensions for Java, can one not simply extend Java itself? Is a distributed Java at all possible?

Distributed programming languages

This question of how a "distributed programming language" might look has been discussed for tens of years, not only after Java came about. There is a rather substantial number of such distributed programming languages, which try to hide the aspect of distribution as far as possible and attempt to integrate its handling as seamlessly as possible into the programming language itself. Object-orientation has proved to be quite suitable, and most approaches build on it. An up-to-date list and classification of such languages can be found in [Briot *et al.* 1997]. Java is not only object-oriented, but offers several additional advantages in distributed systems, in particular platform-independence and the possibility of migrating code. Thus Java itself brings in a whole lot of positive features for creating a distributed programming language on its basis. The second part of this book is dedicated to the search for such a language.

Is Java a distributed programming language?

But what does such a "distributed programming language" look like? What properties and advantages does it have over "normal" programming languages, such as Java? Or is Java, together with the mechanisms introduced in Part I, already a distributed language *per se*? To clarify this question, we will briefly present such a language, Emerald. In this language, an attempt is made to treat all objects, whether remote or local, in the same way, so that the distribution becomes transparent. This approach has been highly acclaimed and has something very elegant and appealing. But it has also been heavily criticized. The criticism has been formulated in a particularly pointed manner by Jim Waldo, one of the main developers of Java RMI, and will be discussed subsequently. After having developed and critically reviewed some ideas about distributed programming languages, we will analyze whether Java matches such ideas. We will try and find an alternative which includes the advantages of Emerald, but also meets the criticism. For this purpose, we will analyze the concept of concurrency proposed by Bertrand Meyer for the Eiffel language. Finally, the idea of a distributed Java is put in more concrete terms by defining requirements to be met by a distributed Java.

13.1 A distributed programming language: Emerald

Emerald is an object-oriented language, which was developed in the late 80s for programming distributed applications at Washington University. The main emphasis during its development focused on the aspect of distribution. With regard to object-orientation which, on the whole, was still rather young in those days, Emerald shows some peculiarities that make this programming language appear a bit strange. Thus, Emerald does not have classes. Objects are created by executing a *constructor*, instead. This constructor resembles a class insofar as it disposes of all necessary information regarding the object (local data, interface definition, and source code).

Peculiarities of Emerald

Nevertheless Emerald is, in a certain way, a very pure object-oriented language. It is based on a unique object model for all language constructions: all constructions and data types are represented by objects. Polymorphism is achieved in Emerald through the usage of type conformity. Emerald is a strongly typed language, whose type system is based on the concept of the *abstract type*. The abstract type defines the interface of an object. An object *conforms* to an abstract type, when it implements at least the interface of the abstract type. If an object is to be replaced by another object, the new object must conform to the given abstract type. In Emerald it is even possible, at runtime, to add a new object implementation for an already existing object, as long this conforms to its abstract type. However, this form of polymorphism is achieved at the cost of source code repetitions, as Emerald does not have any inheritance and thus no overloading of properties.

Unique object model

Another peculiarity of Emerald is the so-called *process*. This is a block of source code which is asynchronously started during the creation of an object. The execution takes place in concurrency with other processes. Objects that dispose of a process are called *active*, whereas all other objects are considered as *passive*.

Processes

Emerald has attracted particular attention as a *distributed* object-oriented language, and will therefore be mainly presented under this aspect. The following three design objectives are of special interest:

Distribution aspects
Distribution in Emerald

1. **Network transparency**. There is no difference at the language level between a local and a remote method call.

2. **Mobility at object level**. Objects can at any time be migrated beyond the local computer boundaries. This includes the case that an object migrates itself.

3. **Efficiency**. Access to local objects is to be carried out as directly and efficiently as possible, which means, for example, that the decision (to be made by the runtime system) as to whether a call is local or remote should be taken without involving network traffic.

Network transparency

In Emerald, every access to an object is carried out via a reference. A reference to a local object does not differ from a remote reference. Thus the distribution of objects becomes transparent. It is not relevant for the access to an object whether the object is local or remote, and the usage is the same in both cases. This also applies to the passing of parameters in method calls, which is simply done by passing a reference in the same way as in a local program.

Mobility of objects

There are, however, situations where it is advantageous to be able to explicitly select the location of an object, for example, to minimize the number of remote method calls by transferring the target object in question into the local environment of the calling object. To make this possible, Emerald has the capability of migrating objects. The following commands are available for this purpose:

- **move X to Y** moves object X to the computer on which object Y is located. As a computer too is represented by an object, the target may also be a specific computer.
- **fix X at Y** moves object X to the computer on which object Y is located. In addition, object X is fixed in that location to prevent it from being moved away.
- **unfix X** allows object X to be moved again.
- **refix X at Z** cancels the fixation of object X, moves it to where Z is located, and subsequently fixes it there. This is an indivisible (atomic) action.

With regard to the move command it should be noted that rather than being a command, it is a *suggestion*. The system is not obliged to execute the migration (for example, because the object is fixed), and in the same way, the object is not obliged to remain at the target location. The remaining three commands, in contrast, are binding for both system and object. Thus, after successful execution of the fix or refix command, the object stays at the target location until it is explicitly released.

A further expression of mobility can be found in connection with the passing of parameters in method calls. Usually, the parameters are passed in the form of references (*call by reference*). Under certain circumstances this can, however, lead to an increased communication cost. If, for example, the calling object and the called object are located on different computers, the target object must initiate a remote method call for each access to a parameter object. In order to prevent or at least restrict this, Emerald provides three variations of the classic *call by reference*. It is, however, left to the programmer to make use of this feature or not.

Call by reference

The first two variations regard the individual parameter objects. When a parameter is prefixed with the keyword move, the corresponding parameter object is moved to the computer of the called object when the method is called (*call-by-move*). The same thing happens when the keyword visit is used (*call by visit*). However, in this case the parameter object is moved back to the caller after termination of the method call. The third variation, instead, regards the return value of a method call. If the call is prefixed with the keyword move, the result object is automatically moved to the caller (*call by move return*).

Call by move

To achieve the highest possible efficiency, there are some additional special features. Thus objects can be marked as unchangeable. This suggests itself, for example, for objects that merely provide functions or contain only constant data. With this, the system can carry out a runtime optimization and copy such objects into the local environment instead of remotely accessing them.

An important aspect in connection with object migration is the question of the volume of the migration or its *granularity*. This means whether, besides the object in question, any other objects need to be migrated as well. If, for example, only one single object is migrated and, in doing so, is possibly torn out of a group of objects that belong together, this can result in a greatly increased communication traffic. This can be circumvented by keeping objects together that stand in a close relation with each other.

Granularity of migration

To make this possible, the programmer must explicitly state which objects are to form a group with regard to mobility. For this purpose, Emerald provides the keyword

attached

attached, which is put before an object reference. When an object is migrated, all objects referenced in this way will follow it automatically. This relation is transitive, but not symmetric. This means that when an object A, with a reference to an object B marked as **attached**, is moved, object B will follow automatically. However, when object B is migrated, A stays where it is.

On the whole, network transparency and object migration have been very impressively demonstrated in Emerald and mimicked in several languages such as Trellis/DOWL and Beta. However, this approach has also been fundamentally criticized, as we will see in the next section.

13.2 The vision of *unified objects*

The aim pursued in Emerald and other similar languages of making the difference between local and remote objects disappear as far as possible, so that distribution becomes transparent in the end, is known as the vision of *unified objects*. In a frequently quoted and highly respected scientific report,

"A Note on Distributed Computing"

"A Note on Distributed Computing" [Waldo *et al.* 1994], Jim Waldo and three of his colleagues discuss this vision, analyzing projects such as Emerald, Arjuna and Clouds, but also CORBA and similar RPC systems. The discussion in this section essentially follows the argumentation of this particular report.

There are several issues which make the approach of unified objects very attractive:

- Whether a call is local or remote has no influence on the *formal correctness* of a program. When an object possesses a specific interface and this interface is supported in a *semantically* correct way, the location of an object has no effect on the correctness of the program.
- The interface of an object is independent from the context in which it is going to be used. The interface need not be designed following the criteria of locality.

- This allows distributed applications to be developed with the same object-oriented design methods as local applications.
- Failure and performance aspects can be taken into account in the implementation of an application component. In the initial design, consideration of these aspects may be omitted.

The fact that there are language systems that actually implement this vision – such as Emerald – shows that it is definitely possible to put this vision into practice. However, the applications that could be constructed with it were always of a limited size. Critics of this vision such as Jim Waldo argue that this fact covers the flaws of the vision which will come to light once the application exceeds a certain size. In realistic scenarios, this vision fails to meet reality and is therefore not a desirable solution. This will be discussed under various aspects in the next sections.

13.2.1 Differences between local and distributed programming

Since the 70s there have been approaches to integrate additional communication mechanisms into programming languages, so that distributed applications too could be developed directly with those languages. They followed the current programming paradigms of their time and were in part extensions of existing or even newly developed languages. In the 70s these were *message-based* languages (such as Occam or CSP). In the '80s they were mostly based on the *remote procedure call* (RPC), and in the '90s finally on the object-oriented remote method call. The early approaches had only a very limited success and remained difficult and prone to errors in their handling. Today the hope of reaching this vision lies for many people in the component-based approach, which extends object-orientation with additional modularity and integration concepts.

However, there are also less optimistic ways of viewing things which do not give this vision a chance. Here the argument is that every attempt to unify local and remote access must fail because the programming of distributed applications is simply not the same as the programming of non-distributed applications. Mere integration of communication mechanisms does not make the programming of distributed applications any easier, because communication between the parts of a distributed application is not the real problem. Indeed, the essential problems of distributed programming regard totally different areas, such as the handling of partial failures and the lack of a central resource manager. Furthermore, ensuring adequate performance and handling of concurrency represent substantial problems. And finally the differences in memory access of local and distributed devices must be solved. Experience has proved that the emphasis in developing distributed applications was on the above problems, not on working with a mere communication mechanism. These differences between local and distributed execution will now be discussed in more detail, in particular with a view to the aspects of latency time, memory access, partial failure, and concurrency.

13.2.2 Latency time

To begin with, we will discuss the subject of latency time, which represents the most obvious difference between local and remote calls. The latency time is the time used for the call of a method without its execution, that is, a measure for the communication and transmission cost. The latency time of remote calls is usually 4 to 5 orders of magnitude higher than that of local calls. Taking the proportional relation into account with which processor speed and network speed are currently developing, this figure is not likely to decrease, not even in the long run. It can rather be expected to grow.

When these differences in performance between local and remote calls are ignored in the development, this leads to applications which, with a relatively high probability, will have to struggle with performance problems and be sufficiently robust only in small, elementary applications. The advocates of unified objects meet this argument as follows:

- Even if the speed of hardware increases faster than the speed of transmission technology, arguments of efficiency will lose significance because a substantial increase in speed can already be noted. The same can be observed with other new technological developments, which initially had problems of efficiency as well, but have finally gained acceptance through optimization and the corresponding increase in performance.

- Development and use of appropriate tools will allow communication patterns between objects to be shown. This newly gained information can then be used to group objects in such a way that closely related objects stay together in the same address space, while objects with little communication between each other can be placed remotely. The important factor remains, however, that the application functions correctly in the first place, before people begin to worry about efficiency.

Whether it will be possible to cover up the differences in efficiency between local and remote calls to a sufficient extent strongly depends on the application in question and the future technological development. But even if this becomes possible, other, more relevant problems are to be faced.

13.2.3 Memory access

Pointers

Another equally obvious difference between local and remote execution regards memory access, in particular through the use of *pointers*. Such pointers, whose scope is limited to the local address space, can be used to directly access specific memory areas. If an attempt is made to transfer such a pointer into another (remote) address space, this will cause unforeseeable effects. One programming language that allows a mixture between pointers and objects is C++. As long as the programmer does not exclusively work with the object-oriented concepts and can alternatively continue to use, or newly introduce pointers, that is, make use of direct memory access, there is a huge potential for problems to arise.

One possible way out is the use of *distributed shared memory* which, however, makes sense only in the context of relatively closely coupled systems. The other alternative is a clean application of the object-oriented paradigm, accessing all objects via logical references instead of physical addresses. Java itself follows the second alternative, but even inside a clean object-orientation, a number of memory-related problems occur.

References

- Many object-oriented languages provide an automatic memory clean-up (garbage collection) which, however, functions only within one local address space or, as in Java, within one virtual machine. As soon as an application is distributed across several address spaces or virtual machines, this mechanism is much harder to implement.
- Passing of parameters in a method call, in the local case, usually means passing references to objects, so that both the calling and the called party access the same object, and changes to the object are visible to either of them. In the remote case, however, for reasons of efficiency (due to the much longer latency time) copies must be passed. In this way, copies of an object are created which are rather difficult to keep consistent. Changes to a copy are not visible in the original, and vice versa.

With memory access too, as with the latency time, it is still imaginable to cover up the difference between local and remote memory access. The problems presented in the next sections, however, which can arise through partial failure and concurrency in the context of distributed execution, raise the question of whether unification will conceptually still be feasible at all.

13.2.4 Partial failures

Failure of technical components or elements is unfortunately bound to occur in all computer-based systems, both in local and in distributed execution. The difference between the two ways of execution is that in distributed execution usually only partial failures occur, while in local execution failures are either complete, that is, all components that work together for an application are affected, or the failures can be detected by a central instance which manages all local resources, for example, the local operating system.

Such a thing is not possible in the context of distributed execution, as here individual components may fail, such as computers or network connections, while the remaining components continue to function. These failures of distributed components generally occur independently from each other. Furthermore, there is no global instance capable of determining which component has failed and then notifying the other components of this fact. No global state exists that could be analyzed to find out exactly which failure has occurred. In a distributed system, the failure of a network connection cannot be distinguished from the failure of a processor in another computer.

When such failures occur, the error cannot be simply caught by an *exception* as is possible in local execution. Instead, complications arise when the target object of a call simply disappears and the flow of control does not return. This means that it must be one of the main concerns of a distributed execution to guarantee that the system state is consistent after such a failure. This kind of problem does not occur to such an extent in the context of local execution.

The effects of partial failures are far-reaching. They affect the design of interface as well as the semantics of operations of such interfaces. Partial failures add a further aspect to the art of programming whose handling is all but trivial. Such cases cause a system to become non-deterministic. In contrast to local execution, where information can be gathered about different states of the system, for example before and after a failure, obtaining such information is not possible in distributed execution. This requires adaptation of the interfaces used for communication tasks in such a way that objects affected by partial failures can still react consistently.

If, in spite of partial failures, one wishes to obtain robust applications, this presumes specific extensions to the interface area. Mere touching up of the implementation is not sufficient. Instead, the interfaces must be modified in such a way that they become capable of naming the cause of a failure or, if this is not possible, at least support putting the system back into a sensible state.

The existence of partial failures in distributed execution should, however, not be interpreted in the sense that there cannot be a common object model for both local and distributed execution. But instead of asking *whether* one can make remote method calls look like local method calls, one should rather ask what the *cost* for such an enterprise would be. According to [Waldo *et al.* 1994] only two approaches are capable of realizing such a unified model.

In the framework of the first approach, all objects are treated as if they were exclusively *local*. This means that the interfaces of these objects must completely ignore any aspect of distribution. Distributed systems developed under this approach reveal fundamental deficits. Their behavior in case of partial failures is non-deterministic, which has the consequence that such systems are very much prone to errors and therefore not very robust. Emerald follows this approach. For closely coupled distributed systems, this approach can, as demonstrated by Emerald, be absolutely sufficient.

In contrast to the first approach, the second approach treats all objects as if they were exclusively *remote*. This becomes particularly perceptible in the interface design. Now, all objects, including those that will never be used remotely, include additional security aspects in their interface descriptions. Furthermore, it should be noted that this approach, in a similar way to the problem of memory access, only functions when the programmer sticks precisely to the specifications, that is, uses only distributed objects, or the programming language is adapted accordingly.

However, use of this approach would achieve the exact opposite of what the original aim of a unique object model for local and remote execution had been. After all, the true reason for attempting such a unification is to take the development of distributed applications nearer to the development of local applications and thus facilitate the development of distributed applications as a whole. This is not achieved by the second approach, although it is secure and robust. Instead, even the current simple development of local applications is made unnecessarily complex.

13.2.5 Concurrency

In many distributed systems one does not only have to struggle with problems of distribution, but also with problems of concurrency. In languages such as Java, these aspects need to be tackled with independent concepts, for example, threads on the one hand, and RMI on the other hand. RMI itself is not concurrent, but executes strictly sequential and synchronous remote calls. Threads themselves, instead, have nothing to do with distribution. However, in order to be able to make use of the advantages of distributed systems, both must be used together, for example, to issue an asynchronous remote call running in parallel with other functions.

Concurrency has its own very specific problems with integration into an object-oriented language. In some projects, the aspect of concurrency is integrated into a language independently of the distribution, for example, to find employment in clusters or parallel computers, where completely different assumptions of latency time, memory access, and partial failure can be made than in distributed systems. The following problems arise:

- With the introduction of concurrency, non-determinism will enter the language or the system. The sequence of execution of concurrent parts of a program can no longer be guaranteed or must be forced through additional measures such as synchronization.

- Finding a suitable synchronization mechanism is difficult. There is obviously the possibility of using constructions such as semaphors, locks, or similar items, but this leads to difficult ad-hoc programming of new solutions for every problem. A fully integrated mechanism would be most desirable.

- Exclusive reservation or locking of resources, which goes hand in hand with synchronization, opens up the risk of deadlocks. A suitable synchronization mechanism must be capable either to prevent or to recognize and eliminate these.
- A difficult problem in the integration of a synchronization mechanism into object-oriented languages is represented by the notion of inheritance. In many approaches, synchronization is defined at the class level, by introducing rules for concurrent or sequential execution of methods. When a further class is derived from such a class, this can completely confuse the existing synchronization. This problem is also known as inheritance anomaly.

For the integration of concurrency into a distributed language, this means in particular that local objects are sequential and remote objects potentially concurrent to each other. Thus, concurrency must be dealt with for remote objects. To achieve the goal of unification of remote and local objects in the sense of the unified objects, this means that, as with partial failures, that the argumentation used for partial failures can also be applied to concurrency. Either all objects take concurrent semantics into account, or they consciously disregard this problem and are prepared to bear the consequences.

13.2.6 Maintaining the difference

The previous discussion clearly suggests that a unification of the local and distributed programming models in the sense of the unified objects is not sensible. The original aim can only be reached in two ways. Both have in common that in the implementational context only objects of one kind can exist, either local or remote. Otherwise, there would no longer be a unified model.

The decision of treating all objects as though they were local opens the door to incalculable risks through non-observation of important aspects of distribution, such as partial failure and non-determinism. The opposite approach of treating all objects as though they were exclusively remote entails an unnecessary complexity. Here, objects are affected that are not at all intended for remote use. These objects would have to implement distribution aspects they will never need, unnecessarily complicating their development. Generally it can be said that the development of applications, whether local or distributed, would be much more complex in the framework of this approach than would normally be necessary.

It would be much more sensible, instead, to accept the irreconcilable differences between local and distributed programming and to be aware of such differences during all phases of development and implementation of distributed applications. This can be achieved through a differentiated treatment of local and remote objects which, for this purpose, must be distinguishable from each other.

Accept the difference

This leaves the simplicity of developing the local aspects of a distributed application unchanged. With regard to aspects of distribution, the programmer can consciously focus on the different distribution problems, such as partial failures or nondeterminism, because of this distinction. But how can such a distinction between local and remote objects or calls be made?

13.3 Is Java a distributed programming language?

With this discussion in mind, Jim Waldo has played a decisive role in the development of Java RMI. RMI is integrated closely enough into Java to be able to call it a part of the language. Is Java with RMI already the answer to our question? Is Java itself a distributed programming language? In RMI, remote objects are uniquely identified by the type system they inherit from the RemoteObject class, and the remotely accessible interface must be defined in an interface that is derived from the Remote interface. Thus remote references are uniquely and sufficiently identified, and RMI meets the requirements of the above discussion.

Disadvantages of RMI

However, RMI shows disadvantages and limitations which make the classification of Java as a "distributed language" questionable:

- As remote objects can only be accessed via an interface, RMI shows all of the limitations that interfaces are subject to. This means that only methods declared as public can be called remotely. It may certainly be argued that this is sufficient; however, it represents a restriction which clearly contradicts a full integration into object-orientation. No access is possible to default, protected, or static methods.

- RMI does not allow migration of objects. Although copies of objects can be passed as parameters of a method call, so that objects can in a certain sense be moved from one computer to another, the objects cannot maintain their identity in this process – they are just copies. One might think that copying an object onto a remote computer and deleting its original is sufficient for a simulation of migration; however, references that point to the original cannot be re-routed to the copy, which is instead mandatory for a true migration.

- Objects can also not be generated on a remote computer. Existing remote objects can be accessed through the name service, but a direct generation of remote objects is not possible. For this purpose, so-called factory objects must exist on a remote computer, which can then generate an object – in their view local – and return a reference to it.

- Asynchronous calls are not possible. These must be simulated with great effort by means of threads. However, without asynchronous calls, an important advantage of distributed systems, their natural parallelism, is lost.

- On the whole, RMI does not provide support for concurrency. Integration of both concurrency and distribution in a direct and simple way is, however, a great hope tied to the concept of a "distributed programming language".

To remedy at least some of these disadvantages, the possibility exists to extend the mechanism of RMI itself. One project that has followed this approach quite successfully is JavaParty [Philippsen and Zenger 1996]. Here, remote objects are not identified by inheritance from special classes and interfaces, but by an additional keyword which is written as a class modifier in front of the declaration of a class. Thus not only the public but all methods and variables of a class are available remotely as well. Even migration of objects and remote generation are possible. The price to be paid is that for each potentially remote class about 10 additional classes need to be generated by a compiler that is comparable to the rmic compiler. Again, aspects of concurrency are not dealt with.

JavaParty

CORBA essentially follows the same approach as RMI but is, in addition, also suited for linking of programs in other languages and for legacy applications. However, the points of criticism that apply to RMI are also valid in this case. Furthermore, for CORBA they are more difficult to overcome. The advantages of Java are being lost and platform independence and mobility of code can no longer be built upon, so that object migration and remote generation actually seem impossible. Although efforts are being made, for example for migration, they are even more forcibly restricted to making a copy and deleting the original.

CORBA

Substantial progress is represented by Voyager. Migration as well as remote object generation are possible without problems, and method calls do not have to be synchronous, but can be asynchronous or even run without any coupling (oneway). Thus Voyager provides a minimum of support of concurrency, although it still lacks concepts for synchronization.

Voyager

However, Voyager has other disadvantages which prevent the Java-Voyager combination from being awarded the predicate of distributed language:

- Remote access to Voyager objects is also restricted to one interface and does not allow the complete range of interfaces to be used.
- Although Voyager provides an asynchronous call, the syntax of this call does not follow object-oriented

principles. The interface to be used for such a call looks as follows:

```
Future.invoke(Object object, String method_name,
Object[]param);
```

Thus, to begin with, no method of the remote object is called, but a static method of the Future class. The method name is merely indicated as a string. The responsibility that the specified target of the call, object, actually contains this method lies completely with the programmer and cannot be verified by a compiler. The parameters too are passed as an array of objects, which makes them lose their type information. Therefore, the type security for such calls is lost as well.

- In the migration of objects, referential integrity must be maintained, that is, all objects that can be reached via references must be equally reachable after their migration. As local references cannot be automatically converted to remote references, all locally referenced objects (the transitive shell) must be created as copies on the new computer. This can have the consequence that the migration of one single object requires an entire object graph to be moved across the network.

- The transitive shells of two objects can overlap: an object C, which is referenced by two objects A and B, belongs to the transitive shells of both A and B. In the case of migration of A or B, a copy is made of C, so that afterwards two versions of this object exist whose consistent state cannot be guaranteed.

Thus we are far from having reached the end of our search for a distributed Java. Let us now have a closer look towards concurrency. As distributed systems harbor concurrency in themselves, one possible approach is to look at concurrent languages and concepts and extend these with aspects of distribution. A proposal of such an approach will be presented in the following section.

13.4 A concept for concurrency: Eiffel SCOOP

Java is one of the first widely diffused languages that directly integrates threads. This has been widely acclaimed and indeed greatly simplifies concurrent programming. Synchronization mechanisms are also directly integrated by means of a monitor for each object.

However, threads are a basic mechanism, in a similar way as sockets are a basic mechanism for remote communication. In the area of communication mechanisms, research has not stopped at this level, but has searched for possibilities of a more suitable integration of this mechanism into the object-oriented paradigm, developing mechanisms such as RPC, RMI and even unified objects. For concurrency too, a construction at a higher level of abstraction would be desirable.

In his book *Object-Oriented Software Construction* ([Meyer 1997], pp. 951-1036) Bertrand Meyer impressively discusses the possibilities, but also the limitations of unifying concurrency and object-orientation. He begins his elaboration with an analysis of previous approaches.

Concurrency via processes

A frequently employed approach is based on the notion of *processes*.These are often used for the programming of non-object-oriented concurrency. A process is a program unit that executes a specific algorithm, usually repeating it until it is terminated by an external event. Processes build on autonomous, encapsulated modules, store values until the next call, provide a clearly defined interface and use a mechanism for communication which might generally be called *message passing*. This makes them quite similar to the objects themselves. What distinguishes them from objects is that they are *active*: they have their own flow of control and run though a loop where they provide a specific functionality. Through these properties they provide the possibility of concurrency.

Objects instead are *passive*: they wait until someone calls a method and passes them a control flow. After appropriate execution, they return the control flow and change back to their waiting state. A popular idea is now to make the objects equal to processes by giving them their own control flow. Such objects are known as *active objects*.

Active objects

This leads, however, to problems in connection with inheritance, which is a fundamental criterion of object-orientation. Generally, new methods are added to inheriting classes. These new methods would obviously have to be taken into account in the definition of the process part and for synchronization, which may entail a reorganization of the entire module. This phenomenon is known as inheritance anomaly. Therefore, in many projects that follow this approach, the whole concept of inheritance (and thus object-orientation itself) has been challenged. However, Meyer argues that the source of the problem is not constituted by object-orientation, but by the active objects.

Inheritance anomaly

He proposes a different concept, which solves the problems of inheritance anomaly, harmonizes well with object-oriented concepts, and impresses us with its simplicity. The proposal is based on the *Eiffel* programming language, which closely resembles Java in many important aspects.

This proposal, known as *SCOOP* (Simple Concurrent Object-Oriented Programming), seems to be suited not only for Eiffel, but also for other languages and – what is much more important in this context – also appears to be a concept well-suited for distribution. Let us begin by introducing the concept.

13.4.1 Concurrency through processors

The aim of concurrency is to be able to execute different calculations at the same time. For the execution of one (sequential) calculation, only a single CPU is needed (which is frequently called a processor; however, we will shortly see that this term is reserved for a higher principle). If, instead, several calculations are to be executed simultaneously (in true parallelism), an appropriate number of CPUs is required. Meyer bases his concept of concurrency on this image and transfers it to object orientation: instead of sticking to the idea of a *process* from which the active objects with their relative control flows have been derived, he follows the concept that a self-contained execution unit (similar to a CPU) manages passive objects and can take on their execution. He calls this execution unit a *processor* and defines the concept as follows:

Processor

> A processor is an autonomous control flow capable of executing the sequential elaboration of instructions in one or more objects.

A concurrent object-oriented system may consist of an arbitrary number of such processors; in a sequential system only one processor is required. This processor must *not* be confused with a physical processor (CPU). Instead, a processor of the kind presented above can be implemented in various ways:

- through a *computer* (with its CPU) in the network,
- through a *process* as supported by some operating systems (such as Unix, Windows, etc.),
- through a *coroutine* (which simulates concurrency via alternate/rotating use of the CPU),
- through a *thread* as supported by multi-threaded operating systems (such as Solaris, Windows NT, etc.).

One of the tasks of a processor is the execution of calculations. A calculation takes place when a processor performs a specific action in a specific object. This makes it quite evident that every method call in an object must be executed by a processor. To make this possible, the processor has to become a kind of manager of objects.

When an object is created, it is automatically assigned a processor with which it will stay for the rest of its lifetime. This processor is then responsible for the execution of method calls in this object.

To create concurrency, several processors are employed. This lays the foundation for a concurrency mechanism. But only the use of asynchronism makes it really possible to draw an advantage out of this. Synchronous calls leave the system with one single flow of control, which only extends over several processors without, however, achieving concurrency. With asynchronous calls, instead, the calling object continues its calculations as soon as it has issued the method call to the target object. To make this work, however, the two objects need to be located in different processors. Meyer integrates the two forms of call into his concept as follows:

- If two objects O1 and O2 are managed by the same processor, a method call from O1 to O2 takes place in a *synchronous* way. This means that object O1 must wait with the execution of further calculations until the method call in object O2 is terminated.
- If two objects O1 and O2 are managed by two different processors, a method call from O1 to O2 is executed in an *asynchronous* way. Object O1 can thus continue with its calculations as soon as it has initiated the method call in object O2.

To make this semantic difference of the calls apparent in the source code, the programming language needs to be modified. In the *Eiffel* programming language, this is solved by introducing the keyword separate. A declaration of the form

separate

```
x : SomeType
```

corresponds to the usual synchronous semantics. Use of the following declaration, instead,

```
x : separate SomeType
```

is meant to express that the object is located in another processor and that method calls in object x are taking place asynchronously.

Because of the different call semantics for separate and non-separate objects, it must be ensured that a reference which points to a non-separate object can never be assigned a separate object. A reference which has erroneously been declared as non-separate, but points to an object in another processor is, in Meyer's words, called a *traitor*. To prevent the occurrence of such *traitors*, Meyer has set forth four consistency rules which must be adhered to by the programmer and which can be summarized as follows:

Traitor

- In assignments, the target must be declared as separate if the source is declared as separate.

- If a separate reference is passed as a parameter, the parameter variable of the interface must also be declared as separate.

- separate return values can only be assigned to separate variables.

With an asynchronous call, it is possible to continue with the calculation after the initiation of a method call. To obtain the result of the call, Meyer proposes the concept of *wait by necessity*. The aim of this concept is to relieve the programmer from the burden of having to go and fetch the results of an asynchronous call. It is assumed that the result of a method call is usually not needed straightaway. At the point where the result of a method call is concretely needed, such as for an assignment or a call to this object, the result is waited for automatically.

Wait by necessity

13.4.2 Concurrency and synchronization

Every concurrent language, whether object-oriented or not, must provide mechanisms which allow concurrent executions to be synchronized, thus defining chronological dependencies between these executions.

Meyer analyzes various (partly non-object-oriented) synchronization solutions, which he subdivides into synchronism- and communication-based procedures. The first group includes, for example, semaphors, critical zones, monitors, and *path expressions*. Once the problems of synchronism are solved, the question still remains of how the concurrent units are to communicate with each other. If, on the other hand, one has developed a good communication mechanism, this can at the same time be used to solve the synchronism problem, because communication implies synchronization. Thus, if the communication mechanism is flexible enough, it automatically provides the complete synchronization that is needed.

Communication-based procedures have been first presented by Hoare in Communicating Sequential Processes (CSP) [Hoare 1985]. In this procedure, communication takes place with the aid of so-called channels through which information is exchanged. If, with this background in mind, one looks at the fundamental way of proceeding of object-orientation, namely to call a method, with parameters where required, in an object, one will find that this is a communication-based procedure. From this fact Meyer concludes that synchronization can be directly integrated into object-orientation.

Thus synchronization occurs through method call and parameter passing. To obtain exclusive access to an object declared as **separate**, this must be used as a parameter in a method call. The method is only executed when the **separate** object is available, that is, not reserved by anyone else. This has the consequence that **separate** objects are available for exclusive use. Synchronization with the return of the result occurs precisely when the result is needed for further elaboration, a mechanism which, as already mentioned, is known as *wait by necessity.*

Under certain circumstances it should, according to Meyer, also be possible to *interrupt* the method execution. In this case, an *exception* is generated, so that the object which originally initiated the method call is made aware of this and can initiate the appropriate corrective measures, such as a repetition at a later point in time.

13.4.3 Distribution

This relatively simple mechanism is well suited for concurrency. However, this mechanism can also be employed with distributed systems, and Meyer outlines some thoughts in this direction. But he rather aims at closely coupled distributed systems, such as clusters. Although he refers to the possibility of migrating processors, he makes no precise statement about how such a mechanism might look. However, due to the restriction that an object stays with its processor all life long, there is no possibility of migration of individual objects. Objects should always be migrated together with their processor.

On the whole, the concept as presented by Meyer rather remains a concept of concurrency, which is only to a certain extent suited for distribution in closely coupled systems with a relatively static distribution. Taking the *Eiffel* programming language as an example, Meyer has shown how these two concepts might be implemented in the framework of object-orientation. Unfortunately, however, there exists no concrete implementation as yet. Nevertheless, this mechanism might be the key to a distributed Java.

13.5 Requirements for a distributed Java

What kind of conclusion can be drawn from the discussion conducted in this chapter? Let us summarize the desirable properties and unsolved problems we mentioned in a list of requirements:

1. Access to remote objects should obviously be possible via the usual, object-oriented mechanism of method calls. However, the visibility of the full interface should be maintained, as in the local case, and not be restricted by the distribution mechanism.

2. Generation of objects on a remote computer should be possible. The fact that a remote computer must first be started through a daemon, as in Voyager, is acceptable and even necessary for reasons of security. Also, prior setting of appropriate privileges, or the registration of code servers, are not deficiencies, but necessities.

3. Local and remote references to objects should be clearly distinguishable from each other, as Waldo demands. This distinction should be as simple and intuitive as possible and let itself integrate well into the language. Nevertheless, the difference should always be identifiable for the developer in order to make correct design decisions and be able to handle exceptions in the appropriate way. The difference should also be identifiable for the compiler and

the runtime system, so that they can check the correct and consistent application of remote accesses and as far as possible support the programmer.

4. When the aspects of distribution are not needed, the programs should remain as unaffected as possible by the existence of such aspects, so that the development of local applications does not change.

5. Automatic garbage collection should also be maintained in the distributed case.

6. Migration of objects should be feasible and easy to handle. The identity of an object should be maintained to its full extent. This means that references to remote objects do not lose their validity even after a migration.

7. There should be a grouping mechanism for objects, for example, to migrate them together. In Emerald, objects can be moved individually or bound to each other via a transitive operation (*attach*). However, this mechanism is too expensive and interferes too strongly with the code of an application. The migration of the transitive referential shell, as in Voyager, however, also has its problems, in particular because the transitive shells may overlap.

8. Methods should be callable synchronously or asynchronously. However, the object-oriented notation should be maintained, to avoid having to give up type security at compile time, as in Voyager in the case of the asynchronous call.

9. On the whole, a mechanism for the handling of concurrency should exist, since this is a natural fact and a big advantage of distributed systems. It should be integrated into the programming language as directly and simply as possible and reflect the principles of object-orientation as proposed, for example, in Eiffel SCOOP.

10. This also requires the integration of synchronization into the language. As Bertrand Meyer argues, this should

build on the communication mechanism and not constitute an additional mechanism.

All of these points are individually fulfilled in different systems and are therefore no Utopian demands. However, none of the systems under analysis can fulfill all of these points together. Let us therefore search for a mechanism that can fulfill as many of these requirements as possible.

But how can a concept look that meets these high demands? Let us have another look at the mechanisms we analyzed. It can be noticed that Voyager and Eiffel SCOOP each fulfill many of these points. Is it possible to unify these two approaches in a sensible way, thus combining their positive features? This will be examined in the next chapter.

13.6 References

Distribution as well as concurrency are often treated in connection with object-orientation. A good overview and classification of distributed and concurrent object-oriented programming languages can be found in [Briot *et al.* 1997].

Specific information on the Emerald and Eiffel languages can be best obtained from the developers themselves. Emerald has seen the light in two doctoral dissertations by Norman Hutchinson [Hutchinson 1987] and Eric Jul [Jul 1989]. A good description can be found in [Jul *et al.* 1987]. Eiffel has been developed by Bertrand Meyer and is one of the most elegant object-oriented languages. The book [Meyer 1997] describes Eiffel and is regarded as a standard textbook on object-orientation. The concurrent extension of Eiffel, SCOOP, was first presented in [Meyer 1993]. An ample discussion can be found in [Meyer 1997], Chapter 30.

14 Virtual processors

In this chapter we search for a concept that is capable of facing the discussion of the previous chapter and fulfills the demands. We are looking for an abstraction that blends distribution and concurrency into a unique concept. Abstraction is one of the most important keys to progress in computer science (and not only there). Let us quote three examples of such abstractions, which have been prerequisites for the development of a language such as Java or have at least facilitated it:

Abstraction as a key

1. In procedural programming, data, functions, and modules represent fundamental, but separate constructions. In object-orientation, these are abstracted to one single construction, the class.

2. Only the abstraction from physical memory addresses (*pointers*) to logical references has made automatic garbage collection and the concept of remote references possible.

3. One of the most important abstractions with regard to Java is the virtual machine – an abstraction from the actual *physical* machine, the computer. It hides the differences that different platforms tend to have. Thus Java is platform-independent, and the executable code can be migrated from one machine to another. The most well-known example of this are applets, whose classes can be downloaded from a Web server and started in a browser on an arbitrary platform.

What would be the advantage of an abstraction of concurrency and distribution? Let us look at an example which is often used in either area and which we have briefly mentioned

The dining philosophers …

in Chapter 2: the problem of the dining philosophers. Five philosophers sit around a table, as shown in Figure 14.1, and dine together. They have a common bowl of rice from which they can eat with the aid of two chopsticks, but each chopstick must be shared between two philosophers. The philosophers can either think, with the chopsticks put on the table, one to their left and one to their right side, or they can eat, for which they need to obtain both the left and the right chopstick.

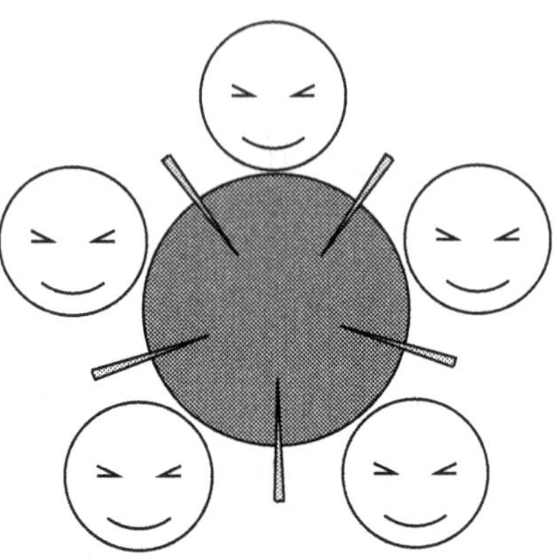

Figure 14.1 *The dining philosophers sitting at their table.*

… concurrent, …

… distributed …

… or abstracting.

This example can be implemented with the aid of threads, with each philosopher receiving his own thread. All threads are running concurrently on one virtual machine. However, it can also be put into practice in a distributed system where (for example) all philosophers are located on different computers and remote communication can be implemented via sockets, RMI, CORBA or Voyager. However, these two approaches do not have much in common. Making the concurrent version distributed *a posteriori* basically means to rewrite the program completely. The same applies to a conversion from the distributed version to a local one. If one had an abstraction capable of expressing both distribution and concurrency,one would need to implement this problem only once and could decide at runtime whether it should be executed locally (all philosophers on one computer) or distributed (each philosopher on a separate computer). One could even change this at runtime, by simply letting the philosophers freely migrate from one computer to another. They could all be created and started on one computer, begin their meal, and be moved at any time from there to another computer without having to interrupt their meal.

And how can such an abstraction be found? Let us take another look at Java's virtual machine. The virtual machine is, as the name says, a virtual concept. It does not correspond to an underlying physical reality. On one computer, none, one, or more virtual machines can be started, as shown in Figure 14.2.

Virtual machines are …

Two virtual machines run in concurrency with each other. When they are located on the same computer, they run in two different processes. When they are started on two different computers, they are truly parallel to each other.

… concurrent, …

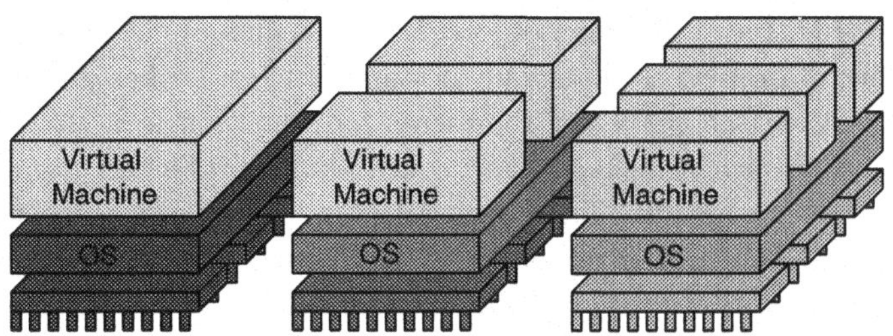

Figure 14.2
The virtual machine hides platform differences.

They are also distributed. To be able to communicate from one virtual machine to another, remote communication must be employed. It does absolutely not matter where the two communicating virtual machines are physically located (as long as they can be reached via a network). They can be located on the same computer or on two different continents – for the communication mechanism this is of no concern. Obviously, transmission time and stability of the connection will change, but otherwise the two are reachable for each other in exactly the same way.

… distributed, …

Unfortunately, however, a virtual machine cannot migrate. It is firmly tied to the location from where it has been started. Individual objects can, as demonstrated by Voyager, be migrated into it or out of it, but the machine itself is static and immobile. This fact cannot be altered, because virtual machines are themselves platform-dependent.

… but cannot migrate.

But maybe an abstraction layer can be drawn between the virtual machine and the objects which permits precisely this: an equally virtual construction with similar capabilities as those of the virtual machine, of which none, one, or more can exist in a virtual machine and which can migrate. In analogy to the fact that physical machines can have one or several (even lots of) CPUs, and inspired by the concept of processor as defined by Meyer (see previous chapter), we will call this concept a *virtual processor*.

14.1 The concept of virtual processor

Before any confusion is created: a virtual processor is neither a piece of hardware or a chip, nor a simulation or an emulator of a CPU, but a common object. However, this object has some special properties that make it stand out from other objects.

A virtual processor represents an execution unit. It is an active object, that is, it has a control flow of its own and manages other objects. The execution of methods (more precisely, of remotely called methods, more about this later) is managed by the virtual processor. Obviously, the actual execution is still performed by the virtual machine; however, the virtual processor lies as a control layer between the virtual machine and the objects. Inside a virtual processor, objects can be used in exactly the same way as in a virtual machine. They can be generated, referenced, called, and copied. They are also collected by the garbage collector when they are no longer needed (the virtual processor additionally takes care of a distributed garbage collection).

Every object is contained in exactly one virtual processor. Thus the object space is uniquely subdivided, so that two objects are located either in the same or in two different virtual processors. The virtual processor can be migrated from one computer to another (more precisely, it can be moved from one virtual machine to another, which may as well be located on the same computer). It is always moved as a whole, and all objects contained in it migrate with it. For this purpose it is very important to be able to determine to which migration unit (that is, to which virtual processor) an object belongs. Figure 14.3 shows a virtual processor.

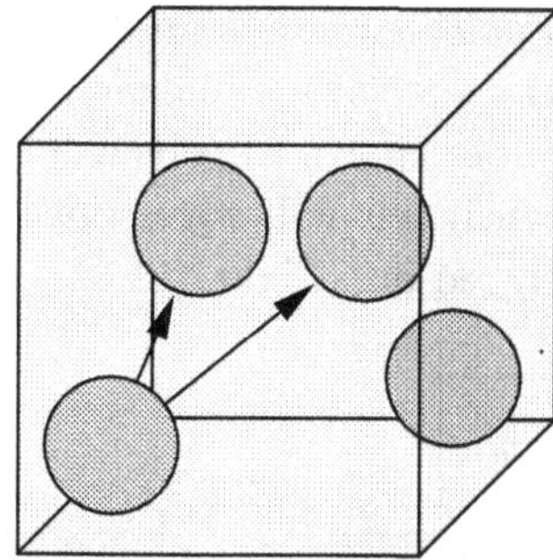

Figure 14.3
The virtual processor with objects contained in it.

However, before we can introduce the virtual processor as a complete concept, we need some middleware which provides a communication infrastructure between the individual virtual machines of a distributed Java system. It must also supply a mechanism for the migration of objects. Such a layer widely covers the physical location of the virtual machines. Middleware with these capabilities is available with Voyager. This is not the only conceivable alternative, but currently the one that best meets the demands made on such middleware. Voyager alone has the disadvantages discussed in the previous chapter, but as an underlying infrastructure for a superior layer of virtual processors it can be of very valuable service.

Voyager as an infrastructure

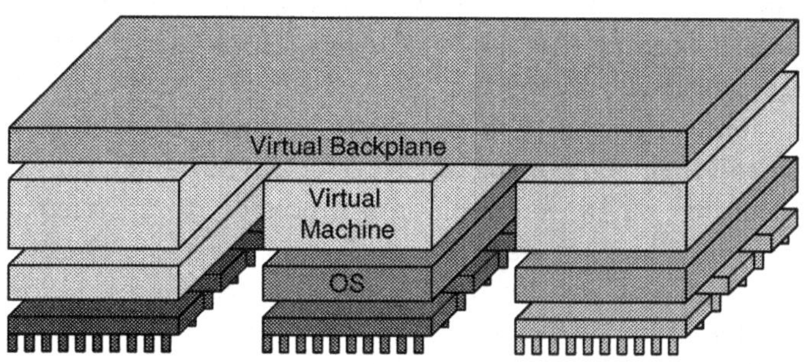

Figure 14.4
The virtual backplane, a layer extending over several VMs.

To match the concept of virtual processors, this layer will be called *virtual backplane*. The concept of *backplane* is usually employed in the hardware area and denotes a board that provides several slots for CPUs. Abstracting from the hardware aspect, we obtain a plane that extends over several virtual machines and, so to speak, provides slots for virtual processors.

To make a virtual machine become part of a *virtual backplane*, it is sufficient to start a Voyager daemon and make its IP address and port number known (details will be given in the next chapter). Subsequently, virtual processors can be generated on this layer and "plugged in" (Figure 14.5).

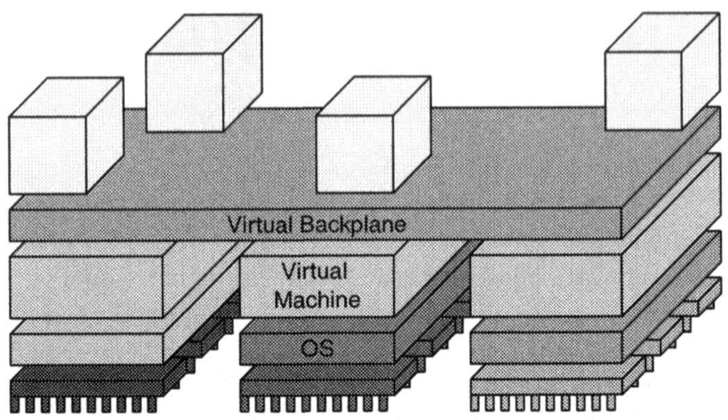

Figure 14.5
Virtual processors on the virtual backplane.

Thus the virtual processors contain objects and can be migrated together with these objects. The objects inside a virtual processor can perfectly normally reference and call each other. But how can objects in one virtual processor access objects in another virtual processor? For this purpose, we introduce a special kind of references, which we will call "remote" references, in contrast to the usual references, which we will now also call "local" references .

Remote references

Remote references allow objects in other virtual processors (we call them remote virtual processors, even though they may be located on the same physical processor) to be referenced as usual. Thus, for example, methods of a remote object can be called or a remote reference can be assigned to another variable.

Differentiating between local and remote references

Remote references must be distinguishable from local references. Developers, as well as compilers or similar tools, should always be able to tell a local reference from a remote one. This can be achieved through various mechanisms. One solution would be to derive such objects from a special interface or class. RMI requires both: inheriting from RemoteObject and implementation of the Remote interface. This has the disad-

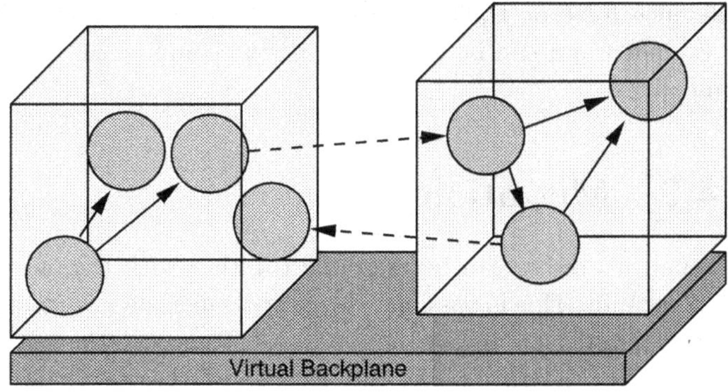

Figure 14.6
Local and remote references.

vantage that only the capabilities of interfaces are available and private methods, for example, cannot be called remotely. Furthermore, this requires an additional programming effort when developing a class. Eiffel SCOOP suggest prefixing a special keyword (separate). This allows the labeling of individual references and does not require a modification of the classes, however, additional rules must be introduced to prevent, for example, remote references being assigned to local variables, which is not allowed.

Differentiation by type

We propose, instead, to generate a special type for each class to be used remotely. As we will see, this generation can be carried out automatically by a compiler, and the generated type can be given a slightly modified name with respect to the original class, for example, "Remote_A" for the A class. Both remote and local references have a type. These two types can be used to document the difference between remote and local references: if a reference is of the normal type (A), it is local, if it is of the generated type (Remote_A), it is remote. In the language presented in the next chapter – called Dejay – the generated types will bear the prefix "Dj", matching the name of the language, for example DjA for the A class. This allows both local and remote references to be generated from one class, without having to invest additional efforts as with RMI. Furthermore, no additional assignment rules are needed because the type conformity rules of Java are fully sufficient, and incorrect usage, such as an assignment of a remote reference (of type DjA) to a variable of the normal type (A), is excluded and can be recognized by the compiler at compile time.

14.2 Migration

Virtual processors can be migrated together with the objects they contain. This is possible whenever no method is currently being executed on any of these objects. To enable the virtual processor to determine this, all method calls to objects under its management are redirected to it. It handles these method calls and forwards them one by one to the originally called object. Thus only one method at a time is executed inside the virtual processor. When the migration order arrives, this call too is placed in the queue, and when its turn arrives, it is certain that no other method call is being executed inside the virtual processor. Then the virtual processor can be packaged (serialized) and transmitted to another computer where it is unpacked (deserialized). Subsequently, the method calls that were in the queue after the migration order can be executed and new calls accepted.

Remote references remain valid

Remote references to objects in the just migrated virtual processor remain valid in spite of the migration. This might be implemented in such a way that access is first attempted at the old location, where it obviously fails because the object has been migrated. However, in the error message, the *virtual backplane* notifies the caller of the new location, so that the caller can issue a new call to that location and find the object. This works even with multiple consecutive migrations of a virtual processor. All this happens "under cover" and remains hidden to the programmer.

Thus, the physical location of virtual processors can be changed without affecting the logical structure of a program using such references. To guarantee this, virtual processors must only be moved as a whole, not in the form of individual objects. However, it is possible to make a copy of an object, even remotely, copying, for example, an object from one virtual processor into another. This is, however, different from migration

Remote copying of individual objects

(although it sometimes serves the same purpose). In a migration, the identity of an object is maintained while, in copying, a new object is created with its own identity. Thus the unit (or granularity) of migration is always the virtual processor. Through this mechanism, the problems caused by migration in Voyager or Emerald can be avoided. In Voyager, as discussed in Chapter 6, unwanted copies may appear and cause inconsistencies. In Emerald, instead, the granularity of migration is so fine that the programmer must use relatively costly attachments to hold correlated objects together. In the concept of virtual processors, each object is contained in exactly one virtual processor, and no copies are created by a migration. All locally referenced objects lie together in one virtual processor, which is equivalent to a simple grouping mechanism.

14.3 Distribution and concurrency

With remote references, a very simple concept for remote communication is available. Objects can be addressed and called across computer boundaries in exactly the same way as local objects: via references. With the aid of the virtual processors, objects can even be migrated. They can even be created remotely, by creating a virtual processor on a remote computer in which a normal object is generated whose remote reference is then returned.

However, virtual processors are also a concept for expressing concurrency. Virtual processors cannot only be created remotely, but also on the same computer. Two such virtual processors are then concurrent to each other and can simultaneously work on two different tasks. One might even push this as far as to do without using Java's own integrated threads; however, we do not want to go this far.

It is much more interesting to see that distribution and concurrency are now flowing together into one concept. Several virtual processors which work together in one application can, as shown in Figure 14.7, be created on one computer and carry out their work concurrently.

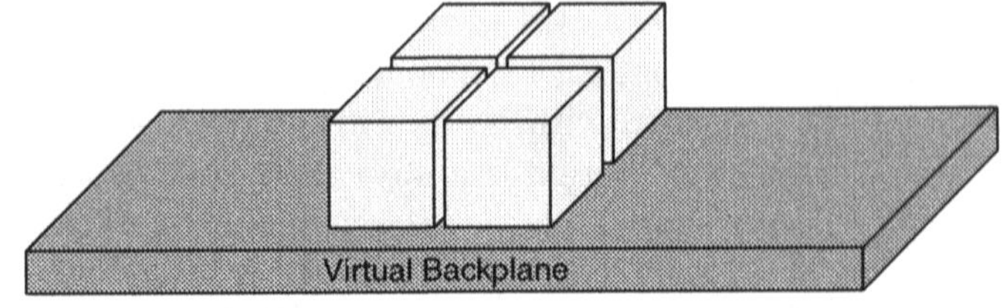

Figure 14.7
Virtual processors concurrent...

At any given time they can then be moved to another computer through the possibility of migration. This may even happen during normal operation, while the objects in their virtual processors call each other and carry on with the application. This is shown in Figure 14.8.

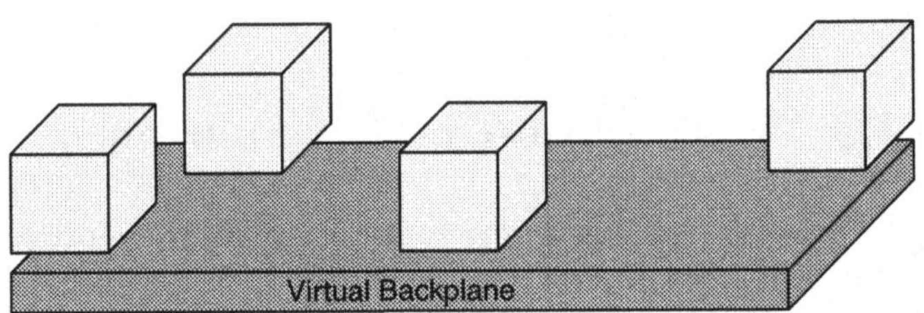

Figure 14.8
... and distributed.

Let us take another look at the example of the dining philosophers. We had seen that they could be implemented either concurrently or distributed, but that a change of one implementation into the other had a very high cost. With the concept of virtual processors it is now possible to write this application in such a way that it runs either locally and concurrent or distributed and truly parallel. The application need not be changed, nor is any additional effort required in its development. Only, the philosophers must be created in different virtual processors and point to the chopsticks assigned to them via remote references (see Figure 14.9). During the development phase, one can completely ignore whether the program will later be executed concurrently or distributed. This can be decided dynamically at the start of the application. It can even be changed dynamically at runtime, by simply migrating the philosophers.

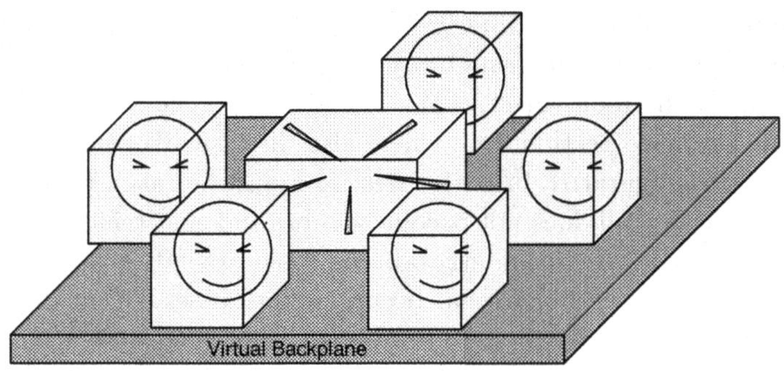

Figure 14.9
The philosophers in virtual processors.

Both alternatives have their advantages. When the virtual processors are moved as closely together as possible, the latency times are substantially reduced and the communication effort is smaller. When two virtual processors run on one virtual machine, communication even takes place via local method calls and not over the network or across process boundaries. Here, both virtual processors need the same CPU – they run concurrently, but not in parallel. When, in contrast, they are moved onto different computers, communication becomes more expensive, but the load is distributed equally across several computers, and the execution is truly parallel.

14.4 Persistence

A problem which resembles migration in many respects is that of persistence. Although, in persistence, objects are not moved, they must, however, be serialized for some persistence mechanisms, exactly as in migration. The serialized form is then not transmitted over the network, but stored on a hard disk. When these objects are reloaded, they must be deserialized again, as in migration. For this reason, persistence might also be understood as a migration in time.

Persistence as migration in time

But there are still more similarities. One common approach in object-oriented databases is to specify a root object and store all objects together that can be reached from this object via references. This guarantees that all references that were valid before making the object persistent will again be valid after reloading the object. This is also known as referential integrity. Thus the granularity of persistence is the transitive shell of the root object. This reminds one of the migration in Voyager (see Section 6.3), where also the transitive shell of an object is migrated. In both cases care must be taken that this transitive shell does not become too big and that references to objects that are not going to be included are cut.

Granularity of persistence

A further problem that occurs in both cases is that of unwanted copies. When an object (let us call it A) can be reached from two objects (B and C), that is, lies in the transitive shell of two different objects, it is made persistent twice. Let us assume that, first, one of the two root objects is made persistent. Obviously, A is stored together with it. It must, however, also remain in memory to enable the other root object to make use of it. Thus there exist two copies of A. When now the other root object is put in the database as well and both are loaded again after a while, two objects for A will be created. This can be prevented by using a common root object instead of the two objects B and C, but this potentially makes the transitive shell become very big, and the granularity of persistence becomes quite unmanageable. It would therefore be preferable to have a mechanism in which the granularity can be more flexibly adapted to the requirements.

If the problems are so similar, could a solution for migration also be a solution for persistence? Can virtual processors be used as a mechanism for the storage of objects? Yes, they can. When the virtual processor is passed as a root object to an object-oriented database, it is made persistent together with the objects it contains. Objects located in other virtual processors can be managed via remote references and need not be discarded. The remote objects are not dragged into the database. They can be stored together with their surrounding virtual processor. Since objects are always contained in only one virtual processor, no unwanted copies can appear, and inconsistencies are avoided.

Virtual processors for persistence

And what happens to the remote references? Exactly as in migration, they maintain their validity. When both the referenced and the referencing object are loaded, things are easy:

the references can continue to be used normally. Things become slightly more difficult when a remote reference is used to access an object that is not present in memory, but in the database. In this case, the required persistent virtual processor can be automatically reactivated, and the object is available again. This happens in a similar way as in migration: the referencing object attempts to call the referenced object. As this is not available, but persistent, an exception is generated. Through an appropriate exception handling, the persistent object is reactivated. Then the call is repeated, this time with success (see also Section 9.5). This happens behind the scenes and remains invisible to the programmer.

The fact that in this concept only one object type, namely the virtual processor, is used as root object, allows practically the entire persistence mechanism to be hidden behind this object, so that the programmer only needs to specify the name of the database and the moment in time when the objects are to be made persistent.

Databases can thus be integrated into the *virtual backplane*, and virtual processors can, upon demand, be moved into virtual memory, reloaded, or automatically reactivated. This is shown in Figure 14.10.

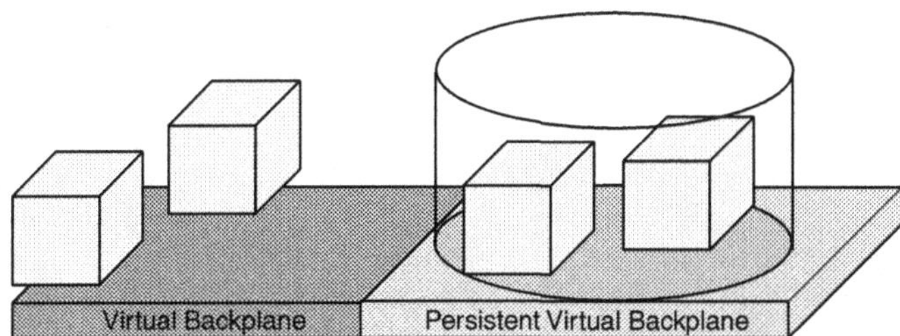

Figure 14.10 *Virtual processors as a mechanism for persistence.*

Summary

With the concept of virtual processor presented in this chapter, an abstraction has been found in which the aspects of concurrency and distribution are blended together. On this basis, all requirements made in Section 13.5 can be met. Furthermore, this concept is also a mechanism for persistence, suitable for easy storage and automatic activation of objects and object groups. The three aspects of distributed systems mentioned in the introduction of this book, namely concurrency, distribution, and persistence, can thus be combined into one concept. This frees a great potential for the simplification of programming distributed systems which now needs to be used. The following chapter introduces a language which implements this concept.

14.5 References

The concept of virtual processor is modeled on the proposals for a concurrent Eiffel, presented in [Meyer 1997] and known as Eiffel SCOOP, but never implemented as yet. Further information on this concept can be found in the publications that emerged from the Dejay project ([Boger 1998], [Boger *et al.* 1999a, 1999b]), and on the Web site http://www.dejay.org.

15 Dejay: a distributed Java

"There is a difference between knowing the way and going the way"
Morpheus in the film "The Matrix"

The concepts introduced in the previous chapter are not only theoretical considerations, but have been implemented in an existing and freely available programming language. This programming language bears the name of *Dejay* and stands for *Distributed Java*. The aim followed with Dejay is the development of a Java-based programming language that facilitates the programming of distributed and concurrent applications. The language is being developed under the author's direction in the framework of a research project at Hamburg University. A fully functional prototype is ready and freely available to the public, including the source code. All necessary classes and the compiler are available via the Web pages for this book or the domain of the Dejay project and can be downloaded from the Internet. The language constructions discussed in the following chapter have been fully implemented; however, the user should be aware that this is still a prototype where some rough spots may occur. The development is not yet concluded and will be continued as an open source project with the publishing of this book. People who wish to participate in the further development, who have questions regarding Dejay, or who just want to take a look at the project will find the necessary information on the project's Web site under www.dejay.org.

15.1 A simple example

Let us begin the introduction to Dejay with a simple example. If you know Java, you already know most of the things you need to know about Dejay. Dejay is read and written in exactly the same way as Java, but makes the aspects of concurrency, distribution, and persistence substantially easier. The syntax of Dejay is identical with that of Java. You just need to use another compiler and differentiate between remote and local references. The underlying concept is the virtual processor – more about this later.

HelloWorld

The first example in practically every programming language is the so-called HelloWorld program. This is not different here. The following class provides the functionality of creating a class, Hello, and calling a method, sayHello(), which outputs a greeting message on the screen.

```
// Hello.dj
public class Hello implements java.io.Serializable {

  public Hello() {
  }

  public void sayHello(java.lang.String name){
    System.out.println("Hello " + name);
  }
}
```

dejayc

This class is a legal Dejay program. It would also be a legal Java program, like all Dejay programs that contain only local references, but we will store it in the file Hello.dj instead of Hello.java. Instead of the javac compiler we use the dejayc compiler and obtain two output files instead of one.

```
lin> dejayc Hello.dj
lin| Hello.class
lin| DjHello.class
```

Now we need a class which can create an object out of this class and then call it. This task will be carried out by a Startup class which looks as follows:

```
// Startup.dj
public class Startup {
```

```
  public static void main( String argv[] ) {
    Hello hello = new Hello();
    hello.sayHello( "Thorsten" );
  }
}
```

We compile this class too by means of the dejayc compiler (however, since we need this class only locally, with the parameter -l, which suppresses the creation of the DjStartup class – more about this in Section 15.8) and start it. By the way, Dejay programs generate normal Java byte code, so they can be executed by any Java interpreter.

```
lin> dejayc -l Startup.dj
lin| Startup.class

lin> java Startup
lin| Hello Thorsten
```

So far, so good. But we could have obtained the same effect using plain standard Java. So far, there is no difference. However, now we will try to run this program the distributed way: starting from the lin computer, an object is to be created on the sun computer, where it will then be called and where it will also produce its output. Now the concept of virtual processors and remote references comes into play. References have a type which they are attributed during their declaration. Remote references are attributed a type whose name is made up by putting the prefix Dj before the name of the class. For the Hello class, for example, local references have the type Hello, while remote references have the type DjHello.

Distributed execution

Remote references

The Startup program is modified as follows: we create a virtual processor on the sun computer and obtain a remote reference (of the DjProcessor type) in return. In this processor we then create the Hello object and obtain a remote reference to it (of the DjHello type). This reference can be used in a perfectly normal way; however, the remote object is called, and the output is carried out on the remote computer. The code for the Hello class need not be present on the sun computer; all that needs to be done is start a Voyager daemon (details are given in Section 15.9).

```
// Startup2.dj
public class Startup2 {
  public static void main( String argv[] ) {
     DjProcessor p1 = new DjProcessor("sun:8000");
     DjHello hello = new DjHello(p1);
     hello.sayHello( "Thorsten" );
  }
}
```

```
lin> dejayc -l Startup2.dj
lin| Startup2.class
```

```
sun> voyager 8000 -c http://lin:7042
```

```
lin> java Startup2
```

```
sun| Hello Thorsten
```

Now, this object can even be migrated from one computer to another, let's say to the win computer, and create an output there as well. Once more, we extend the program and also start a Voyager daemon on the win computer:

```
// Startup3.dj
public class Startup3 {
  public static void main( String argv[] ) {
     DjProcessor p1 = new DjProcessor("sun:8000");
     DjHello hello = new DjHello(p1);
     hello.sayHello( "Thorsten" );

     hello.moveTo( "win:9000" );
     hello.sayHello( "Jan" );
  }
}
```

```
lin> dejayc -l Startup3.dj
lin| Startup3.class
```

```
sun> voyager 8000 -c http://lin:7042
```

win> voyager 9000 -c http://lin:7042

lin> java Startup3

sun| Hello Thorsten

win| Hello Jan

With this, we now have a program capable of remotely creating, referencing, and calling objects, and of migrating them as well. References to remote objects are maintained even after a migration (otherwise we would not have been able to call the sayHello() method a second time), the necessary code is automatically migrated if it is not locally available in the first place, and distributed garbage collection functions too.

15.2 Virtual processors

The foundation for the possibilities of Dejay lies in its virtual processors. All objects of a Dejay application exist in a virtual processor. The first virtual processor is created implicitly and without any further intervention by the programmer at the start-up of a Dejay program. Therefore, in a locally and sequentially executed program without distribution, this concept is transparent to the programmer, and every Java program is automatically also a Dejay program. You merely need to adjust the file name extensions and recompile the files. However, as soon as concurrency or distribution are desired or needed, further virtual processors need to be created explicitly.

Processor

In principle, a virtual processor is a perfectly normal object of the Processor class, which can be created remotely (among other things, which will be discussed later). It manages objects which are, so to speak, "in it". Since for other objects it is a remote object, it is handled through a remote reference which, in conformity with the naming convention for remote objects in Dejay, is of the DjProcessor type. A new virtual processor is instantiated by applying the new operator to the DjProcessor type.

DjProcessor

```
// create a new virtual processor
DjProcessor p = new DjProcessor("//sun:8000");
```

The above example creates a new virtual processor on the sun computer on port 8000. The prerequisite is a running Voyager daemon on this port. The address of the new virtual processor can be any valid IP address (134.100.15.1) or a logical computer name (sun.informatik.uni-hamburg.de or, inside a local network, simply sun). The specification of a port is mandatory, since the Voyager daemon to be addressed is reachable only on the corresponding port. It is also possible to start several daemons of this kind which can then be addressed between each other via localhost:<port_number>. In addition to the address, the following optional parameters are admitted in the creation of a new virtual processor:

- A value of Boolean type which can be used to control the output of debugging information. When this parameter is not specified, no debugging information is output.
- A value of String type which informs the Voyager daemon on which the virtual processor is created about where to look for missing classes. On the specified computer, the CLASSPATH environment variable is used to find the appropriate classes and load them. The string must contain a valid http address. When this parameter is not specified, localhost is assumed as the source for missing classes.

Both parameters are optional and can be arbitrarily combined. The Boolean value must, however, be specified before the string value.

```
// create a new virtual processor with all parameters
DjProcessor p = new DjProcessor("//localhost:8000", true, "http://www.dejay.org/");
```

The newly created virtual processor is located on the local computer on port 8000 and is set to output debugging information. Missing classes are automatically searched by Voyager on the www.dejay.org Web server.

The virtual processor possesses some more methods that can be used to access local information.

- void printAddress(String) displays the current address of the specified virtual processor on the console of the computer on which the virtual processor is located. The local name of the remote virtual processor is specified as the parameter.
- String getAddress() returns the current address of the virtual processor. The return string contains an address of the form tcp://<computer_name>:<port_number>.
- void printStorage() supplies a string representation of the references contained in the virtual processor, that is, a list of all objects that belong to this processor. The output is shown on the console of the computer on which the virtual processor is located.

The possibilities of moving a virtual processor from one computer to another, of calling already existing objects, and of making a virtual processor persistent are described in detail in Sections 15.4, 15.5, and 15.6. First, however, we will discuss creation and use of remote objects.

15.3 Remote objects

In Dejay, objects can be created either locally or remotely. The creation of a local object is carried out exactly as in Java by means of the new operator. The new operator is equally used for the remote creation of a new object, although on another type. For the creation of an object of type A, the type is used with the prefix Dj, thus resulting in DjA. All constructors of A are also available for DjA, and the parameters of these constructors remain the same, except for the addition of a parameter used to specify in which virtual processor the object is to be created.

```
DjA a1 = new DjA ( <Parameter1, ..., ParameterN,> DjProcessor );
```

The result is a remote reference to the newly created remote object. The mechanism of remote references is implemented with the aid of proxies so that, precisely speaking, one does not get a remote reference, but a local reference to an automatically generated proxy which provides the functionality of remote usage. In Dejay this mechanism is hidden as far as possible, giving the programmer the feeling of actually handling remote references. Only at a few places these proxies emerge and require a different treatment than true references. An example is the comparison of references. In the comparison of remote references, for example

Comparison operations

```
DjA a2 = a1;
if (a1 == a2) ...
```

it is therefore checked whether both references locally point to the same proxy, not whether they point to the same remote object. As this check too can be useful, it has been kept. To verify the *equality* of contents of two different remote objects, the equals() method has been overloaded in order to act remotely. For a test of whether two remote references point to *the same* remote object, the isRemoteIdentical() method is available:

```
if ( a1.isRemoteIdentical(a2) ) ...
```

To obtain two different references to the same remote object, that is, two different proxies and not two local references to one proxy, a further constructor exists (the copy constructor) which, as a parameter, contains a remote reference to an object.

Copy constructor

```
DjA a2 = new DjA ( a1 );
```

Once remote objects have been created, they can be used. The examples of the previous section have already shown the first simple calls of methods in local and remote objects. There is no difference between the call of sayHello() in the local and the remote object, neither in the call syntax nor in the output. Only the place of the output is different.

Remote calls

```
Hello hello_local = new Hello();
hello_local.sayHello( "Toby" );

DjHello hello_remote = new DjHello(p1);
hello_remote.sayHello( "Thorsten" );
```

Parameter passing

Parameters too can be passed as usual in the method calls. When a local reference to a parameter is specified, the parameter is copied into the address space of the remote object. Existing methods need not be modified, so that for example all objects and their methods of the JDK or of existing projects can simply be used without having to change or to recompile them. When a remote reference is passed, the parameter is accessed remotely. It is, however, not possible to obtain a remote reference to a local object.

Return values

The return value of a remote call is, if possible, supplied as a remote reference to the remote result. This functions if and only if the remote type for the return value exists and the corresponding code can be reached by the surrounding virtual processor. The remote type, for example DjA for the A class, is generated by the dejayc compiler. The remote type can also be generated for a class that is present in byte code, so that the class definition need not be available as source code in order to be used remotely. When the virtual processor finds the remote type, it returns a remote reference to the result object.

If no corresponding proxy class exists, a copy of the result object is returned. This is possible if all affected classes are serializable, which is the case for practically all standard classes. Thus, for example, for a method that returns a string, a copy of the string is returned which can then be processed locally on the caller's side. User-defined classes too should always be serializable, which can be achieved by adding implements java.io.Serializable to the definition.

Creating local copies

Although it is usually desirable to obtain a remote reference to an object, it will sometimes become necessary to create a local copy of that object. For this purpose, a getCopy() method exists for each remote reference, which does just this.

```
// creating a local copy of a remote object
DjA a_remote = new DjA(p1);
A a_local_copy = a_remote.getCopy();
```

Call semantics

Dejay differentiates between three kinds of call semantics: synchronous, asynchronous, and one-way calls. With synchronous calls, the calling object waits until the called object has returned the result, as is always the case with local calls. With asynchronous calls, the calling object only waits for an acknowledgement that the call has arrived at the called object. Subsequently, the control flow returns, and the program continues to run. When the result of the call is needed, that is, when methods are called in this object, to read the results, for example, a check is made as to whether the result is already present or not. If the result has not arrived at this point in time, the calling process stops and waits, in the blocking manner. This kind of semantics is known as "wait by necessity".

Wait by necessity

With one-way calls, the call is issued without waiting for an acknowledgement or a result. Therefore, this kind of call is only sensible when no return value is expected. The calling object completely ignores the further processing of the call. In particular, this also applies to the case that the call could not be properly forwarded, for example because of network problems. Therefore, this is also known as "fire and forget" semantics. In return, no waiting times are created for the calling object. Thus, although this kind of call is not too reliable, it is very fast and can be very useful in some cases.

Fire and forget

The call semantics of a method call can be specified by means of an additional parameter. By default, Dejay uses synchronous calls which therefore need not be labeled any further. For asynchronous or one-way calls, a constant from the Dejay class is specified as additional parameter. Such a constant also exists for the synchronous call, but need not be specified.

```
DjA a = new DjA("lin:8000");

// synchronous call
B b1 = a.method1( 42 );
```

```
if (b1 instanceOf DjB)
  DjB b2 = (DjB) b1;

// asynchronous call
DjB b3 = a.method1( 42, Dejay.ASYNC );

// one-way call
a.method1( 42, Dejay.ONEWAY );
```

Concurrent execution

Asynchronous and one-way calls cause concurrent execution. Thus, with asynchronous method calls, the result can be requested before it is actually ready. Normally, at the first use of the result, waiting takes place with blocking. However, there are mechanisms that allow a more flexible and controlled reaction to this situation. For this purpose, the result of an asynchronous call must be returned as a remote reference. This makes it possible to inquire about the presence of the result, which is known as *polling*, or to wait at a defined place without using the result itself. For this purpose, the remote reference types provide the methods isAvailable() and waitForResult(). isAvailable() returns **true** if the result is present, **false** otherwise. Thus it can be dynamically decided whether the result is to be processed or something else should be processed during the waiting time. With waitForResult() it is possible to wait explicitly for the result. It always returns **true**, but blocks until the result is available. The following two examples are equivalent in their behavior. In both of them, an asynchronous remote call is issued, and the result is waited for. While the first example is very easy to write, the second one allows the control flow to be handled in a much more flexible way.

```
// example for wait by necessity
DjB remote_result = a.method1( 42, Dejay.ASYNC);
remote_result.method2();

// example for polling and explicit waiting
DjB remote_result = a.method1( 42, Dejay.ASYNC);
```

```
if ( remote_result.isAvailable() ) {
  remote_result.method2();
} else {
  remote_result.waitForResult();
  remote_result.method2();
}
```

Different virtual processors are concurrent with respect to each other, as each virtual processor possesses its own control flow. Use of several virtual processors allows things to be executed concurrently or in parallel. Asynchronous calls make use of this possibility. This means that Dejay makes concurrency usable in a very simple way. From the point of view of the Dejay program, it does not matter whether this is only apparent concurrency or true parallelism.

15.4 Migration

The previous section has shown how in Dejay remote objects can be created and called and concurrency expressed with the aid of virtual processors. This is sufficient to allow distributed applications to be programmed in a very simple way. Until now, we had assumed that remote objects and virtual processors are created in a specific location and remain there during the whole runtime of a program. In distributed systems, however, it is often desirable that objects change their location. This is known as object migration – we have already encountered it in the sections on Voyager and Emerald. However, in both approaches problems occurred that were chiefly due to the granularity of migration.

In Dejay, the unit of migration is the virtual processor. This means that a virtual processor can be migrated, taking with it all objects it contains. Thus, all local references to the objects contained in it remain valid. And remote references too retain their validity, as we will see.

To initiate a migration, a moveTo() method is available for remote reference types. It can either be called in a virtual processor or in any (remotely referenced) object inside it. In both cases the entire virtual processor moves with all contained objects. The moveTo()method exists in several versions that can be called with different parameters.

- moveTo(String) causes a move to the address and port number specified in the parameter. The address must contain a valid IP address or a valid logical computer name. A Voyager daemon must already be running under the specified address.
- moveTo(DjProcessor) causes a move to the address under which the specified virtual processor can be reached.
- moveTo(DjObject) causes a move to the address under which the virtual processor that contains the specified object can be reached.

This results in a number of alternatives to achieve the same effect, as shown in the following examples. We assume that a Voyager daemon each has been started on the local computer (ports 7000 and 8000) and on the sun computer (ports 8000 and 9000).

```
// different alternatives for calling moveTo()
DjProcessor p1 = new DjProcessor( "//localhost:8000" );
DjProcessor p2 = new DjProcessor( "tcp://sun.uni-hamburg.de:7000" );
DjHello hello1 = new DjHello( p1 );
DjHello hello2 = new DjHello( p2 );

// move p1 from port 8000 to port 9000
p1.moveTo( "//localhost:9000" );

// move p2 from port 7000 to port 8000
hello2.moveTo( "tcp://sun.uni-hamburg.de:8000" );

// move p1 to tcp://sun.uni-hamburg.de:8000
hello1.moveTo( p2 );
```

```
// move p2 from tcp://sun.uni-hamburg.de to localhost
p2.moveTo( "//localhost:8000" );

// move p1 from tcp://sun.uni-hamburg.de to localhost
hello1.moveTo( hello2 );
```

Individual objects cannot be migrated. Instead, a local copy of a remote object can be made, in which not only the individual object, but its transitive shell is copied. Subsequently, the copied objects have an identity of their own, and references to the original still point to the original. Copying of objects can be very sensible to avoid expensive remote calls, in particular if these objects are only to be accessed in reading.

```
Hello copy_of_hello1 = hello1.getCopy();
```

15.5 Name service

In most communication mechanisms, such as RMI or CORBA, it is not possible to create objects remotely. Instead, objects must first be created on a remote computer, then registered through an appropriate mechanism, and finally contacted. A frequently used mechanism for this purpose is the name service. In Dejay, not only remote creation is possible, but also the connection to existing objects. Dejay too provides a name service, for which different implementations are possible, for example, a network-wide name service as made possible by CORBA or Jini, or a computer-related service which can only manage objects on one computer (or for one virtual machine) as in RMI and Voyager.

Two-level name service

The variation currently implemented in Dejay has two levels. Since objects in Dejay are always surrounded by a virtual processor, the first level of the name service manages only virtual processors, currently limited to those virtual processors that run on a Voyager daemon. A virtual processor can thus be given a name under which it can be registered and, when required, deregistered with the local name service. Both registration and deregistration can be carried out remotely. For registering both local and remote references to a virtual processor, the registerByName() method is available.

Inside a virtual processor we find a second level of the name service through which the contained objects can be internally bound to a name. This is also carried out by means of a registerByName() method. Thus, a registration might look as follows:

```
DjProcessor p1 = new DjProcessor("lin:8000");
DjA a1 = new DjA(p1);
a1.registerByName("DemoA");
p1.registerByName("DemoProcessor");
```

Now, another computer can make use of the name service to access this virtual processor and, subsequently, the object A. For this purpose, the Dejay class provides the static method getProcessorByName(), while the virtual processor provides the method getObjectByName().

```
DjProcessor q1 = Dejay.getProcessorByName("DemoProcessor","lin:8000");
DjA a2 = (DjA) q1.getObjectByName("DemoA");
```

The references a1 and a2 now point from different computers to the same object of class A on the lin:8000 computer.

15.6 Persistence

In Dejay, objects can be made persistent in a simple way. As with migration, the whole virtual processor is made persistent together with all objects that are contained in it. Thus local references continue to remain valid, as all locally referenced objects are always located together in memory or in persistent storage. However, remote references too retain their validity. When a remotely referenced object is not present in memory, but has been made persistent, it is automatically reactivated. Both the storage mechanism and the activation mechanism used in Dejay are based on Voyager.

To make a virtual processor persistent, it must be prepared and assigned a name (memento) and the name of a database. This happens already at creation time by a special constructor. Subsequently, its contents can be stored in the database by calling the persist() method. The isPersistable() method can be used to verify whether a virtual processor has been appropriately created or prepared.

```
DjProcessor p1 = new DjProcessor("PersistProc","ProcessorDB","lin:8000");
DjA a1 = new DjA();
if ( p1.isPersistable ) {
  p1.persist();
  p1.flush();
}
```

After having been made persistent, the processor remains in memory, and its objects can continue to be accessed. Frequently, however, persistence is employed to free the memory from rarely needed objects. With the flush() method, the virtual processor can be released for automatic garbage collection so that the memory occupied by it can be freed.

When a remote object now accesses an object in a virtual processor treated in this way, the object is either still in memory and can be used directly, or it is no longer in memory but in the database; then it is automatically reactivated and available again after a short delay. In the above example, this means that the reference a1 can be reused at any point in time, even when the corresponding object is no longer present in memory. This is even possible when the virtual machine or even the computer have been shut down in the meantime, and only

Backplane

the *virtual backplane* has been set up again. However, in order to re-enable activation, mere starting of the Voyager daemon is not sufficient: the Backplane class must be started, instead.

Another alternative resembles the name service. After having been made persistent, the remote references to a virtual processor can be discarded. At a later time, the virtual processor can be called back from the database by name, using the getProcessorFromDB() method of the Dejay class. Objects inside the virtual processor can then be reached again via the standard internal name service.

```
DjProcessor q1 = Dejay.getProcessorFromDB("PersistProc","ProcessorDB","lin:8000");
```

15.7 Exception handling

In the handling of exceptions, Dejay differentiates between two kinds of exception. On the one hand, there are those defined in the interface of an object and can regularly be generated or "thrown" by an object. Obviously, these exceptions must also be intercepted and handled in the distributed case. With method calls to remote objects they must be caught, exactly as with local calls, by a corresponding try-catch block. Also some methods that are only made available through remote referencing, such as the moveTo() method, can create exceptions, in accordance with the definition of their interface in the remote type.

On the other hand, there are exceptions that are not defined in the interface of the object, but may emerge only through remote access, for example a network fault. Such errors can be, but do not need to be, handled. In applications that must show a high robustness, such exceptions can be explicitly reacted to. However, in cases where one can well enough rely on the network, or where the increased cost for exception handling cannot be justified, this is not mandatory. This makes learning Dejay and creating small sample applications much easier than for example RMI, where every remote call must be surrounded by a try-catch block.

The area of exception handling is still under development, so that the final set of exceptions cannot yet be given. Until now, the following additional exceptions have been defined – by way of example, so to speak – in Dejay:

- StartProgramFailedException: execution of the main() method or creation of the first implicit virtual processor have failed.

- ConstructProcessorFailedException: the creation of a virtual processor has failed.

- NoRemoteReferenceClassException: in an asynchronous call the result could not be returned as a remote reference, for example because the Dj type was not available.

15.8 The dejayc compiler

Dejay has its own compiler called dejayc which is used very much like the javac compiler of the JDK. It translates Dejay classes from a file that bears the name of the class it contains plus the extension .dj into Java byte code. During this process it creates two Java classes which are then automatically translated further into byte code. By means of directives, the compiler can also be set to exclusively generate Java code or to keep this code for later use. By default, however, it will create the two classes Hello.class and DjHello.classfrom the file Hello.dj.

```
lin> dejayc Hello.dj
lin| Hello.class
lin| DjHello.class
```

The class Hello.class corresponds to the class of which a local instance is created. The class DjHello.class corresponds to a proxy that enables remote access to an object. When a class is to use the particular features of Dejay, such as migration and asynchronous calls, it must be compiled in this way in order to function appropriately. It is also possible to integrate Java classes into Dejay, for example the classes of the JDK. They can even be given remote references, for example as parameters in a method call, and thus use part of Dejay's functionality. Method calls are then executed remotely without preparing the Java class explicitly for distribution. However, they cannot use migration or asynchronous method calls, and access to arrays of data is not possible.

It is also possible to create remote references to existing Java classes. The Dejay compiler is capable of creating the proxy class only from the .class file of a Java class, it need not even be present in source code. One can, for example, create a proxy of the java.util.Vector class and use it to create, access, and migrate vectors remotely.

```
lin> dejayc java.util.Vector.class
lin| DjVector.class
```

There is, however, a restriction: this is not possible with classes that cannot be derived any further (final), such as the java.lang. String class.

15.9 Program start

The generated classes can subsequently be executed by any common Java interpreter. However, the class that contains the main() method to be run must have also been compiled with dejayc. The directive -l can be used to specify that this class is only to be used locally and not referenced remotely.

```
lin> dejayc -l Startup.dj
lin> java Startup
```

The main() method is modified by the Dejay compiler in such a way that, automatically, a Voyager daemon is started and a virtual processor is created in it, which makes the creation of the first virtual processor transparent to the programmer. The -p <port> parameter can be used to specify the port of this Voyager daemon.

```
lin> java Startup -p 8000
```

When the -p parameter is not specified, the Voyager daemon is started on Port 7042. Obviously, additional parameters can be passed which are then read and processed by the main() method, but this parameter must be the first one if specified.

For a distributed execution of the program, Voyager daemons must be started on the appropriate ports on all computers involved. This can be done either from within a Dejay program or from the command line. The following command can be used to start the Voyager daemon from the command line.

```
sun> voyager 8000
```

Voyager makes use of the CLASSPATH environment variable on the local computer to find class code. As in distributed applications it may be sensible not to distribute the source code of the classes across all computers involved, there is a possibility of specifying additional sources for the search for classes. These sources can be directories on the local computer as well as remote computers. Remote computers must, however, be accessible via http and, for example, run a Web server or another Voyager daemon on the appropriate port. In the following example, the search alternatives for the Voyager daemon are extended with the local directory /home/my-code and the remote computer lin.

```
sun> voyager 8000 -c file:///home/my-code/ -c http://lin:9000
```

15.10 Limitations

The previous sections have dealt with the extensions of Java. In most cases, the authors of Dejay have succeeded in keeping the handling as intuitive as possible and orienting the semantics towards what one would expect to see as a Java programmer. However, there are cases where this could not be achieved, for technical reasons or lack of time; furthermore Dejay has several limitations with respect to the normal use of Java. The following list cannot claim to be exhaustive, but tries to put together as many of the known peculiarities as possible.

- Many classes in Java's standard libraries cannot be derived any further (they are final), for example the String class. Since the mechanism used in Dejay to generate proxy classes is based on derivation from the local class, it cannot be employed for non-derivable classes. Accordingly, no remote references of these classes can be created. To circumvent this restriction, the use of wrapper classes becomes necessary. In this case, an instance of the real class (for example String) is managed by aggregation in a surrounding class (for example, an Address class). The surrounding class emulates the interface of the real class or provides a similar interface. From outside, only the surrounding class with its public interface can be used. A method call can be forwarded by the surrounding class to the corresponding method call of the real class. In the distributed program, instances of the wrapper class are used for which now remote references (for example DjAddress can be created.

- Equally, methods declared as final are not contained in the interface of a proxy class.
- Variables of an object cannot be accessed directly because the proxy class provides only methods for remote access. However, direct access to variables is strongly discouraged anyway.
- The scope of static variables is the virtual machine. They are not migrated. Thus, after a migration, access to such static variables may result in different values being output.
- The methods of the Object class are all overridden by a proxy class and forwarded to the remote object. This is one of the reasons they look like remote references; however, the usual semantics of these classes has changed.
- Java enables concurrency by splitting off threads from the real control flow. In Dejay, concurrency is usually replaced with virtual processors. For reasons of compatibility with Java and out of practical considerations (programming of user interfaces in Java, for example, makes extensive use of threads) use of the Thread class continues to be possible in Dejay as well. However, the use of

threads in a virtual processor leads to the fact that several control flows exist in this virtual processor. Sequential processing of incoming calls is therefore no longer guaranteed. Problems occur with migration: migration of a virtual processor leads to different behavior, depending on whether the virtual processor is moved to another computer or physical processor or not. When the virtual processor stays on the same computer, the connection to the split-off control flow is maintained. When, on the other hand, the virtual processor changes over to another computer, the thread object too changes computer, but the original thread stays on the old computer. The connection with it is lost. Therefore, migration of virtual processors that contain threads should be avoided.

- With the introduction of JDK 1.1, the use of inner and local classes was defined for Java. These special classes are currently not handled adequately in Dejay.

- Synchronization has been dealt with in Dejay only to a limited extent. The existing synchronization mechanisms are based on those of Java so that, for example, the keyword synchronized acts on the proxy and not on the remote object. It is planned to make synchronization act on the remote object as well.

- In the case that an object is only referenced locally, but a remote reference is required, for example as a parameter in a remote method call, there is currently no possibility to obtain a remote reference because objects do not know their virtual processor. This can only be achieved remotely via the copy constructor for already remotely referenced objects.

- Proxy classes inherit from the class they are to remotely reference. This has many advantages, but also a couple of disadvantages. Thus, for example, at the call of new DjA, the constructor of a class A is executed twice, once during the creation of the object DjA which (locally) executes the constructor of its superclass, a second time during the remote creation. This causes for example output of the constructor to be displayed both locally and remotely. Output or creation of GUIs should therefore not take place in the constructor.

15.11 References

Dejay is freely available and can be downloaded together with the source code from the Web site http://www.dejay.org. There you will also find further documentation, implementation descriptions, examples, benchmarks, and much more. Dejay is a project that is still under development, and you are welcome to contribute actively to this development. Interested parties will find additional information under the specified URL or can participate in the developers' mailing list dejay-dev@egroups.com. People who would only like to be informed about news on Dejay can register with the mailing list dejay-news@egroups.com.

16 Examples

In this chapter, Dejay will be demonstrated with the aid of three concrete examples. All three are small enough to discuss them in this framework, but also big enough to show a practical relevance. The emphasis lies on highlighting the aspects of concurrency, distribution, and persistence, and to demonstrate the advantages of Dejay. All of the examples bear characteristics of all three aspects, but each example particularly focuses on one of these aspects.

One example each for distribution, ...

The first example presents a scenario that deals with negotiating and signing a contract. The parties involved are spatially separated from each other, so that the object of negotiation, the contract, needs once to be remotely accessed and once to be migrated. Here the special emphasis lies on distribution and migration.

... concurrency, ...

The second example is a typical case for concurrent calculations: the Mandelbrot set. The Mandelbrot set is a geometrical figure (a fractal) which is the result of a simple algorithm with special properties. The algorithm is very calculation-intensive, but is well suited for parallelization. This is implemented in the example by means of a distributed network (or cluster), so that concurrency is combined with distribution.

... and persistence.

The third example is intended to demonstrate the advantages of Dejay for the aspect of persistence. A personal appointment assistant is introduced which can manage appointments, addresses, and a task list. This can either be remotely accessed over a network, or it can be migrated. When it is not needed, it can be stored (made persistent) in a very easy way. When it is needed again, it can be reactivated, which will be our main concern in this example.

16.1 Distribution

Let us imagine a scenario where several parties want to reach an agreement on a specific project and seal it with a contract. The parties, which we will call partners for the purpose, are either unable or unwilling to meet personally, maybe because they live very far away from each other. Or they have already met and want to negotiate the final details from their offices. For this purpose they use a network which can be the Internet, an intranet, or an extranet, depending on the requirements and given conditions. As a coordinator who guides and checks the course of negotiation they nominate a notary. In our example, this notary (like all parties involved) is simulated by a program, but could operate fully automatically in the real world as well.

The notary

The notary should guide the course of negotiation and the conclusion of the contract; he is, so to speak, our principal actor. In the absence of a real or even only virtually existing world, the notary must first create the partners and the contract, which are each represented by one object. He assigns the partners to the contract and submits the contract to each of them for perusal, correction and, finally, the signature. To avoid inconsistencies, only one copy of the contract should exist. However, to accelerate the access to the contract object during elaboration, the contract is always moved to the partner who is currently allowed to view, correct, or sign it. Finally, the notary should check that all partners have signed the contract.

The partner

The partner has a name and a "home address", represented by a URL. Any further information is omitted for sake of simplicity. For the same reason, neither checking nor correcting of a contract will be demonstrated – we will only concentrate on the signature. The partner has one essential method, the one used for signing. Thus the notary can submit the contract to be signed. The partner will want to sign the contract only when the contract is at the same place (the same URL) as he himself. The reason for this might be that during the signature a password or a key is passed, and the partner will have a justified interest in not transmitting such confidential data over the network. It is therefore important that the partner checks whether the contract is present before signing it. If this is not the case, he tells the notary (via the return value false) that he does not want to sign the contract. The notary then moves the contract to the partner and calls the method again. Now the partner will sign.

The contract

The contract represents the central element of the example, at which remote access and migration will be demonstrated. It is created by the notary who can anytime access and move the contract via a remote reference. Also the partners involved can be reached from the contract via a remote reference.

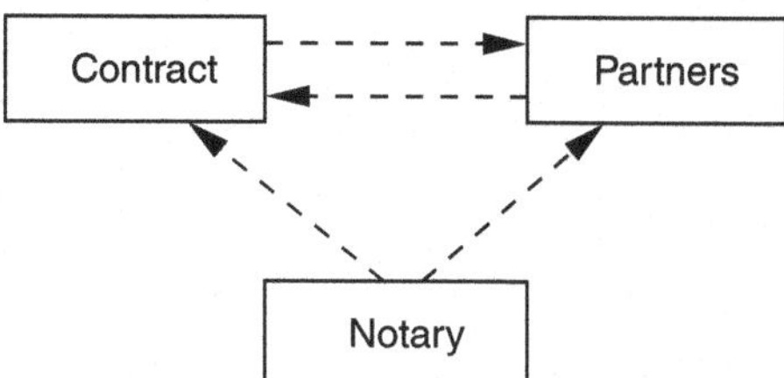

Figure 16.1
The classes of the contract scenario.

The contract

Now the individual classes will be presented in detail. We begin with the contract. The content of the contract is of no relevance and is therefore simply represented by the denominator string. The only other field is a vector, partnerList, in which the partners of the contract are stored. The partners are inserted into the contract by the notary, making use of the newPartner() method. The method iSign() is called by the partners when they want to sign the contract. Obviously, this method does not generate a signature in the sense of cryptography (the password is not used at all, the partner is identified by his name, ...) but, for our purposes, it is sufficient.

Signing the contract

The hasEverybodySigned() method can be used to check whether all of the partners have signed the contract. For this purpose, an Enumeration of all partners represented in the partner list is gone through, checking the hasSigned field for each of them. The loop stops when one partner has not signed and returns **false** as its return value. If, however, all partners have signed, the loop runs through to the end and returns **true**.

The most important feature of this method is that no complete partners are stored in the partner list, but remote references to these partners DjPartner. This means that the remote partners are accessed to determine the current value of hasSigned.

Remote reference to the partner

Last not least, a method called sendWord() is used to make the contract issue a message in order to find out its location during program execution.

```
public class Contract {

  public Vector partnerList;
  public String denominator;

  public Contract(String denominator) {
    this.denominator = denominator;
    partnerList = new Vector()
  }

  public void newPartner(DjPartner newPartner) {
    System.out.println("new Partner "+newPartner);
    partnerList.addElement(newPartner);
  }

  public void iSign(String signing, String password) {
    Partner nextPartner;
    for(Enumeration e = partnerList.elements(); e.hasMoreElements();) {
       nextPartner = (DjPartner)(e.nextElement());
       if(nextPartner.giveName().equals(signing)) {
         System.out.println(nextPartner.giveName() + " signs.");
         nextPartner.setHasSigned(true);
       }
    }
  }

  public boolean hasEverybodySigned() {
    DjPartner partner;
```

```
    System.out.println("Have all "+ partnerList.size() + " signed?");
    for(Enumeration e = partnerList.elements(); e.hasMoreElements();) {
      partner = (DjPartner)(e.nextElement());
      System.out.println("Check "+partner.giveName());
      if(!partner.giveHasSigned()) {
        System.out.println(partner.giveName() + " has not signed.");
        return false;
      } else {
        System.out.println(partner.giveName() + " has signed.");
      }
    }
    return true;
  }

  public void sendWord() {
    System.out.println("-------------- The contract "+denominator+" is here!");
  }
}
```

The partner

The partner has only three fields. The hasSigned field is by default set to false. Name and homeAddress are set by the constructor. For each of these fields there is a method to read its content. This is particularly important for remote access, because only methods can be remotely accessed, not the fields themselves. The all-important method of this class is sign(). Here, a contract passed as a parameter is to be signed. The contract is passed as a remote reference, so that the contract is accessible, but not necessarily local. Therefore, the address of the contract is determined by means of contract.getRemoteAddress(). Only when this address matches the home address is the contract signed. From the return value, the notary can see whether the contract has been signed or not and, if required, ask the partner once more to sign the contract. As with the contract, a sendWord() method can be used to display a message showing where the partner currently is.

sign()

```
public class Partner {

  public String name;
  public String homeAddress;
  public boolean hasSigned;

  public Partner(String name, String homeAddress) {
    this.name = name;
    this.homeAddress = homeAddress;
    this.hasSigned = false;
    System.out.println("I am " + name);
  }

  public String giveHomeAddress() {
    return homeAddress;
  }

  public String giveName() {
    return name;
  }

  public void setHasSigned(boolean hasSigned) {
    this.hasSigned = hasSigned;
  }

  public boolean giveHasSigned () {
    return hasSigned;
  }

  public boolean sign(DjContract contract) {
    String contractAddress = contract.getRemoteAddress();

    if(contractAddress.equals(homeAddress)) {
      // here comes the section where "confidential" data is transmitted
      contract.iSign(name, "myPassword");
      System.out.println("I sign the contract "+contract);
      return true;
```

```
    } else {
      System.out.println("The contract is not here, I do not sign it!");
      return false;
    }
  }

  public void sendWord() {
    System.out.println("———————— Hello, I am "+name+", I am here!");
  }
}
```

The notary

The notary is the central control instance of our example. We need it to test the functionality of the individual classes and methods. Since this example is mainly concerned with remote creation and mobility of objects, in this case the mobility of the contract, we will focus on this problem and only marginally comment on the remaining code.

Remote creation

First of all, three DjProcessors are created. On one of them, the contract is started, on the other two the partners are created who are then added to the contract. Now we want the partners to sign the contract. The sign(contract) method is called twice for each partner, since the first call will fail because the contract is not on the same computer. Then the contract is moved (or, more precisely, the DjProcessor in which the contract is located), and the method is called again. This time the partner will sign. After the move, the contract should send word, so we can see where it is (see program output). Finally, we can check whether all partners have signed the contract and terminate our test program.

```
public class Notary {

  public static void main(String args[]) {
    DjContract contract;
    DjPartner partner1;
    DjPartner partner2;
```

```
String address0 = "tcp://sun:8000";
String address1 = "tcp://lin:8000";
String address2 = "tcp://win:8000";

DjProcessor proc0 = null;
DjProcessor proc1 = null;
DjProcessor proc2 = null;
try {
  proc0 = new DjProcessor(address0);
  proc1 = new DjProcessor(address1);
  proc2 = new DjProcessor(address2);
} catch (ConstructProcessorFailedException e) {
  System.out.println("no processor!"+e);
}

// create the contract
contract = new DjContract("MS License agreement", proc0);

// create the partners
partner1 = new DjPartner("Toby",address1,proc1);
partner2 = new DjPartner("John",address2,proc2);

System.out.println("Partners are added.");
contract.newPartner(partner1);
contract.newPartner(partner2);
if (!(partner1.sign(contract))) {
  contract.moveTo(partner1);
  contract.sendWord();
  partner1.sign(contract);
}

//check whether partner1 has signed
System.out.println(partner1.giveHasSigned());

//same for partner2
if (!(partner2.sign(contract))) {
  contract.moveTo(partner2);
  contract.sendWord();
  partner2.sign(contract);
}
```

```
    System.out.println(partner2.giveHasSigned());

    contract.moveTo(address0);

    if (contract.hasEverybodySigned()) {
      System.out.println("OK!!!");
    } else {
      System.out.println("Not OK!!!");
    }
    System.exit(0);
  }
}
```

Program output

This program can now be compiled with the dejayc Dejay compiler. The generated code must be available to each computer involved or be downloadable from a code server as described in the previous chapter.

```
sun> dejayc Notary.dj Contract.dj Partner.dj
```

Building up the virtual backplane

To be able to run the program, we must first build up the underlying infrastructure, the *virtual backplane*, by starting a Voyager daemon on each of the computers involved, in our case sun, lin, and win.

```
sun> voyager 8000

lin> voyager 8000

win > voyager 8000
```

On the notary's computer, the Voyager daemon is started automatically, since the notary contains the main program and the Dejay compiler prepares main programs in this way. We start the notary on the sun computer. The following output lines are ordered by their sequence in time, it should be noted, however, that they appear on different computers.

```
sun> java Notary
sun| Address - main : tcp://sun.informatik.uni-hamburg.de:7042

lin| I am Toby

win| I am John

sun| Partners are added.
sun| new Partner Partner@80d3460
sun| new Partner Partner@80d25f3
```

On the sun computer, a Notary and a Contract have been created, each in their own virtual processor, while the two Partners have been created, again in one virtual processor each, on the lin and win computers. Figure 16.2 shows this scenario. The contract contains remote references to the two partners (not shown in the figure).

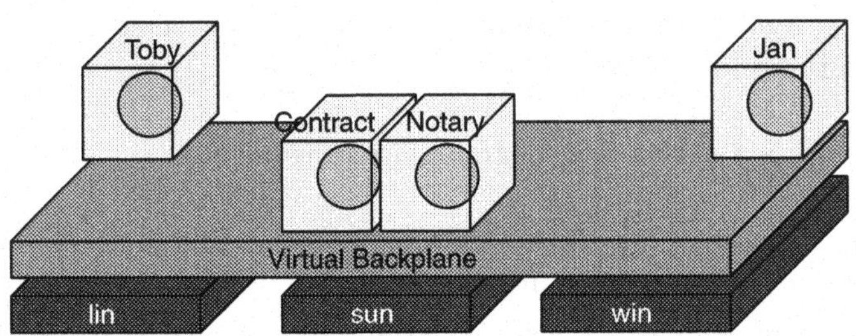

Figure 16.2
The scenario after initialization.

Toby is asked to sign the contract, but since the contract is not locally present, Toby declines. Consequently, the notary moves the contract. The corresponding output appears on the notary's console. Then the contract is with Toby, and he signs it. Finally, the notary checks whether Toby has actually signed, which leads to output at the notary's place. The current situation is shown in Figure 16.3.

```
lin| Contract is not here, I do not sign it!

sun| Previous address is tcp://sun.informatik.uni-hamburg.de:8080
sun| New address is tcp://lin.informatik.uni-hamburg.de:8000
```

```
lin| -------------- The contract MS license agreement is here!
lin| Toby signs.
lin| I sign the contract Contract@80d2264

sun| true
```

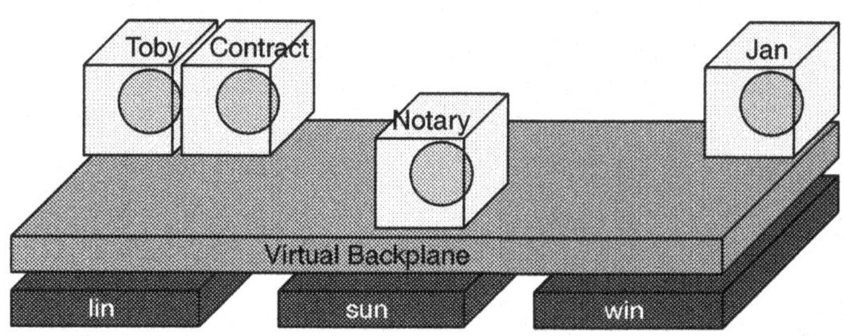

Figure 16.3 *The contract is moved to Toby.*

The same happens with John.

```
win| Contract is not here, I do not sign it!

sun| Previous address is tcp://lin.informatik.uni-hamburg.de:8000
sun| New address is tcp://win.informatik.uni-hamburg.de:9000

win| -------------- The contract MS license agreement is here!
win| John signs.
win| I sign the contract Contract@80d250d

sun| true
```

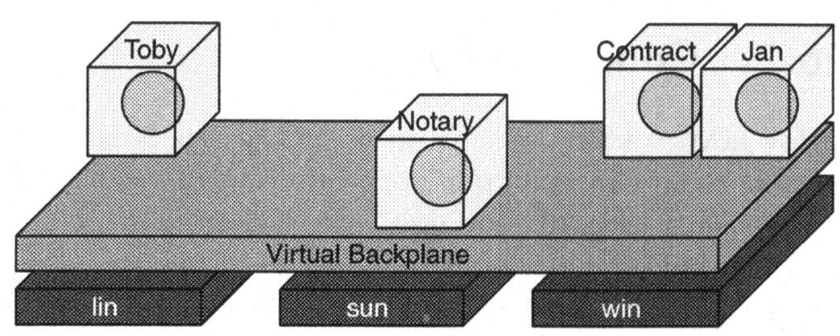

Figure 16.4 *The contract is moved to John.*

Subsequently, the notary fetches the contract back and checks whether all partners have signed, finding that everything is

OK. This check causes a remote access to the corresponding partners.

```
sun| Previous address is tcp://win.informatik.uni-hamburg.de:9000
sun| New address is tcp://sun.informatik.uni-hamburg.de:8080
sun| Have all 2 signed?
sun| Check Toby
sun| Toby has signed.
sun| Check John
sun| John has signed.
sun| OK!!!
```

What does this example show us? The migration of objects is very simple in Dejay, and remote references are maintained. The Contract has both its own, local objects (such as the partnerList as a vector or the denominator as a String object) and references to remote objects, namely the Partners. Each object is located in a virtual processor. When an object is told to move, the entire virtual processor is moved in which it is located, including all objects to which local references may exist, plus all objects that may have local references to the object to be moved. The problem of inconsistency of data no longer occurs. In our example this means that the contract, when it is moved, always carries its denominator string and the partnerList vector with it. The remote references to the partners are maintained even when the contract is migrated.

16.2 Concurrency

In the next example, we will focus on the aspect of concurrency in Dejay. An important application area for concurrency are problems which require great calculation efforts, but can be easily split up into partial problems. Then the partial problems can be calculated in parallel, on different computers or processors at the same time, and subsequently recombined. Examples include weather forecasts, physical simulation (for example, simulation of nuclear tests), or graphical algorithms (for example, animation of comics). One example that possesses these properties is the calculation of a fractal image: we are going to look at the so-called Mandelbrot set. The advantage of this problem is, on the one hand, that although the algorithm is very compact and easy to program, it creates a high demand on computing power; on the other hand, that in an appropriate interpretation, the result creates a – very well known – fascinating image. The algorithm is based on a recursive formula which is passed two parameters as starting values. For each calculation, the resulting value can either tend towards infinity (diverge) or approach a determined value (converge). To be able to decide whether the value diverges or converges, a variable number of recursions must be passed through. In the graphical display, the starting values (the two parts of a complex number) are used as coordinates and the depth of recursion is converted into a color value, so that an image is created. At the borders of the emerging figure, one can arbitrarily refine the calculation, that is, one can "zoom in" on the image to an arbitrary degree, making more and more spiral ornaments visible that resemble each other in a most surprising way. Further information on the fascinating subject of fractal images and their calculation can be found in [Peitgen *et al.* 1992]. The calculation of the image can be split into many individual problems which can be calculated individually and in a distributed fashion until finally the whole image can be put together. These calculations should be carried out by several servers which receive their tasks from a client. Furthermore it is possible to run several clients at the same time.

The Mandelbrot set

Program structure

The program code for this example, particularly for the graphical representation, is too voluminous to be printed in full. The complete version can be found on the Web server for this book. However, all essential parts, in particular the ones that are important for distribution and concurrency, will be shown. Basically, we need the following classes:

- a client (MandelbrotClient) which requests the calculations and reassembles them,
- the corresponding user interface (MandelbrotGUI),

- a calculation server (Server) that executes the algorithm,
- a task description of the partial tasks (Task),
- the result of the calculation (Result)

The user interface

Let us begin with the user interface (GUI). Figure 16.5 shows the GUI after the complete calculation. Its most important task is obviously the representation of the Mandelbrot set. However, it is also used to control the whole application. From here, the calculation is started, the course of the calculation shown, and the server managed. From here, new calculation servers can be added and deleted and – since with Dejay remote creation of objects is possible, which will be discussed later – newly created. Servers can also be moved, even during operation, which we will also consider at a later stage. The servers involved are displayed together with the information of how many parts of the whole image they have already calculated. In our screen shot there are two servers which have each calculated about half of the 128 partial images. The program code of the GUI is not shown, as it has nothing to do with the concurrency or the distribution. It is, however, available on the Web server for the book.

The client

The most important class in this example is the MandelbrotClient. This class is called to start the program, from here the GUI and the servers are created, and here is where concurrency control and remote communication take place. On the one hand, the MandelbrotClient takes care that the user interaction is put into practice, on the other hand, it manages the Servers and processes the Results. For this purpose, the MandelbrotClient uses two Hashtables. In the first one, myServers, all Servers are stored, with the key being a consecutive numbering. In the second one, myResults, the Results are stored, using the same key.

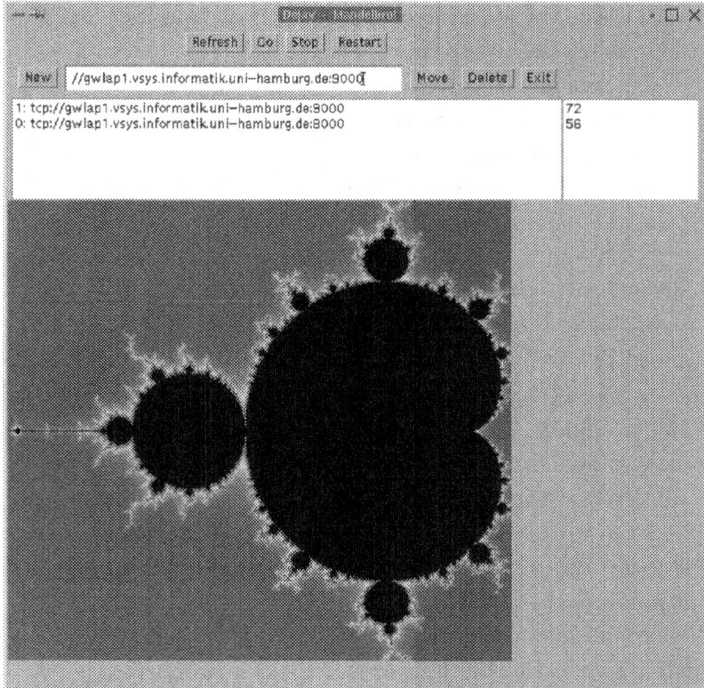

Figure 16.5
The MandelbrotGUI with the completely calculated image.

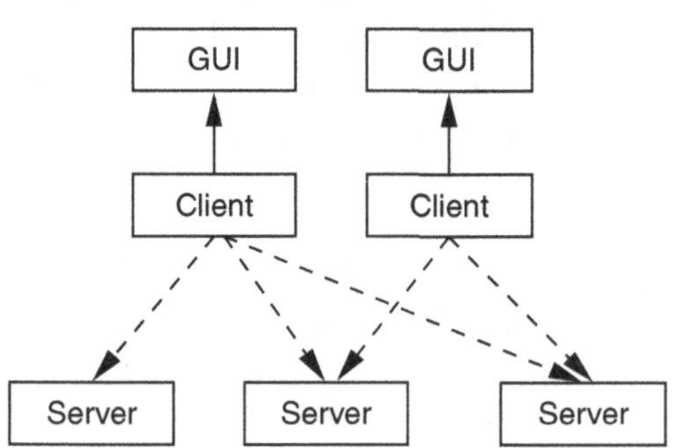

Figure 16.6
The client is the central class.

The MandelbrotClient uses the following essential methods to manage the Servers:

- newServer()
- moveServer()
- giveNewTask()

With these, the MandelbrotClient can create new Servers, move them, and assign them new tasks.

newServer()

To generate a server (remotely, mind you!), the MandelbrotGUI calls the newServer() method, passing it an address where a DjProcessor and, inside it, a Server are created. If a calculation is running and further rectangles are to be calculated, the new Server is immediately assigned a Task.

moveServer()

Although this section mainly deals with the aspect of concurrency, we also mention migration, which is implemented by means of the moveServer() method. This method is simply passed two strings, one to identify the server to be moved, the other one as the target address to which it is to be migrated. This method can be called during normal operation, and the server moves from one computer to the other between one calculation and the next.

giveNewTask()

Now to the calculation itself. The giveNewTask() method assigns a server a task. To allow the calculation to be executed in parallel, the call of the server must not block and wait for the result like a normal method call. Therefore, the decisive call (server.calculate()) is executed asynchronously, which is achieved by specifying the additional parameter Dejay.ASYNC. Subsequently, isAvailable() can be used to find out whether the result of the call is already available, or the result can explicitly be waited for with waitForResult(). The easiest solution is, however, to simply use the result when it is needed (wait by necessity). In this example, the result is simply put in a hash table and accessed only at a later stage.

run()

The client itself is implemented as a thread to be able to run in concurrency with the GUI. The run() method of the MandelbrotClient contains several loops, the first of which runs once through the list of servers and gives each of them something to do as long as rectangles, and thus tasks to be calculated, are still available. Since the giveNewTask() method sends an asynchronous call to the server, the loop can be cycled through without having to wait. The subsequent second loop cycles through the list of results as long as further results are expected, and uses isAvailable() to check whether they have been calculated and arrived at the MandelbrotClient.

The call result.isAvailable() returns false when an already issued asynchronous call (in giveNewTask()) has not yet been answered. Once the result has arrived, it is converted into a piece of graphics, and the entry in the Hashtable is deleted. When there are any rectangles left, the server is immediately passed a new Task. Whenever a task is assigned, the variable numb is incremented, and when a result has been processed, it is decremented. As soon as numb reaches zero, all tasks have been processed and the image is ready. Here are some excerpts of the code:

```
import java.util.*;
import dejay.base.*;

public class MandelbrotClient extends Thread {

   MandelbrotGUI gui;

   Hashtable myServers = new Hashtable();
   Hashtable myResults = new Hashtable();
   Hashtable myRResults = new Hashtable();

  public void newServer(String where) {
    DjProcessor processor = null;
    DjServer server = null;
    String key = "";
    if(where.length() > 0) {
      try {
        String address = "tcp://"+where;
         processor = new DjProcessor(address);
         server = new DjServer(processor);
        key = myServers.size() + "";
        myServers.put(key, server);
        if (myThread.isAlive()) {
          if (Rectangle.size() > 0)
            giveNewTask(key);
        }
      } catch (Exception e) {System.out.println(e);}
    }
  }
```

```
public void moveServer(String which, String whereto) {
  int position = which.indexOf(":");
  String numm = which.substring(0,position);
  DjServer server = (DjServer)myServers.get(numm);
  server.moveTo("tcp://"+whereto);
  System.out.println("Nr. "+numm+"moved to " + whereto + "...");
}

public void giveNewTask(Object key) {
  Result result;
  Rectangle rect = (Rectangle)(Rectangles.firstElement());
  Recangles.removeElementAt(0);
  DjServer server = (DjServer)myServers.get(key);
  Task task = new Task(rect, myZoom, xs, ys, myIterationDepth);
  result = server.calculate(task, Dejay.ASYNC);
  myResults.put(key, result);
}

public void run() {
  int numb = 0; //issued tasks
  int rectangles= Reactangles.size();;

  // first run (through the servers)
  for( Enumeration e = myServers.keys(); e.hasMoreElements(); ) {
    if (Rectangles.size() > 0) {
      Object key = e.nextElement();
      giveNewTask(key);
      numb++;
    }
  }

  // all further runs (through the results)
  do {
    for( Enumeration e = myRResults.keys(); e.hasMoreElements(); ) {
      Object key = e.nextElement();
      DjResult result = (DjResult) myResults.get(key);
      if(result.isAvailable()) {
        convert (result.getCopy());
```

```
            if(Rectangles.size() > 0) {
              giveNewTask(key);
              numb++;
            }
          gui.draw();
          numb--;
        }
      }
    }
}
```

The server

The Server is a rather simple object. The only relevant issue is the calculate() method, which is called by the client. It is passed a Task object as a parameter and returns an object of the Result type. This Result holds a SerialArray which contains a color value for each pixel of the calculated partial image. The code is not listed here as it does not show any peculiarities of Dejay, but can be written as if it was used locally.

16.2.1 Implementation techniques

This example is very well suited to compare different implementation techniques. It is nice and simple, but nevertheless requires a whole lot of communication. It has therefore been programmed and tested in several variations. In the following paragraphs we will (at least briefly) analyze the speed of execution on the one hand, and the complexity for the programmer on the other. The execution speed can easily be measured and objectively compared. Things are more difficult with regard to complexity. As an objective measure, we will use the length of the required code. Even if such numbers convey only a partial picture, they still give an impression of the result. We have tried to be as fair as possible and not cheat with devious implementations, omission of comments or empty lines. Specifically, the following communication mechanisms were considered:

- Sockets
- RMI
- Voyager (in two variations)
- Dejay

To achieve as fair a comparison as possible, the Dejay code has been taken over as directly as feasible into the socket, RMI and Voyager implementiation. The communication mechanism was used in the most commensurate fashion. In most variations, a thread needed to be added on the client's side to take on the asynchronous communication with one server each. In Dejay, this function is already made available by the asynchronous call and the "wait by necessity". Voyager too provides an asynchronous call through the Future concept. Therefore, the implementation of Voyager was programmed once with Futures and once similarly to the socket and RMI implementation.

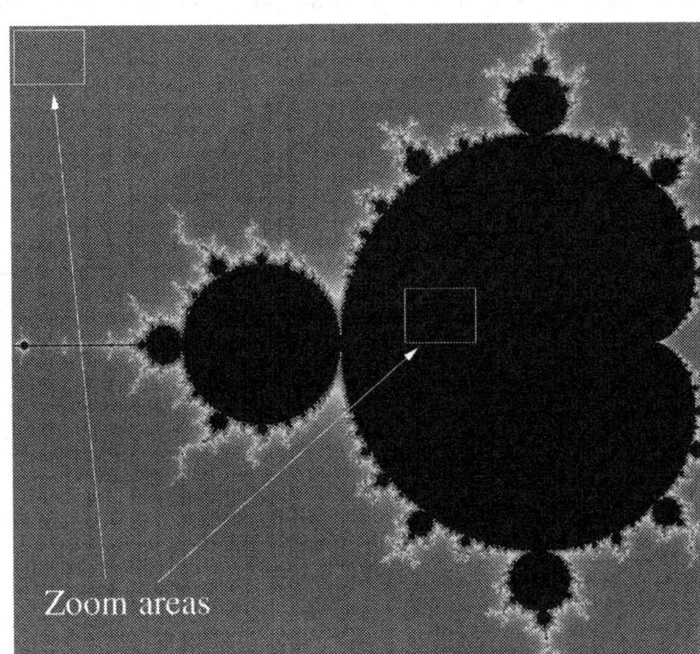

Figure 16.7
Different zoom areas.

First some remarks on execution speed. To look at different scenarios, a fractal image offers good opportunities. The calculation of the pixels of a fractal takes a different time depending on how often the recursion must be performed to reach a limit. By "zooming in" on different areas of the picture one can therefore obtain calculations of different degrees of complexity.

Different areas in a fractal image

If, for example, you zoom in on the border of the picture, you get a single-color red image which is, however, calculated very quickly (about 10 milliseconds) because only one iteration needs to be performed for each pixel. Thus this is a very communication-intensive scenario, nearly every 10 milliseconds a remote call takes place. If, instead, you zoom in on an area in the middle of the picture, the entire image is black. For each pixel, the recursion must be performed down to the maximum iteration depth (in this example, 401). Here the communication mechanisms have longer pauses of about one and a half seconds each. However, as with the "red" image, exactly 128 results are generated and transmitted.

Hardware used

The computers available for this test included three PCs with 333 MHz Intel Pentium II processor, connected with each other via a 10 MBit Ethernet with a switch, and running either the client or one of the servers. The result can be seen in Figure 16.8. It shows the minimum time in milliseconds the program needed with the respective mechanism to calculate one entire image, one red image, and one black image.

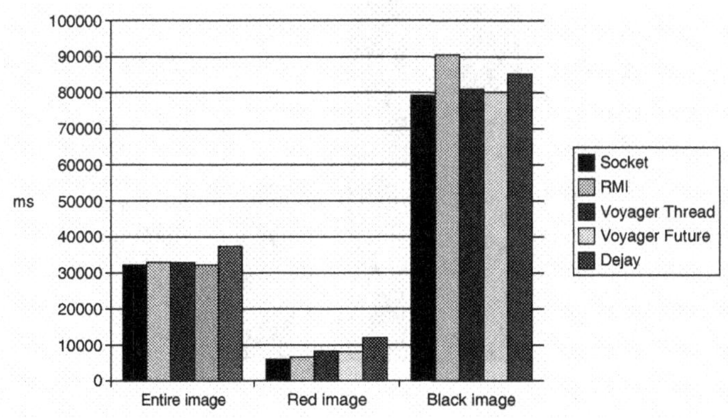

Figure 16.8
Calculation times with two remote servers.

The results show that, although Dejay is slower, it nevertheless achieves acceptable results. Dejay is based on Voyager and can therefore not be faster than a corresponding implementation in Voyager. And both Voyager and RMI use sockets for transmission, so that it can be expected that the socket implementation is the faster one. For communication-intensive scenarios (as in the red image) an implementation with sockets will pay off. However, in scenarios where a certain amount of calculation performance is unfolded on the servers, as is the case in most practical applications, the additional expenditure of time through Dejay is modest (under 15% for the entire image and 9% for the black one).

It is worth noting that the overhead of Dejay with respect to Voyager is more or less constant for all scenarios. This is due to the additional creation of objects, which is very time-consuming and has not yet been optimized. Here, Dejay can still be improved, so that it will on the whole draw nearer to the results of Voyager.

However, the aim of the design of Dejay was not to be particularly fast, but to simplify the programming of distributed systems. Let us therefore consider the effort for the programmer, expressed in lines of code. The client and server sides are analyzed separately.

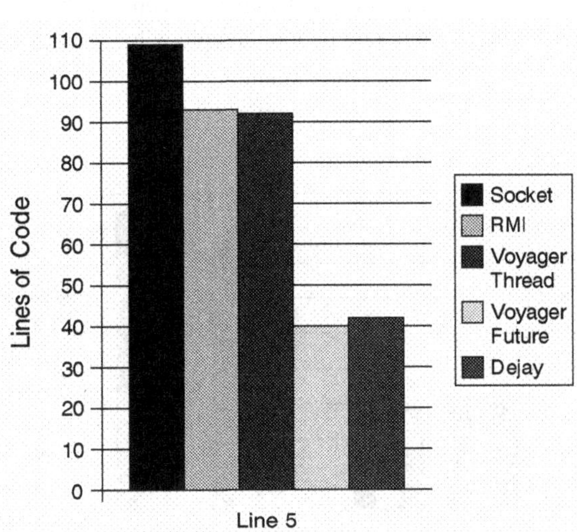

Figure 16.9 *Code length for the client.*

On the client's side, an additional effort is required for the simulation of asynchronous communication through an additional thread in three of the alternatives, namely with sockets, RMI, and the first Voyager variation. Here, a very big difference to Dejay can be seen, which lies between 120% and 160% more code in the relevant methods. The possibility of asynchronous communication, which is available in Voyager (Future variation) and Dejay, thus represents a substantial simplification. This Voyager variation and the Dejay program are more or less of the same length. However, Dejay is much easier in its use. For example, the asynchronous call is significantly easier in Dejay than in Voyager. In Voyager, a static method of the Future class is called, which is passed a reference to the object to be called, the method name as a string, and the parameters as an object array.

```
//Voyager
Result result = Future.invoke(server,"calculate", new Object[]{task});
```

In Dejay, instead, only one additional parameter is specified at the call of a remote object, while the asynchronous call otherwise corresponds to the normal syntax of a method call.

```
// Dejay
DjErgebnis result = server.calculate(task, Dejay.ASYNC);
```

A maybe more objective picture can be obtained on the server side. The code lengths of the communication-relevant parts of the different variations are shown in Figure 16.10. For the socket variation, a considerable effort must be invested for the conversion of the data into a byte stream, so that this variation definitely requires the largest amount of code. For the socket and RMI variations an instance must be created on the server side with which the client can subsequently establish a connection, as in these variations no remote creation of objects is possible. Furthermore, this object must be created by an

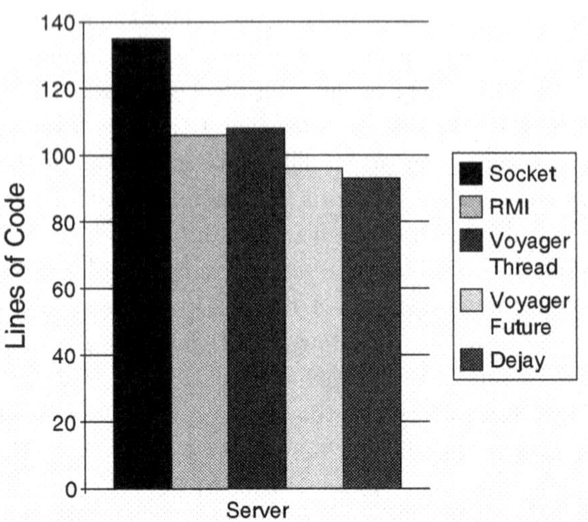

Figure 16.10
Code length of the server (communication-relevant parts.)

administrator, and a name service must be used, which additionally increases the complexity. The first Voyager variation has been kept synonymously to the RMI example, while in the second variation remote creation is used. Then the Dejay and the Voyager programs are of a comparable length. However, for the Voyager server an additional interface (IServer) needs to be created, which has not been taken into consideration in these figures. In Dejay, this step too can be omitted – the server must simply be compiled with the Dejay compiler.

16.3 Persistence

Our example for persistence is a personal appointment assistant. It is designed to manage addresses, appointments, and a task list, be usable from an arbitrary location inside a network and, when it is currently not needed, be persistent. The aim of this example is not to develop a particularly elegant application that can do everything, but to show the advantages of Dejay, especially under the aspect of persistence.

Fundamentally, the application consists of three different applications: an address book, an agenda, and a task list. It should be implemented in such a way that these parts can also be used independently from each other. However, the data they work with are connected in a natural way: a contact in the address book may, besides name, street, etc., also include a date, for example the birthday; a task in the task list may, besides the description, include a date (for example, a delivery date) and a contact; and, finally, an appointment should be able to include contacts or tasks besides its normal entries.

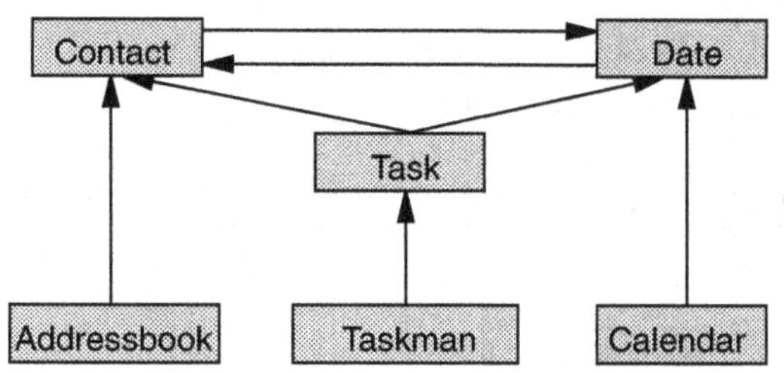

Figure 16.11
Classes of the appointment assistant.

Thus, besides a graphical user interface (GUI), the following classes are needed:

- AddressBook, stores and manages all contacts
- AppointmentCalendar, stores and manages all appointments
- TaskList, stores and manages all tasks
- Task
- Contact
- Appointment

This problem can certainly be solved with JDBC, however, a considerable effort needs to be made to overcome the *impedance mismatch* between relational databases and object-oriented programming. It would be much easier to employ an object-oriented database where the above objects can simply be stored and accessed again when they are needed. In object-oriented databases, a root object is defined for this purpose, and all objects reachable from this object are together made persistent.

The root object must therefore point to the AddressBook as well as the TaskList and the AppointmentCalendar to reach all objects.

Let us assume that the staff management wish to use this system, but require an extension. They would like to be able to take a contact from the address book – for example, an employee – and, from there, directly access the corresponding personnel file. Thus, the Contact class must be complemented with an additional reference to a Person object from which further objects depend, such as PersonnelFile and PersonnelAccounting, as shown in Figure 16.12.

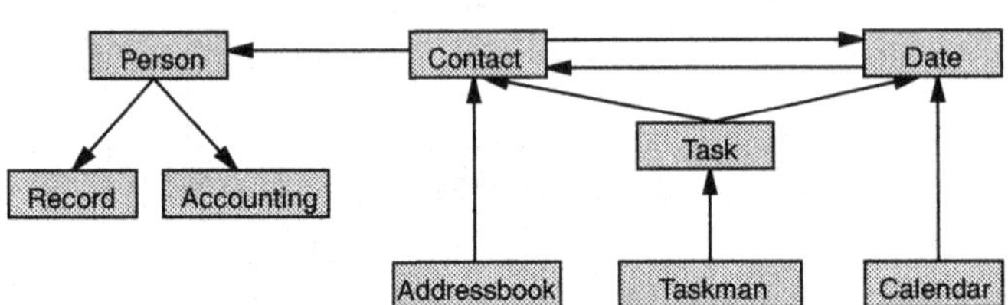

Figure 16.12 *Extension for use by the management.*

However, maybe the personnel data, which can reach a considerable size, is to be stored in a different database than the data of the appointment assistant. With Java and object-oriented databases, this can no longer be achieved in a simple way. It would, for example, be necessary to delete the references from Contact to Person before storing them, and to reintegrate them after loading.

In Dejay, instead, the objects of the appointment assistant and the personnel data are simply placed in two different virtual processors, as shown in Figure 16.13. References from Contact to Person are now remote references. The personnel records can be accessed whenever required, no matter whether they are stored in memory (possibly on a remote computer), or in a database from where they are automatically reactivated upon the call.

A possible graphical interface for this application is shown in Figure 16.14. It allows the user to create and delete new contacts, appointments, and tasks. To store the current state of the appointment assistant, the persist() method must be called in the surrounding processor; in the sample implementation

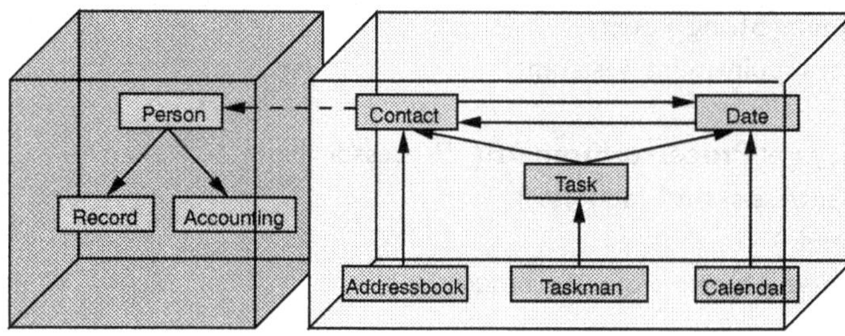

Figure 16.13
Distribution across different virtual processors in Dejay.

this happens at every termination of the program or upon pressing the "Store" button. The application is started from a further class named Assistant, listed below. First, an attempt is made to load an appointment assistant from a database. If this fails, a new appointment assistant is created and, initially without any additional objects, made persistent in the database. Then the GUI is started, which displays the existing data (if present) and offers the possibility to create new data.

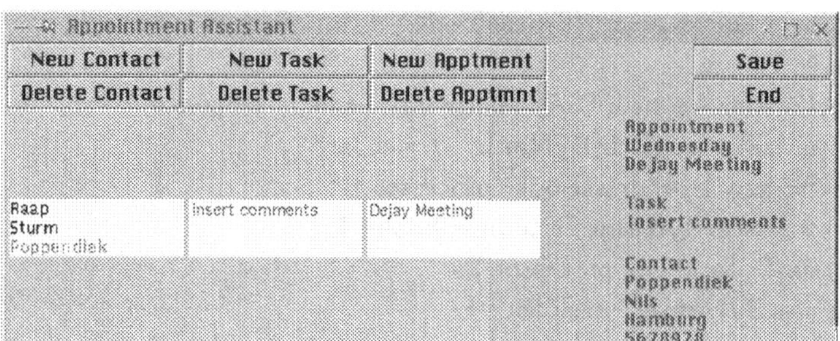

Figure 16.14
The appointment assistant's GUI.

```
public class Assistant implements java.io.Serializable {

  public DjAddressBook addressBook;
  public DjAppointmentCalendar appointmentCalendar;
  public DjTaskList taskList;
  public DjProcessor processor;

  GUI gui = new GUI(this);
```

```
public static void main(String[] args) {
  // load or create appointment assistant

  processor = Dejay.getProcessorFromDB("Processor.db",
      "AppointmentAssistant", address);
  if ( processor!=null ) {
    // fetch the three objects from the processor
    try {
     appointmentCalendar = (DjAppointmentCalendar)
         processor.getObjectByName("calendar");
     addressBook = (DjAddressBook)
         processor.getObjectByName("address book");
     taskList = (DjTaskList) processor.getObjectByName("task list");
    } catch (Exception e) {}
  } else {
    System.out.println("Nothing found in database. Creating a new appointment
        assistant.");

    processor = new DjProcessor("Processor.db", "AppoinmentAssistant",
        address);
    appointmentCalendar = new DjAppointmentCalendar( processor );
    appointmentCalendar.registerByName( "calendar" );
    addressBook = new DjAddressBook( processor );
    addressBook.registerByName( "address book" );
    taskList = new DjTaskList( processor );
    taskList.registerByName( "task list" );

    // first of all make persistent
    processor.persist();

    gui = new GUI( this );
    gui.pack();
    gui.show();
  }
 }
}
```

16.4 References

The code for this example and for additional examples can be obtained via the Web site for this book (see Preface) or via http://www.dejay.org. There you can also find the different variations of the Mandelbrot set. Basis for the Mandelbrot program has been a programming example by Matthias Günter of Bern University, which can be found on the Internet under http://iamexwiwww.unibe.ch/studenten/mguenter/ex/Prozess/Apfel/YAMB.html. In his implementation, the communication between client and server is based on Java sockets.

Appendix A
The chat interface

In several chapters of this book a chat system was presented. Every time, the same graphical user interface has been used. To avoid redundancy, this class is discussed here for all these examples together.

Typically, a chat interface has a relatively large text output field in which the text of the chat can be output and followed, and a text input line in which the user can enter text and send it to the chat. In the following program, a very simple interface for the examples is created with the aid of the Java AWT.

```
import java.awt.*;

public class ChatFrame extends Frame {

  protected TextArea output;
  protected TextField input;

  public ChatFrame (String title){
    super (title);

    setLayout (new BorderLayout ());
    add ("Center", output = new TextArea ());
    output.setEditable (false);
    add ("South", input = new TextField ());

    pack ();
    show ();
    input.requestFocus();
  }
```

```
   public static void main (String args[]) {
      new ChatFrame("Chat");
   }
}
```

When called through the command line via java ChatFrame or from within a program via ChatFrame gui = new ChatFrame("Chat");, this creates the following graphical interface:

Figure A.1 *Graphical chat interface.*

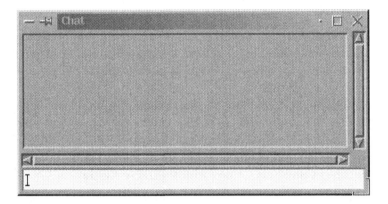

The line at the bottom is used to enter text. This is forwarded to a chat program and appears both in this window and in the upper text field of all other parties involved in the chat. This allows a text-based "conversation" with other people to take place, which is commonly called a chat.

To integrate this interface into a chat program, the program must intercept two events that are created by this interface. This is done by means of EventListeners. These are implemented in Swing, Java's graphical library, via inner classes. Inner classes are classes which are defined inside another class and are valid only in the context of the outer class. This inner class can be passed as an argument to methods such as addKeyListener() or addWindowListener() and is thus registered as EventListener.

The two events that occur in this interface are, first, the input of a line of text in the bottom text field, which is triggered by pressing the Enter key, and second, the closure of the window which is triggered, for example, by a mouse click on the X in the menu bar. The application must react to the first event, and should react to the second one. The AWT provides an event mechanism for this purpose. An application registers an EventListener for a specific type of event with the system, which is then called upon occurrence of this event.

For the "key has been pressed" event, a KeyAdapter exists, which can be appropriately extended by the programmer. As the input of a chat message is terminated by pressing the Enter key, this is used here and implemented as follows: During creation of this object, a reference to the client and to the GUI is passed. The EnterListener needs these to call the sentTextToChat() method at the ChatClient, and to be able to update the GUI. Both are carried out in the keyPressed()method, which is inherited and overridden by the KeyAdapter and called by the system upon pressing a key.

```
import java.awt.event.*;

public class EnterListener extends KeyAdapter {

   ChatClient client;
   ChatFrame gui;

   public EnterListener (ChatClient client, ChatFrame gui) {
      this.client = client;
      this.gui = gui;
   }

   public void keyPressed(KeyEvent e) {
      if (e.getKeyCode()==KeyEvent.VK_ENTER) {
         client.sendTextToChat(gui.input.getText());
         gui.input.setText("");
      }
   }
}
```

Similarly, when a window is closed, the windowClosing method of the WindowAdapter class is called. This is overridden in an appropriate way, so that the ChatClient can de-register properly from the chat system before the application is closed.

```
import java.awt.event.*;

public class ExitListener extends WindowAdapter {

  ChatClient client;

  public ExitListener(ChatClient client) {
    this.client = client;
  }

  public void windowClosing(WindowEvent e) {
    client.disconnect();
    System.exit(0);
  }
}
```

Appendix B
The BulletinBoard interface

In the chapters on persistence, an electronic bulletin board is used as an example. This example is much better suited to explain a persistence mechanism than a chat system, where usually no storage is required. On an electronic bulletin board, messages can be left, and then retrieved and read at any moment in time. In this example, such messages, containing a title and a text body, and referring to a specific subject area, are to be created and called. This requires a slightly more complex graphical interface, which for our purposes has been kept as simple as possible, as the focus of this book is not GUI programming, but concurrency, distribution, and persistence.

The main window of this application is generated and managed by the BulletinBoardFrame class and shown in Figure B.1. The construction of the GUI is chiefly carried out in the initGUI()method. It is subdivided into one output and one input area. The output area consists of three parts which are managed by means of a BoarderLayout. The upper area holds a subject selection list, the center part shows the titles of the messages concerning the selected subject area, while the lower area holds a text field used to display the body of a message. The input area contains two buttons: the first one ("New Posting") to create a new message, the second one to terminate the application ("Quit").

```
import java.util.*;
import java.awt.*;
import java.awt.event.*;
```

```
public class BulletinBoardFrame extends Frame {
  private String title = "";
  private Vector subjects = null, categories = null;
  private BulletinBoard bboard = null;

  private List subjectList = null;
  private TextArea body = null;
  private Button quitButton = null;
  private Button newButton = null;
  private Choice categoryList = null;

  private Frame gui;

  public BulletinBoardFrame(String _title, BulletinBoard _bboard) {
    super(_title);
    gui = this;
    title = _title;
    bboard = _bboard;
    subjects = new Vector();
    categories = new Vector();
    initGUI();
  }

  private void initGUI() {
    categoryList = new Choice();
    subjectList = new List(6, false);
    body = new TextArea(10,60);
    quitButton = new Button("Quit");
    newButton = new Button("New Posting");
    Panel bboardp = new Panel(new BorderLayout());
    bboardp.add(categoryList, BorderLayout.NORTH);
    bboardp.add(subjectList, BorderLayout.CENTER);
    bboardp.add(body, BorderLayout.SOUTH);
    add(bboardp, BorderLayout.CENTER);
    Panel buttons = new Panel();
    buttons.setLayout(new FlowLayout());
    buttons.add(newButton);
    buttons.add(quitButton);
    add(buttons, BorderLayout.SOUTH);
```

```
// the event stuff
addWindowListener( new WindowAdapter() {
  public void windowClosing(WindowEvent e) {
    System.exit(0);
  }
});

quitButton.addActionListener( new ActionListener() {
  public void actionPerformed(ActionEvent e)  {
    if ((bboard != null) && (bboard.handleQuit()))
      System.exit(0);
  }
});

newButton.addActionListener( new ActionListener() {
  public void actionPerformed(ActionEvent e) {
    if (bboard != null) {
      NewPostingDialog d = new NewPostingDialog(gui);
      d.show();
      if (d.ok) {
        int _id = ((Integer)categories.elementAt(
          categoryList.getSelectedIndex())).intValue();
        bboard.insertNewPosting(d.subject.getText(), d.body.getText(), _id);
      }
    }
  }
});

subjectList.addActionListener( new ActionListener() {
  public void actionPerformed(ActionEvent e) {
    System.out.println("--- subject selected, updating body");
    if (bboard != null) {
      int _id = ((Integer)subjects.elementAt(
        subjectList.getSelectedIndex())).intValue();
      body.setText(bboard.getBody(_id));
    }
  }
});
```

```
    categoryList.addItemListener( new ItemListener() {
      public void itemStateChanged(ItemEvent ie) {
        if (bboard != null) {
          int _id = ((Integer)categories.elementAt(
            categoryList.getSelectedIndex())).intValue();
          bboard.reloadSubjects(_id);
          setBodyText("");
        }
      }
    });
    setSize(400,400);
    setVisible(true);
  }

  public void addCategory(int _id, String _cat){
    categories.addElement(new Integer(_id));
    categoryList.add(_cat);
  }

  public void clearSubjects() {
    subjects.removeAllElements();
    subjectList.removeAll();
  }

  public void addSubject(int _id, String _subj) {
    subjects.addElement(new Integer(_id));
    subjectList.add(_subj);
  }

  public void setBodyText(String _body) {
    body.setText(_body);
  }
}
```

The interface crated by this program is shown in Figure B.1.

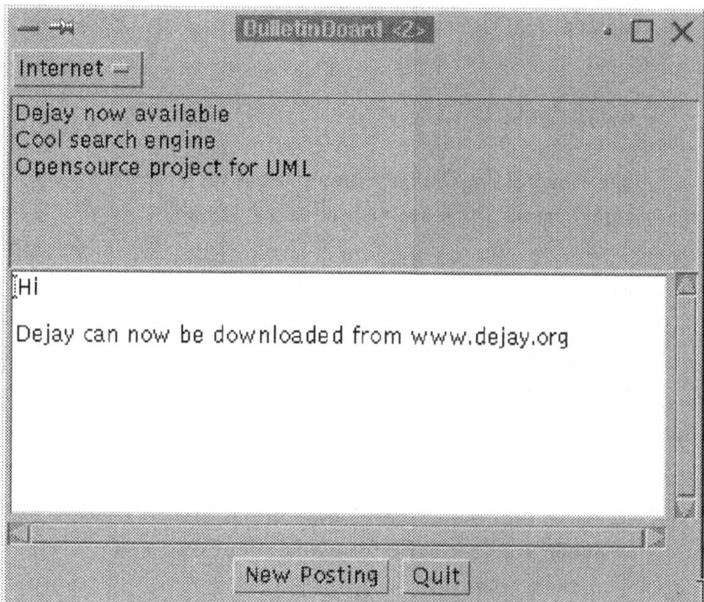

Figure B.1
The main BulletinBoard window.

To create a new message, the "New Posting" Button is pressed, which causes a dialog window to be opened. This dialog window is created and managed by the NewPostingDialog class. It contains a text field, in which the title of the message can be entered, and a TextArea, where the message itself can be typed in. The category of the message is derived from the category currently selected in the main window.

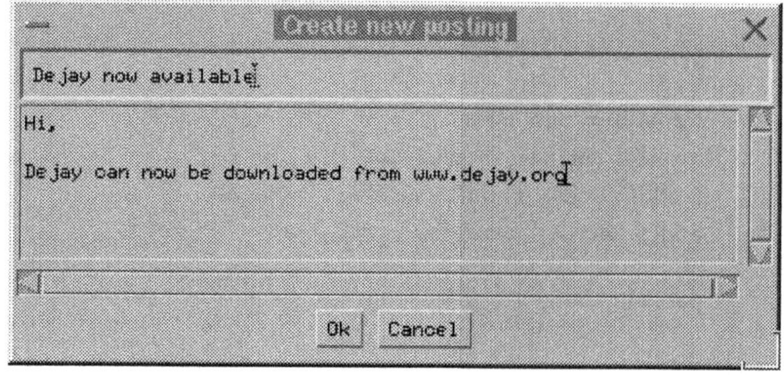

Figure B.2
The dialog window for new messages.

```
class NewPostingDialog extends Dialog {

    protected TextField subject;
    protected TextArea body;

    protected boolean ok = false;

    public NewPostingDialog(Frame parent) {
        super(parent, "Create new posting", true);

        subject = new TextField(60);
        body = new TextArea(6,60);
        setLayout(new BorderLayout());
        add(subject, BorderLayout.NORTH);
        add(body,BorderLayout.CENTER);

        Button b_ok = new Button("Ok");
        b_ok.addActionListener( new ActionListener() {
            public void actionPerformed(ActionEvent e) {
                ok = true;
                dispose();
            }
        });

        Button b_cancel = new Button("Cancel");
        b_cancel.addActionListener( new ActionListener() {
            public void actionPerformed(ActionEvent e) {
                ok = false;
                dispose();
            }
        });

        Panel p = new Panel();
        p.setLayout(new FlowLayout());
        p.add(b_ok); p.add(b_cancel);
        add(p, BorderLayout.SOUTH);

        pack();
    }
}
```

List of Figures

Bibliography

[Achauer 1993] Bruno Achauer. The DOWL Distributed Object-Oriented Language. *Communications of the ACM* **36**(9) (September 1993).

[Agha et al. 1993] G. Agha, P. Wegner, and A. Yonezawa. "Research Directions in Concurrent Object-Oriented Programming". MIT Press (1993).

[Agha and Callsen 1993] G. Agha and C. J. Callsen. ActorSpace: An Open Distributed Programming Paradigm. In "Proceedings of the 4th ACM Conference on Principles & Practice of Parallel Programming" (1993).

[Agha 1986] Gul Agha. "ACTORS: A Model of Concurrent Computation in Distributed Systems". MIT Press (1986).

[Aho et al. 1986] A. V. Aho, R. Sethi, and J.D. Ullman. "Compilers: Principles, Techniques and Tools". Addison-Wesley (1986).

[Altherr et al. 1999] M. Altherr, M. Erzberger, and S. Maffeis. Kommunikation über den iBus. *Java Spectrum* **1/2** (February/April) (1999).

[Andrews 1991] Gregory R. Andrews. "Concurrent Programming: Principles and Practice". Benjamin Cummings (1991).

[Appel 1997] Andrew W. Appel. "Modern Compiler Implementation in Java". Cambridge University Press (1997).

[Arnold and Gosling 1996] Ken Arnold and James Gosling. "The Java Programming Language". Addison-Wesley (1996).

[Atkinson et al. 1996] M. P. ATKINSON, L. DAYNES, M.J. JORDAN, T. PRINTEZIP, AND S. SPENCE. An Orthogonally Persistent Java. *ACM SIGMOD Records* **25**(4) (December 1996).

[Atkinson and Jordan 1998] M. P. ATKINSON AND M.J. JORDAN. Orthogonal Persistence for Java - A Mid-term Report. In "3rd Int. Workshop on Persistence and Java, Tiburon, CA" (September 1998).

[Atkinson 1991] COLIN ATKINSON. "Object-oriented Reuse, Concurrency and Distribution". Addison-Wesley (1991).

[Bacon 1997] JEAN BACON. "Concurrent Systems. Operating Systems, Database and Distributed Systems: An Integrated Approach". Addison-Wesley, Second edition (1997).

[Bal 1990] HENRI BAL. "Programming Distributed Systems". Prentice Hall (1990).

[Ben-Ari 1990] M. BEN-ARI. "Principles of Concurrent and Distributed Programming". Prentice Hall (1990).

[Bernstein 1996] P. A. BERNSTEIN. Middleware. *Communications of the ACM* **39**(2) (February 1996).

[Birman and van Renesse 1994] K. P. BIRMAN AND R. VAN RENESSE, editors. "Reliable Computing with the Isis Toolkit". IEEE Computer Society Press (1994).

[Birman 1993] KENNETH P. BIRMAN. The Process Group Approach to Reliable Distributed Computing. *Communications of the ACM* **36**(12) (December 1993).

[Birman 1996] KENNETH P. BIRMAN. "Building Secure and Reliable Network Systems". Prentice Hall (1996).

[Black et al. 1986] A. BLACK, E. J. HUTCHINSON, H. LEVY, AND L. CARTER. Object Structure in the Emerald System. In "Proceedings of Conference on Object Oriented Programming Systems" (October 1986).

[Black et al. 1987] A. Black, E. J. Hutchinson, E. Jul, H. Levy, and L. Carter. Distribution and Abstract Types in Emerald. *IEEE Transactions Software Engineering* **13**(1) (1987).

[Boger et al. 1999a] Marko Boger, Frank Griffel, and Winfried Lamersdorf. Dejay: Unifying Concurrency and Distribution to Achieve a Distributed Java. *Integrated Computer-Aided Engineering (ICAE)* (1999).

[Boger et al. 1999b] Marko Boger, Frank Wienberg, and Winfried Lamersdorf. Dejay: Unifying Concurrency and Distribution to Achieve a Distributed Java. In "Proceedings of Technology of Object-Oriented Languages and Systems TOOLS Europe 99, Nancy" (1999).

[Boger et al. 1999c] Marko Boger, Frank Wienberg, and Winfried Lamersdorf. Dejay: Concepts for a Distributed Java. In "Proceedings of Distributed Computing on the Web (DCW´99), June 99, Rostock" (1999).

[Boger and Gellersen 1996] Marko Boger and Hans-Werner Gellersen. On Models in Object-Oriented Methods - Critique and a new Approach to Reversibility. In "Proceedings of Technology of Object-Oriented Languages and Systems TOOLS 19, Paris" (1996).

[Boger 1998] Marko Boger. Migrating Objects in Electronic Commerce Applications. In "Proceedings of Trends in Distributed Systems for Electronic Commerce" (1998).

[Brandt and Madsen 1993] S. Brandt and O.L. Madsen. Object-Oriented Distributed Programming in BETA. In "Proceedings of Object-Based Distributed Programming, ECOOP'93 Workshop, Kaiserslautern, Germany, Lecture Notes in Computer Science, Vol. 791, Springer-Verlag" (1993).

[Brenner et al. 1998] Walter Brenner, Rüdiger Zarnekow, and Hartmut Wittig. "Intelligente Softwareagenten - Grundlagen und Anwendungen". Springer-Verlag (1998).

[Briot et al. 1997] J. BRIOT, R. GUERRAOUI, AND K-P. LÖHR. Concurrency, Distribution and Parallelism in Object-Oriented Programming (December 1997). Technical Report B-97-14, FU Berlin, FB Mathematik und Informatik.

[Brose et al. 1997] G. BROSE, K.-P. LÖHR, AND A. SPIEGEL. Java does not distribute. In "Proceedings of Technology of Object-Oriented Languages and Systems TOOLS Europe '97, Paris" (1997).

[Buschmann et al. 1996] FRANK BUSCHMANN, REGINE MEUNIER, HANS ROHNERT, PETER SOMMERLAD, AND MICHAEL STAL. "Pattern-Oriented Software Architecture: A System of Patterns". John Wiley & Sons (1996).

[Caglayan and Harrison 1997] ALPER K. CAGLAYAN AND COLIN G. HARRISON. "Agent Sourcebook - A Complete Guide to Desktop, Internet, and Intranet Agents". John Wiley & Sons (1997).

[Cardelli 1997] LUCA CARDELLI. Ambit (1997). www.luca.demon.co.uk/Ambit/Ambit.html.

[Caromel 1989] DENIS CAROMEL. Service, Asynchrony and Wait-by-Necessity. *Journal of Object-Oriented Programming* **2**(4) (November 1989).

[Caromel 1993] DENIS CAROMEL. Toward a method of object-oriented concurrent programming. *Communications of the ACM* **36**(9) (September 1993).

[Carriero and Gelernter 1989] NICHOLAS CARRIERO AND DAVID GELERNTER. Linda in Context. *Communications of the ACM* **32**(4) (April 1989).

[Carriero and Gelernter 1990] NICHOLAS CARRIERO AND DAVID GELERNTER. "How to write Parallel Programs". MIT Press (1990).

[Chandy and Misra 1996] MANI CHANDY AND JAYEDEV MISRA. "Parallel Program Design". Addison-Wesley (1996).

[Coad and Yourdon 1991] P. Coad and E. Yourdon. "Object Oriented Analysis". Prentice Hall, Second edition (1991).

[Cockayne and Zyda 1998] William R. Cockayne and Michael Zyda. "Mobile Agents". Manning (1998).

[Codd 1970] E. F. Codd. A Relational Model of Data for Large Shared Data Banks. *Communications of the ACM* **13**(6) (June 1970).

[Coleman et al. 1994] Derek Coleman, Patrick Arnolds, Stephanie Bodoff, Chris Dollin, et al.. "Object-Oriented Development: The Fusion Method". Prentice Hall (1994).

[Corbett 1996] J. C. Corbett. Evaluating deadlock detection methods for concurrent software. *IEEE Transactions on Software Engineering* **22**(3) (March 1996).

[Coulouris et al. 1994] G.F. Coulouris, J. Dollimore, and T. Kindberg. "Distributed Systems, Concepts and Design". Addison-Wesley, Second edition (1994).

[Date 1995] C.J. Date. "An Introduction to Database Systems". Addison-Wesley, Sixth edition (1995).

[Dijkstra 1968] Edsker W. Dijkstra. "Programming Languages", chapter Cooperating Sequential Processes. Academic Press (1968).

[Dijkstra 1972] Edsker W. Dijkstra. "Operating Systems Techniques", chapter Hierarchical Ordering of Sequential Processes. Academic Press (1972).

[Downing 1998] Troy Brian Downing. "Java RMI: Remote Method Invocation". Prentice Hall (1998).

[Eckel 1998] Bruce Eckel. "Thinking in Java". Prentice Hall (1998).

[Ehmayer and Reich 1998] Gerald Ehmayer and Siegfried Reich. "Java in der Anwendungsentwicklung". dpunkt.verlag (1998).

[Farley 1998] JIM FARLEY. "Java Distributed Computing". O'Reilly (1998).

[Foster 1995] IAN FOSTER. "Designing and Building Parallel Programs". Addison-Wesley (1995).

[Foundation 1992] OPEN SOFTWARE FOUNDATION. "Introduction to OSF Distributed Computing Environment". Prentice Hall (1992).

[Fowler and Scott 1997] MARTIN FOWLER AND KENDALL SCOTT. "UML Distilled - Applying the Standard Object Modelling Language". Addison-Wesley (1997).

[Friedman and van Renesse 1996] R. FRIEDMAN AND R. VAN RENESSE. Strong and Weak Virtual Synchrony in Horus. In "1996 IEEE Symposium on Reliable Distributed Systems". IEEE Press (October 1996).

[Frølund 1994] SVEND FRØLUND. "Constraint-Based Synchronization of Distributed Activities". PhD thesis, University of Illinois at Urbana-Champaign (1994).

[Frølund 1996] SVEND FRØLUND. "Coordinating Distributed Objects. An Actor-Based Approach to Synchronization". MIT Press (1996).

[Gamma et al. 1995] ERICH GAMMA, RICHARD HELM, RALPH JOHNSON, AND JOHN VLISSIDES. "Design Patterns. Elements of Reusable Object-Oriented Software". Addison-Wesley (1995).

[Gelernter 1985] D. GELERNTER. Generativ Communication in Linda. *ACM Tansactions Programming Languages and Systems* **7**(1) (1985).

[Goldberg and Robson 1989] ADELE GOLDBERG AND DAVID ROBSON. "SmallTalk-80. The Language". Addison-Wesley (1989).

[Gosling et al. 1996] JAMES GOSLING, BILL JOY, AND GUY STEEL. "The Java Language Specification". Addison-Wesley (1996).

[Gries 1981] DAVID GRIES. "The Science of Programming". Springer-Verlag (1981).

[Griffel 1998] FRANK GRIFFEL. "Componentware. Konzepte und Techniken eines Softwareparadigmas". dpunkt.verlag (1998).

[Guerraoui et al. 1993] RACHID GUERRAOUI, OSCAR NIERSTRASZ, AND MICHEL RIVEILL, editors. "Object-Based Distributed Processing". Springer-Verlag (1993). LNCS 791.

[Hafner and Lyon 1997] KATIE HAFNER AND MATTHEW LYON. "ARPA Kadabra. Die Geschichte des Internet". dpunkt.verlag (1997).

[Hall 1997] D. A. HALL. "Applying Mobile Code to Distributed Systems". PhD thesis, University of Cambridge (June 1997).

[Halls et al. 1996] D. HALLS, J. BATES, AND J. BACON. Flexible Distributed Programming using Mobile Code (1996). www.cl.cam.ac.uk/users/dah28/sigops96.ps.gz.

[Hamilton et al. 1997] GRAHAM HAMILTON, RICH CATTELL, AND MAYDENE FISHER. "JDBC Database Access with Java". Addison-Wesley (1997).

[Hartley 1998] STEPHEN J. HARTLEY. "Concurrent Programming. The Java Programming Language". Oxford University Press (1998).

[Henderson-Sellers and Graham 1996] BRIAN HENDERSON-SELLERS AND IAN GRAHAM. OPEN: Towards Method Convergence? *IEEE Computer, Object Technology department* **29**(4) (April 1996).

[Heuer 1997] ANDREAS HEUER. "Objektorientierte Datenbanken - Konzepte, Modelle, Standards und Systeme". Addison-Wesley, Second edition (1997).

[Hoare 1974] C. A. R. HOARE. Monitors: An Operating System Structuring Concept. *Communications of the ACM* **17**(10) (October 1974).

[Hoare 1978] C. A. R. Hoare. Communicating Sequential Processes. *Communications of the ACM* **21**(8) (1978).

[Hoare 1985] C. A. R. Hoare. "Communicating Sequential Processes". Prentice Hall (1985).

[Hughes et al. 1997] Merlin Hughes, Conrad Hughes, Michael Shoffner, and Maria Winslow. "Communicating Sequential Processes". Manning (1997).

[Hutchinson 1987] Norman C Hutchinson. "Emerald: An Object-Based Language for Distributed Programming". PhD thesis, Department of Computer Science, University of Washington (January 1987).

[Inprise 1999] Inprise. Inprise (1999). http://www.inprise.com/.

[Iona 1999] Iona. Iona Technologies (1999). http://www.iona.com/.

[Jalloul 1994] Ghinwa Jalloul. "Concurrent Object-Oriented Systems: A Disciplined Approach". PhD thesis, University of Technology, Sydney (1994).

[Jul et al. 1987] E. Jul, H. Levy, N. Hutchinson, and A. Black. Fine-grained mobility in the Emerald system. In "Proc. of the Eleventh ACM Symposium on Operating System Principles". ACM (November 1987).

[Jul 1989] Eric Jul. "Object Mobility in a Distributed Object-Oriented System". PhD thesis, University of Washington (1989).

[Jul 1998] Eric Jul, editor. "Object oriented Programming: 12th European conference,Brussels, Proceedings ECOOP 98". Springer-Verlag (July 1998).

[Khanna 1994] Raman Khanna. "Distributed Computing". Prentice Hall (1994).

[Kleiman et al. 1996] Steven Kleiman, Devang Shah, and Bart Smaalders. "Programming with Threads". Prentice Hall (1996).

[Knapik and Johnson 1998] MICHAEL KNAPIK AND JAY JOHNSON. "Developing Intelligent Agents for Distributed Systems - Exploring Architectures, Technologies, and Applications". McGraw-Hill (1998).

[Knudsen 1989] JONATHAN B. KNUDSEN. "Java Cryptography". O'Reilly (1989).

[Kredel and Yoshida 1999] HEINZ KREDEL AND AKITOSHI YOSHIDA. "Threads- und Netzwerk-Programmierung mit Java". dpunkt.verlag (1999).

[Laboratory 1998] IBM TOKYO RESEARCH LABORATORY. Aglets Workbench - Programming Mobile Agents in Java (1998). www.trl.ibm.co.jp/aglets/.

[Lange and Oshima 1998] DANNY B. LANGE AND MITSURU OSHIMA. "Programming and Developing Java Mobile Agents with Aglets". Addison-Wesley (1998).

[Lea 1993] DOUG LEA. Objects in Groups (1993). www.cs.oswego.edu/dl/Groups/Groups.html.

[Lea 1997] DOUG LEA. "Concurrent Programming in Java: Design Principles and Patterns". Addison-Wesley (1997).

[Lea 1998] DOUG LEA. Overview of Package util.concurrent (1998). www.cs.oswego.edu/dl/util/concurrent/intro.html.

[Links 1999] CETUS LINKS. Links on Objects & Components (1999). http://www.rhein-neckar.de/ cetus/software.html.

[Linnhoff-Popien 1998] CLAUDIA LINNHOFF-POPIEN. "CORBA - Kommunikation und Management". Springer-Verlag (1998).

[Löhr et al. 1994] K.-P. LÖHR, I. PIENS, AND T. WOLFF. Verteilungstransparenz bei der objetorientierten Entwicklung verteilter Applikationen. *OBJEKTspektrum* **1994**(5) (1994).

[Loomis 1995] MARY E. S. LOOMIS. "Object Databases: The Essentials". Addison-Wesley (1995).

[Lynch 1993] NANCY LYNCH. "Distributed Alogrithms". Addison-Wesley (1993).

[Maffais et al. 1999] SILVANO MAFFAIS, FRIDJOF TOENNIESSEN, AND CHRISTIAN ZEIDLER, editors. "Erfahrungen mit Java - Projekte aus Industrie und Hochschule". dpunkt.verlag (1999).

[Maffeis 1993] SILVANO MAFFEIS. Electra: Making Distributed Programs Object-Oriented. In "Symposium on Experiences with Distributed and Multiprocessor System, USENIX" (September 1993).

[Maffeis 1995] SILVANO MAFFEIS. "Run-Time Support for Object-Oriented Distributed Programming". PhD thesis, University of Zürich (February 1995).

[Maffeis 1997] SILVANO MAFFEIS. iBus- The Java Intranet Software Bus. In "???" (February 1997).

[Magee and Kramer 1999] JEFF MAGEE AND JEFF KRAMER. "Concurrency - State Models and Java Programs". John Wiley & Sons (1999).

[Magic 1998] GENERAL MAGIC (1998). www.genmagic.com.

[Masuoka and Yonezawa 1993] SATOSHI MASUOKA AND AKINORI YONEZAWA. "Research Directions in Concurrent Object-Oriented Programming", chapter Analysis of Inheritance Anomaly in Object-Oriented Concurrent Programming Languages, pages 107–150. MIT Press (1993).

[McHale 1994] CIARAN MCHALE. "Synchronization in Concurrent Object-Oriented Languages". PhD thesis, Trinity College (1994).

[Meier and Wüst 1997] ANDREAS MEIER AND THOMAS WÜST. "Objektorientierte Datenbanken". dpunkt.verlag (1997).

[Meier 1998] ANDREAS MEIER. "Relationale Datenbanken". Springer-Verlag, Third edition (1998).

[Merz et al. 1998a] M. MERZ, F. GRIFFEL, M. BOGER, H. WEINREICH, AND W. LAMERSDORF. Electronic Contracting with COSMOS - How to Establish, Negotiate and Execute Electronic Contracts on the Internet. In "Enterprice Distributed Objects Computing Workshop (EDOC'98), San Diego" (1998).

[Merz et al. 1998b] M. MERZ, F. GRIFFEL, T. TU, S. MÜLLER-WILKEN, H. WEINREICH, M. BOGER, AND W. LAMERSDORF. Supporting Electronic Commerce Transactions with Contracting Services. *International Journal on Cooperative Information Systems, Vol. 7, No. 4* **7**(4) (1998).

[Merz et al. 1999] M. MERZ, F. GRIFFEL, M. BOGER, H. WEINREICH, AND W. LAMERSDORF. Electronic Contracting im Internet. In "GI/ITG-Konferenz 'Kommunikation in Verteilten Systemen' (KIVS'99), Informatik-Aktuell" (1999).

[Meyer 1990] BERTRAND MEYER. Sequential and Concurrent Object-Oriented Programming. In "Technology of Object-Oriented Languages and Systems 91, Paris" (June 1990).

[Meyer 1993] BERTRAND MEYER. Systematic Concurrent Object-Oriented Programming. *Communication of the ACM, Special Issue on Concurrent Object-Oriented Programming* **36**(9) (September 1993).

[Meyer 1997] BERTRAND MEYER. "Object-Oriented Software Construction". Prentice Hall, Second edition (1997).

[Middendorf and Singer 1999] STEFAN MIDDENDORF AND REINER SINGER. "Java- Programmierhandbuch und Referenz". dpunkt.verlag (1999).

[Moldt 1996] DANIEL MOLDT. "Höhere Petrinetze als Grundlage für Systemspezifikationen". PhD thesis, Universität Hamburg, Fachbereich Informatik (August 1996).

[Mowbray and Zahavi 1995] THOMAS J. MOWBRAY AND RON ZAHAVI. "The Essential CORBA". John Wiley & Sons (1995).

[Mullender 1993] S. MULLENDER, editor. "Distributed Systems". Addison-Wesley, Second edition (1993).

[Neimeyer 1998] PAT NEIMEYER, editor. "Core Java Networking". Prentice Hall (1998).

[Nelson 1998] JEFF NELSON, editor. "Programming Mobile Objects with Java". John Wiley & Sons (1998).

[Nierstrasz and Tsichritzis 1995] OSCAR NIERSTRASZ AND DENNIS TSICHRITZIS, editors. "Object-Oriented Software Composition". Prentice Hall (1995).

[Nierstrasz 1992] OSCAR NIERSTRASZ. "Advances in Object-Oriented Software Engineering", chapter A Tour of Hybrid: A Language for Programming with Active Objects. Prentice Hall (1992).

[Oaks and Wong 1997] SCOTT OAKS AND HENRY WONG. "Java Threads". O'Reilly, Second edition (1997).

[Oaks 1998] SCOTT OAKS. "Java Security". O'Reilly (1998).

[ObjectDesign 1998] OBJECTDESIGN. ObjectStore (1998). www.odi.com.

[ObjectSpace 1998a] OBJECTSPACE. Java Generic Library (1998). www.objectspace.com.

[ObjectSpace 1998b] OBJECTSPACE. Voyager (1998). www.objectspace.com.

[OOPSLA 1998] OOPSLA. "Conference proceedings OOPSLA '98, Vancouver, British Columbia, October 18-22, 1998". ACM Press (1998).

[Orfali et al. 1996] ROBERT ORFALI, DAN HARKEY, AND JERI EDWARDS. "The Esssential Distributed Objects Survial Guide". John Wiley & Sons (1996).

[Orfali and Harkey 1997] ROBERT ORFALI AND DAN HARKEY. "Client/Server Programming with Java and Corba". John Wiley & Sons (1997).

[Papathomas 1995] M. PAPATHOMAS. "Object-Oriented Software Composition", chapter Concurrency in Object-Oriented Programming Languages, pages 31–68. Prentice Hall (1995).

[Peitgen et al. 1992] HEINZ-OTTO PEITGEN, HARTMUT JÜRGENS, AND DIETMAR SAUPE. "Bausteine des Chaos. Fraktale". Springer-Verlag (1992).

[Peitgen et al. 1998] HEINZ-OTTO PEITGEN, HARTMUT JÜRGENS, AND DIETMAR SAUPE. "Bausteine des Chaos. Fraktale". Rohwolt Taschenbuch (1998).

[Philippsen and Zenger 1996] MICHAEL PHILIPPSEN AND MATTHIAS ZENGER. JavaParty - Transparent Remote Objects in Java. *Concurrency: Practice and Experience* **9**(11) (November 1996).

[Pree 1994] WOLFGANG PREE. "Design Patterns fo Object-Oriented Software Development". ACM Press (1994).

[Pree 1997] WOLFGANG PREE. "Komponentenbasierte Softwareentwicklung mit Frameworks". dpunkt.verlag (1997).

[Puder and Römer 1998] ARNO PUDER AND KAY RÖMER. "MICO is CORBA". dpunkt.verlag (1998).

[Redlich 1999a] JENS-PETER REDLICH. "CORBA 2.0, eine praxisorientierte Einführung". Addison-Wesley, Second edition (1999).

[Redlich 1999b] JENS-PETER REDLICH. "CORBA 3.0, eine praxisorientierte Einführung". Addison-Wesley Longman, Second edition (1999).

[Reese 1997] GEORGE REESE. "Database Programming with JDBC and Java". O'Reilly (1997).

[Richardson et al. 1993] J. E. RICHARDSON, M. J. CAREY, AND D. T. SCHUH. The Design of the E Programming Language. *ACM Transactions on Programming Languages and Systems* **15**(3), 494–534 (1993).

[Rothermel and Hohl 1998] KURT ROTHERMEL AND FRITZ HOHL, editors. "Mobile Agents - Second International Workshop, MA´98". Number 1477 in LNCS. Springer-Verlag (1998).

[Rothermel and Popescu-Zeletin 1997] KURT ROTHERMEL AND RADU POPESCU-ZELETIN, editors. "Mobile Agents - First International Workshop, MA´97". Number 1219 in LNCS. Springer-Verlag (1997).

[Rumbaugh et al. 1991] JAMES RUMBAUGH, M. BLAHA, W. PREMERLANI, F. EDDY, AND W. LORENSEN. "Object-Oriented Modeling and Design". Prentice Hall (1991).

[Ryan 1997] TIMOTHY W. RYAN. "Distributed Object Technology. Concepts and Applications". Prentice Hall (1997).

[Saake et al. 1997] GUNTER SAAKE, INGO SCHMITT, AND CAN TÜRKER. "Objektdatenbanken - Konzepte, Sprachen, Architekturen". MIT-Press (1997).

[Schaffert 1986] CRAIG SCHAFFERT. An Introduction to Trellis/OWL. In "OOPSLA '86 Proceedings, Portland". SIGPLAN Notices 21 (11) (September 1986).

[Siegel 1996] JON SIEGEL. "CORBA Fundamentals and Programming". John Wiley & Sons (1996).

[Siegmund 1999] GERD SIEGMUND. "Technik der Netze". Hütig (1999).

[Silberschatz and Galvin 1994] AVI SILBERSCHATZ AND PETER GALVIN. "Operating System Concepts". Addison-Wesley (1994).

[Softwired 1998] SOFTWIRED. "Programming iBus Applications". Softwired AG, Zuerich, www.softwired.ch, version 0.5 edition (1998).

[Spence 1997] SUSAN SPENCE. Distribution Support for PJama. In "Workshop on Persistence and Distribution in Java" (1997).

[Stevens and Wright 1994] W. RICHARD STEVENS AND GARY R. WRIGHT. "TCP/IP illustrated". Addison-Wesley (1994).

[Straßer et al. 1996] M. STRASSER, J. BAUMANN, AND F. HOHL. Mole: A Java based mobile agent system. In "Proceedings of the 2nd ECOOP Workshop on Mobile Object Systems". dpunkt.verlag (1996).

[Strom et al. 1991] R. STROM, D. BACON, A. GOLDBERG, A.LOWRY, D. YELLIN, AND S. YEMENI. "Hermes: A Language for Distributed Computing". Prentice Hall (1991).

[Systems 1992] ISIS DISTRIBUTED SYSTEMS. "ISIS User Guide and Reference Manual". Isis Distributed Systems, Inc, 111 South Cayuga St., Ithaca NY (1992).

[Tanenbaum and Woodhull 1997] ANDREW S. TANENBAUM AND ALBERT S. WOODHULL. "Operating Systems. Design an Implementation". Prentice Hall, Second edition (1997).

[Tanenbaum 1992] ANDREW S. TANENBAUM. "Modern Operating Systems". Prentice Hall (1992).

[Tanenbaum 1995] ANDREW S. TANENBAUM. "Verteilte Betriebssysteme". Prentice Hall (1995).

[Tanenbaum 1996] ANDREW S. TANENBAUM. "Computer Networks". Prentice Hall (1996).

[Tanenbaum 1997] ANDREW S. TANENBAUM. "Computernetzwerke". Prentice Hall (1997).

[Tatsubori 1997] M. TATSUBORI. OpenJava (1997). www.softlab.is.tsukuba.ac.jp/ mich/openjava/.

[Technologies 1999] IONA TECHNOLOGIES. Iona Technologies (1999). http://www.iona.com/.

[Tel 1994] GERARD TEL. "Introduction to Distributed Algorithms". Cambridge University Press, Second edition (1994).

[Tokoro et al. 1992] MARIO TOKORO, OSCAR NIERSTRASZ, AND PETER WEGNER, editors. "Proceedings of ECOOP 91 Workshop on Object-Based Concurrent Computing". Springer-Verlag, LNCS 612 (1992).

[van Renesse et al. 1996] R. VAN RENESSE, K. P. BIRMAN, AND S. MAFFEIS. Horus: A Flexible Group Communication System. *Communications of the ACM* **39**(4) (April 1996).

[Vitek and Tschudin 1997] JAN VITEK AND CHRISTIAN TSCHUDIN, editors. "Mobile Object Systems - Towards the Programmable Internet. Second International Workshop, MOS´96". Number 1222 in LNCS. Springer-Verlag (1997).

[Vogel and Duddy 1998] ANDREAS VOGEL AND KEITH DUDDY. "Java Programming with CORBA". John Wiley & Sons, Second edition (1998).

[Waldo et al. 1994] JIM WALDO, GEOFF WYANT, ANN WOLLRATH, AND SAM KENDALL. A Note on Distributed Computing, Technical Report (1994). www.sunlabs.com/technical-reports/1994/abstract-29.html.

[White 1997] J. E. WHITE. "Software Agents", chapter Mobile Agents, pages 437–472. AAAI Press and MIT Press (1997).

[Wilkinson 1997] T. WILKINSON. Kaffe – A Virtual Machine to run Java Code (1997). www.tjwassoc.demon.co.uk/kaffe/kaffe.htm.

[Winston and Narasimhan 1996] PATRIC HENRY WINSTON AND SUNDAR NARASIMHAN. "On to Java". Addison-Wesley (1996).

[Wittmann and Zitterbart 1999] RALPH WITTMANN AND MARTINA ZITTERBART. "Multicast - Protokolle, Programmierung, Anwendung". dpunkt.verlag (1999).

[Wyatt et al. 1992] BARBARA B. WYATT, KRISHNA KAVI, AND STEVE HUFNAGEL. Parallelism in Object-Oriented Languages: A Survey. *IEEE Software* **9**(6), 56–66 (1992).

[Yonezawa and Tokoro 1987] AKI YONEZAWA AND MARIO TOKORO. "Object-Oriented Concurrent Programming". MIT Press (1987).

[Yonezawa 1987] AKI YONEZAWA. "Object-Oriented Concurrent Programming", chapter Modelling and Programming in an Object-Oriented Concurrent Language ABCL/1, pages 55–66. MIT Press (1987).

Index

9 780471 49